MW00632398

Praying for Murder, Receiving Mercy

From At-Risk to At Peace; My Journey from Fear to Freedom

Kelly J. Stigliano

Praying for Murder, Receiving Mercy

From At-Risk to At Peace;
My Journey from Fear to Freedom

Dedication:

Part One of this book is dedicated to women in at-risk relationships and the people who love them. (It's harder to escape than you realize. Judging them helps no one.)

Part Two is dedicated to single mothers who are trying their best, whether they see themselves as successful or not, and the people who love them.

The whole book is dedicated to anyone who needs to receive hope and embrace forgiveness. God has mercy on each of us and forgives us when we ask Him.

∞∞∞∞∞∞∞∞∞∞∞

Whoever conceals their sins does not prosper, but the one who confesses and renounces them finds mercy.
Proverbs 28:13 (NIV)

Note to the Reader:

This is a work of creative nonfiction. It depicts actual events in the life of the author as her recollection permits and/or research can verify. The dialogue is as she remembers and may not be what others remember. The places are real. The names and identifying details of individuals have been changed to respect the innocent and protect the guilty. If you see yourself depicted herein, you may remember differently. This is the author's personal story.

The *Psychology Dictionary* defines brainwashing as that which "manipulates and modifies a person's emotions, attitudes, and beliefs."

∞∞∞∞∞∞∞∞∞∞∞

Dr. Mark R. Banschick, MD said in *Psychology Today*, "The fact is that abusive relationships have a lot in common with cults. In both, victims feel completely demoralized, injured and trapped. . . . abuse victims feel stuck and desperately unhappy."

∞∞∞∞∞∞∞∞∞∞∞

In their article, "Domestic Violence against Women: Recognize Patterns, Seek Help", the Mayo Clinic Staff reported that you might be experiencing domestic violence if you're in a relationship with someone who:
- Calls you names, insults you or puts you down
- Prevents or discourages you from going to work or school or seeing family members or friends
- Tries to control how you spend money, where you go, what medicines you take or what you wear
- Acts jealous or possessive or constantly accuses you of being unfaithful
- Gets angry when drinking alcohol or using drugs
- Threatens you with violence or a weapon
- Hits, kicks, shoves, slaps, chokes or otherwise hurts you, your children or your pets
- Forces you to have sex or engage in sexual acts against your will
- Blames you for his or her violent behavior or tells you that you deserve it

∞∞∞∞∞∞∞∞∞∞∞∞∞

"Somewhere between the playground bully and the monsters who kidnap, torture, and imprison women, lay those who terrorize the 1.3 million women who face some degree of abuse each year. I happened to marry one when I was a teenager." – Kelly J. Stigliano

Table of Contents

Prologue: An Introduction to the Spirit World; How My Rebellion Began

Part One
Pathway to the Courthouse

Chapter One: A New Chapter
Chapter Two: Getting To Know You
Chapter Three: Confusing the Signs
Chapter Four: Independence
Chapter Five: Sowing and Reaping
Chapter Six: A Surprisingly Surprising Beginning
Chapter Seven: The Lights Go Out
Chapter Eight: Searching in the Darkness
Chapter Nine: The List Grows
Chapter Ten: Maybe God Does Care
Chapter Eleven: Leaving the House
Chapter Twelve: Same Show, Different Stage
Chapter Thirteen: The Clouds Are Moving
Chapter Fourteen: Another Word
Chapter Fifteen: Refuge for a While
Chapter Sixteen: A New World
Chapter Seventeen: Exploitation
Chapter Eighteen: Grateful for Life
Chapter Nineteen: Eager to Please
Chapter Twenty: Carry On
Chapter Twenty-One: They Gave Me Apple Butter
Chapter Twenty-Two: Freedom Is a Slippery Slope
Chapter Twenty-Three: Trying It on My Own
Chapter Twenty-Four: Choices
Chapter Twenty-Five: Manifestation
Chapter Twenty-Six: Final Attempt
Chapter Twenty-Seven: Serenity

Part Two
Pathway to the Altar

Chapter Twenty-Eight: Sailing Solo May Be Simple, But Never Easy
Chapter Twenty-Nine: Sinking My Ship
Chapter Thirty: How Low Can I Go?
Chapter Thirty-One: My Fantasy Comes True
Chapter Thirty-Two: Messy Places
Chapter Thirty-Three: New People, Ageless God
Chapter Thirty-Four: Subtle Seduction
Chapter Thirty-Five: A Quiet Whisper
Chapter Thirty-Six: Cleaning up My Act
Chapter Thirty-Seven: He Wouldn't Let Me Go
Chapter Thirty-Eight: Gifts
Chapter Thirty-Nine: A New Reality
Chapter Forty: Unexpected Fòes
Chapter Forty-One: Nothing New Under the Sun
Chapter Forty-Two: Reflection—God in the Midst of the Storm
Chapter Forty-Three: Your Best Decision Yet

Epilogue: Forgiveness

Acknowledgments

Endnotes

Organizations that can help you

Foreword

Heartbreaking, riveting, hopeful and instructional, I couldn't put this book down as Kelly's trials and triumphs kept me glued to the pages late into the night. I emerge from this experience with more compassion and a sad-but-true awareness of the failures of the body of Christ. Most importantly, my spirit is burning to extend more of God's love to every woman I meet. Thank you, Kelly, for baring your soul and your scars so we could better understand the heart of our Loving Father. I highly recommend this book!

- Marnie Swedberg, International Leadership Mentor, www.Marnie.com

Praying for Murder, Receiving Mercy

From At-Risk to At Peace;
My Journey from Fear to Freedom

Prologue: An Introduction to the Spirit World; How My Rebellion Began

1965—Toledo, Ohio

"Go get the dustpan," seven-year-old Sophia ordered.

Only five, I was thrilled my older sister paid attention to me. It didn't matter that we cleaned our bedroom; I relished any time she gave me. When she said we should tidy our room one Saturday, I jumped at the chance.

"Okay." I joyfully ran in my typical hyperactive way. When I opened our bedroom door, I fell backward, almost running into a man—who instantly disappeared. Electricity shot through my body.

Snapping my head toward my sister, I tried to catch my breath. "Did you see that?"

"What?"

"That man in the doorway—red and dark like the devil. I almost hit him. He was there and then—poof—gone." My animation made my normal rapid-fire speech nearly incomprehensible.

"Shut up," Sophia scolded. "Get the dustpan and just shut up." She became solemn and removed, not speaking to me again that day. Clearly, I had frightened her with my enthusiastic description.

1

Thus began my awareness of the supernatural world. I lived with a sense that someone watched me all the time and my interest in the mystical grew. Games that dabbled in the spirit world intrigued me—Ouija Board, Ka-bala, and Magic 8 Ball. I requested and received every one. **(Endnote 1)**

Through these occultic toys, I welcomed rebellion into my life. The possibility of communicating with the dead fascinated me. When we were young teens, my girlfriends and I had séances regularly.

1973—Parkman, Ohio

My best friend Suzie and I were thirteen when we learned of an epitaph on a tombstone in the back corner of the oldest cemetery in town. It belonged to an elderly woman named Phebe Bentley, and we were told that the inscription was similar to one that lore tells is on a tombstone in Tasmania, Australia.

"Stop ye travellers as you pass by; As you are now, so once was I; As I am now, soon you shall be—Prepare yourself to follow me."

Tradition tells of a graffiti response in Tasmania of, "To follow you I am not content— How do I know which way you went?"

Phebe sounded like an interesting woman. We believed the story and chanted the rhyme like a mantra, trying to call her back from the dead as we sat cross-legged in front of a candle in the dark.

That same year, my grandparents took us to a family reunion at a park in Pennsylvania. I had been sitting on a swing, smoking a cigarette when a group of teenage boys came over to talk to us. They were cute, so we listened.

They told us about Jesus and asked us if we wanted to pray to ask Him to come into our hearts. It all sounded interesting; we prayed their prayer. After all, they were boys.

However, I didn't read my Bible or try to grow closer to God, and my rebellious spirit flourished. I carried a razorblade and handwritten will in my wallet at all times. I thought, *just make my day. Give me a reason to check out—I'm ready to go.*

1975—New Year's Eve

We were fifteen years old. Elaine Zeigler, one of the girls from our circle of friends, disappeared while camping in Florida with her family. Throughout our teenage years, we didn't know if our beloved friend was alive or dead. We suspected the worst and tried to call her back at every séance.

Part One – Pathway to the Courthouse

Chapter One: A New Chapter

1983—Chardon, Ohio

I walked out of the small country courthouse; my eyes darted right and left. Was he gone? I shivered. The chilly October wind whipped around my legs, and my long blonde hair blew. Grateful for the stinging breeze, I wiped away the tears.

You've cried enough, I thought.

Dace's favorite slur for me echoed in my mind. "You're a skinny piece of crap."

Relief. Uncertainty. Fear. So much fear. I had fought the urge to run out of the building first, before he left. I waited twenty minutes. Standing in the chill, I looked around, but didn't see him anywhere. His friend was to pick him up. In what?

Still uncertain of his whereabouts, I made a beeline to my ugly, green 1979 Ford Pinto.

Gotta carry on, I encouraged myself.

His whispered taunt, spoken just minutes earlier in the eerie halls of the courthouse, made my skull throb. "Only one person can sail this ship. Now sail your own ship, Captain."

Fragments of conversations from years gone by ricocheted in my head and coupled with this latest mock, repeated in a painful loop in my brain.

Will I be able to sail my children to safety?

The number of single mothers in America continued to increase, but could *I* do it? I'd failed at so many things. Could I succeed in this new chapter of my life? It seemed I could do nothing right. For years, my husband had been quick to remind me of that. Having been hit in the head so often and called worthless had taken its toll.

Maybe I'm too stupid to do this alone.

I had to stop the negative thoughts. I needed to reflect on how I'd gotten there—that day—in that courthouse.

For a diversion, I hurried to the health club. Having taken the day off work for the divorce proceedings, I raced against the clock until the time to retrieve my kids from the day care center.

The drive to the suburbs of Cleveland felt longer than usual. The drab scenery seemed to stretch on forever. Ohio weather can be depressing as winter creeps in. The colorful leaves from just a few weeks earlier now lay in brown heaps against buildings and stuck in the jumbled interior of the shrubbery. The landscape seemed to be a celestial joke simulating my life. *I hope this season isn't long.*

The gym was just what I needed. No working out today—just the desserts: the spa. The clock in the locker room echoed. Moving in robot-like precision, I got into my one-piece swimsuit.

I caught a quick glimpse of my reflection in the glass doors at the pool area.

Maybe Dace is right. You are a skinny piece of crap. I shook my head vehemently. *Skinny maybe, but not crap.*

Sitting at the edge of the pool, I dangled my legs in the warm water.

Not many people here this time of day. Good. I don't feel like talking to anyone.

Having just come from court, I looked like the man-stalkers I despised. The women who supposedly came to work out and wore full makeup and the latest spandex fashions made me queasy. They obviously weren't there to get fit. The endorphins they sought would come from a day of shopping at the jewelry store or an exhausting afternoon of sex with a stranger. Not my bag.

My mind wandered. I was back in Phoenix, Arizona, beside my mother-in-law's pool.

Former mother-in-law. What do I call her now?

The crystal-clear water in Janice's pool had been refreshing, promising hours of fun, someday. That someday never came. Her son saw to that. I had clung to hope for a normal life in Arizona, a life free from the violence that defined our marriage in Ohio. New hope had come with a different job out West. But old patterns eclipsed new hope.

On autopilot, my feet moved in the water. Clouds of recall darkened my thoughts. My mood grew ominous. Memories of one outburst of rage collided with another. Time and place were undefined as shouts, slaps, choking, concern for my kids' safety, and untold embarrassment threatened to pull me under. I stared while my legs hung motionless in the pool.

Splash! A quick splatter of water on my face got my attention. As usual, there was a perfectly-coiffed, big-haired, bleached-blonde bimbo surrounded by three hairy-chested Italians with gold chains around their necks. They were loud and vulgar. Positioned in a close circle, God only knew what their hands did under the water. I got up and entered the sauna.

"Nice legs," one yelled as I passed. I ignored him, and his bimbo slapped his shoulder, recapturing his focus.

Serenity. Heat. I lay back and inhaled deeply, savoring the distinct smell of cedar. Again, I imagined I was in Arizona in March. The tiny alley behind our apartment allowed just enough room for a foldout lawn chair. In my mind, I was working on my tan. Family in Ohio still shoveled snow. It seemed weird, but no weirder than the Christmas light-bedazzled cacti had been.

That apartment had been so hot. Despite the one hundred-plus-degree heat, my husband wouldn't allow me to turn on the air-conditioner until he arrived home from work. "Don't waste it," he'd warn, and I knew better than to disregard that order.

Uncomfortable thoughts morphed into horrific memories of the last night the babies and I were in Arizona. I was screaming as Dace's thumbs pushed into my eye sockets. Darkness, panic, and flashes of light like cartoon stars.

My eyes shot open. I was too hot and seeing stars in the sauna. Numb, I stood and shuffled through the door, trance-like. The cold dip was just outside the sauna. Stepping over the edge, I plunged deep into the frigid water, shocking me back to reality. My mind raced. *It's time to go get the kids.* I needed them to be safe at home with me now.

Hurrying to the locker room, I showered, dressed quickly, pulled my wet hair into a sloppy ponytail, and left the gym.

Gotta carry on. I repeated my mental mantra.

The drive to the day care gave ample time for introspection. How did I ever get into this position? Weren't there warning signs? Of course there were. But who listens to such things when she's just seventeen years old?

7

Chapter Two: Getting to Know You

1977—Middlefield, Ohio

Dace and I met at the end of my junior year at Cardinal High School in Middlefield, Ohio. No one had ever told me I was pretty or desirable. When my friend Christine's twenty-one-year-old brother came home from the navy, I was eager to meet the bad-boy icon I had heard so much about. Tales of this handsome guitar-playing philosopher intrigued me.

I had one week left of a month-long grounding for another infraction of my parents' rules. Chris called to say her brother was in town and I should come over to meet him.

Having driven Mom crazy all month, when I asked her if I could go visit Chris that Saturday afternoon, she gave in. I drove to their house in Parkman.

On my arrival, I found Dace was more handsome than I'd imagined. His curly blonde hair hung over his ears. Piercing blue eyes peeked out from behind tresses that shimmered with hues of gold. Slouched down on the couch with his long, lean legs crossed on the coffee table, his posture projected his comfort and easygoing attitude.

When I entered, he jumped up to greet me. Tall and slim, he thrust his hand out to shake mine, and I blushed.

"Want a Coke, Kelly?" I loved the way he said my name.

"Sure."

He strode into the kitchen, bell-bottoms swishing together, dragging on the floor. The worn leather belt on his low-rise jeans held them firmly to his hips. His knit shirt clung to his torso, accentuating his physique. I ran my hands along my goose-bumped arms.

When he returned, I took the tall glass of icy soda and sat with him and Chris in the living room. I breathed deeply, concentrated on relaxing and tried to control my nervous shivering, attempting to appear cool and composed.

Dace and I hit it off, and he asked me to go to a movie that night. With one weekend left of my punishment, I'd have to lie to get my way. I told my parents I wanted to go to a movie with Chris's family, so they agreed. She picked me up and brought me to their house. Dace and I left in his car.

At the theater, I couldn't concentrate on the film, and sat rigidly in the hard seats, making my back stiff. Afterward, we had pizza nearby.

Eating our pie, I did more listening than talking. He wiped a spot of sauce from my upper lip. His tender touch embarrassed me.

We got home late. He shut the engine off.

"I had a nice time tonight. Did you?"

I smiled and nodded. "I did, thank you."

"Would you like to go out again sometime?"

Once more, I could only smile and nod. He reached forward, gently placed his hand behind my neck, and drew me to him for a deep, soft kiss.

My parents watched at the window. I was in a strange car with a man they had never seen before. Suddenly the passenger door flew open and my arm jerked right. My father had my elbow and yanked me out of the car.

"I don't know who the heck this clown is, but you can tell him good-bye."

"Dad, don't." I stumbled to my feet. Humiliation won out over the anger, and I ran toward the house with my father just inches behind me.

That's how they learned about Dace—not a good first impression.

∞∞∞∞∞∞∞∞∞∞∞∞∞∞

Dace Easton's return ignited my sensual awakening. He was full of compliments, and within days, we were together as one. His intimate experiences encompassed countries renowned for their unconventional practices. My skills were limited to high school exploits in my boyfriend's basement and flirting under the bleachers after twirling my baton in football game halftime shows.

However, familiarity came quickly. One evening in his bedroom, he exploded with frustration. "I thought you were a majorette. You have no rhythm. You're a lousy lay."

I sat in silence and stared at him.

"Did you hear what I just said? You-are-a-lousy-lay. Don't you have anything to say about that?"

Shrugging, my gaze drifted to the floor. I felt my face burn crimson, and tears stung my eyes. He wanted to fight. I didn't. I drew my knees to my chest. I longed to crawl inside myself and disappear.

He took pity on me and heaved a sigh.

"Okay, look. You just stick with me and I'll teach you, okay?" He sat beside me on the bed and put his arm around my shoulders.

I was mortified. I'd never thought about being good in that area of my life. I'd had only one steady boyfriend, and sex had been a quick weekend event, an expected routine.

Maybe I should just walk away from him. He's a jerk and wants to hurt me. Still, maybe he can teach me. I guess that matters.

10

I forced the corners of my mouth up and blinked away tears. Squeezing my shoulders gently, he leaned his head into mine. "Just stick with me. You'll improve." His softened voice lessened the sting a little.

The next time we were together he put large, padded headphones over my ears and blasted Pink Floyd when we made out.

"Just listen to the music," he coached. "Close your eyes. Relax and just let the music take you away."

Letting go in this way was new to me, but I paid attention to his instructions. The headphones helped me overcome my inhibitions, and in a short time, I seemed to be living up to his expectations. Names of other girls dropped off his schedule, which looked more like a scoreboard than a calendar.

Each time we got together, we had sex. His tenderness made it feel more like making love than simply fooling around. Floods of oxytocin overwhelmed me, and I soon confused the hormone rush with love, something I was too immature to handle. It created a union that blinded me to my lover's faults, and I perceived a mutual bond that perhaps didn't exist.

∞∞∞∞∞∞∞∞∞∞∞∞∞∞

Starting in 1974, Belkin Productions hosted the World Series of Rock at Cleveland's Lakefront Stadium, home of the Cleveland Indians baseball team. In August of 1977, Dace scored two tickets. We planned to spend the day listening to Peter Frampton, Bob Seger & the Silver Bullet Band, The J. Geils Band, and Derringer.

Still shy and unsure of myself, I sat in silence throughout the day, grooving to the music and smoking pot.

The break between bands seemed to drag. We amused ourselves by mocking the countless women who

11

fancied themselves Farrah Fawcett-Majors, America's favorite Charlie's Angel. All sported tight spandex clothes, suntan-colored pantyhose, and of course the famous Farrah-do. Bleached-blonde hair feathered out to the side and sprayed stiff crowned the heads of short, tall, thin, heavy, pretty, homely, Caucasian, Asian, even African-American women. Everyone wanted to be Farrah.

When the sun set, the temperature dipped. I grew bored, stiff, and sleepy. I noticed my boyfriend getting edgy. He tapped his foot, squirmed in his chair, and breathed hard. He seethed with hatred and whispered through clenched teeth, "Look at him."

I couldn't see whom he was talking about and he became impatient with me.

"There—that jackhole down there."

At last, I saw the source of his rage. A stoned guy a few rows below us in the bleachers had wrapped himself in an American flag to stay warm.

"He's just cold and wasted." I was calm. I had never seen him so agitated, and while it disturbed me, his patriotism impressed me. *He loves his country*, I concluded, dismissing his demeanor.

After the concert he maneuvered his car through the maze of vehicles exiting the parking lot. We continued to smoke pot. Out on the street, he gained speed. The 8-track stereo blasted Bob Seger.

The road opened before us and he spun around a corner. The passenger door flew open and, not wearing a seatbelt, I felt myself slipping out. Still insecure, I didn't want to yell.

Within the next few seconds, my mind lined up the details of me losing my grip on the console and flying out of the car. I pictured myself hitting the grass alongside the road. How badly would I be hurt? Would he even notice me gone? On impulse, I gripped tighter and raised my voice slightly, "Hey."

Dace looked over and grabbed my arm. "Oh crap." He pulled the car over to let me close the door. "We nearly lost you there. Why didn't you say something?"

"I did," I said quietly. He grinned and I was self-conscious, but felt safe and taken care of.

Time together intensified our relationship. We smoked pot, ate pizza, drank beer, attended concerts, listened to heavy metal music at his home, and talked.

We discussed the boyfriend I'd had since seventh grade and how, after five years, we'd split up. He told me about the woman he left behind in the Philippines who claimed to be pregnant with his child. He denied the validity of her claim and told of leaving her crying, rejected by her family. My heart hurt for her. *Why would she lie about that? Maybe Dace should've stayed to take care of her.*

He regaled me with stories of his time and duties in the navy, describing in detail events that could never have been true. I would've realized the error in the timing of his war tales if I had ever listened in history class or even watched the television news. Still, I hung on his every word, mesmerized by his steel-blue eyes, blonde curls, and full lips.

A rhythm guitar player, he played for long stretches of time when we were together. With a physical resemblance to Jimmy Page, lead vocalist of Led Zeppelin, he focused much of his time playing their songs. He had a good voice and above-average guitar skills, and I enjoyed my private concerts. However, sometimes I just wanted to watch TV. Music was very important to him, and he talked about someday being in a band. He often described what their album covers would be like, drawing every detail. I couldn't wait to see where he would go with his music.

It wasn't just Led Zeppelin's music that intrigued him. Band members Robert Plant and Jimmy Page were interested in the occult. Page once lived in Satanist Aleister Crowley's house, the Boleskine House, in the Scottish Highlands.

Dace spent hours investigating "Zofo" (also read as Zoso), Page's emblem on the inner jacket of Led Zeppelin's unnamed fourth album. Each band member had a symbol many believed to be runes—alphabet characters used by ancient Germanic peoples, often associated with magic. Dace was obsessed with Zofo, often referring to himself that way. (Years later, in secret defiance, I mentally changed the name to Bozo, the iconic clown.)

Christine shared stories about her brother with me for two years before I'd met him. I knew he had a bad temper and drank too much. She told me how he and their stepfather, Lino, had physical confrontations and court battles.

She told about a large cardboard box full of pornography, including some child porn, brought into the courtroom. According to Christine, Lino said the magazines had belonged to Dace. "You found them in *his* apartment, didn't you?" her brother had declared with the self-righteousness of a teenager who had one up on his authority.

The judge had given Dace the choice of joining the military then or risking another infraction, which would land him in a juvenile detention center. He joined the U.S. Navy.

I learned about how, in a drunken rage while home on leave, he vandalized the turn-of-the-century one-room schoolhouse that sat in their backyard. I saw none of this in Dace. Aside from yelling at me in the bedroom and being mad at the stoner at the concert, he seemed calm and in control all the time. *Probably the booze. I'm so glad he's not like that anymore.*

Throughout high school, I had loved to spend time at Christine's house. The classic northeastern Ohio Century Home had part of the Underground Railroad in the basement.   The brightly lit laundry room in the basement felt safe, with no oppressive darkness or apprehension there. Bricks concealed the entrance to part of the secret route used by slaves during the nineteenth century. Some of the bricks had been removed revealing a dark passageway.

I begged to see where it led. "Chris, grab a flashlight; let's go in there."

"No way. Lino would have a fit. He said it's dangerous and we might get killed in there."

Still my curiosity burned and awakened a desire to explore the tunnel.

Although he seemed nice, I never felt safe around Lino. I made sure to never be alone with him. After all, Chris had accused him of some heinous crimes.

He owned three grocery stores, the original one was housed in an older building with wooden floors, in a town an hour away. The initial charm disappeared when the smell of stale lunchmeat wafted from the small meat department in the corner. The produce section held two coolers displaying in-season crops. A rack of the latest comic books obscured steep wooden stairs to a basement.

"See those steps?" Chris whispered as we looked at the comic books one day.

"Yeah. What about 'em?"

"That's where he takes them."

15

"Takes who?"

"Shhhh. I'll tell you later."

Lino approached us. "Take this rib roast home to your mother, Chrissie. You girls can each get a candy bar on your way out. Be careful going home."

We thanked him, chose our favorites, and left.

On the way home, Christine explained. "Whenever he catches a girl shoplifting, he takes her into the basement of the store and makes a deal with her."

"What do you mean?" I thought I understood, but couldn't fathom it.

"He tells them that he won't tell the police or her parents if she . . . you know, lets him."

"Are you *sure*?" My mind whirled with disbelief, concern for girls who, like me, had shoplifted.

"Yep. You know Barb—the girl from school with the big boobs who lives across the road?"

I nodded, dreading the rest of the report.

"Well, he found us smoking pot in the barn. He told her he wouldn't tell her parents if she'd let him feel her up. She told me about it later. He's messed with me before too. He has big fat hands," Chris murmured, drifting off in thought.

"Just watch the road." I didn't want to believe her. It had become common knowledge among our school friends that you don't believe 80 percent of what Christine said and you question the other 20 percent.

Considering there might be some fact to what she said, her brother's accusations of this man's involvement in a child pornography ring made sense to me now. Dace always called him "Fat Arse." I wondered if Lino had ever molested him. I appreciated my boyfriend never leaving me alone with him. *Just another way he takes care of me. That's a good sign that he loves me.*

16

Chapter Three: Confusing the Signs

Junior year ended and summer vacation began.

I drove to Janice and Lino's house to see Dace. Turning my stereo down, I maneuvered my parents' old matador-red Oldsmobile around the circular driveway, trying not to kick up dust.

I stopped at the side door and clicked open my seatbelt. Just as I shut the engine off, my car door flew open. Dace grabbed my wrist and pulled me out, jerking my shoulder.

"What are you doing?" I tried not to be frightened. He flung the screen door open and dragged me upstairs. I stumbled, laughed and struggled to keep up.

Once we were in his bedroom, he slammed the door behind us. "How long have you been on the Pill?" he gasped, winded from running up the stairs.

"What? Why?" My head spun and I squinted to bring him into focus.

"How long?" he demanded.

"Since I was about fifteen, why?"

"You have to stop taking it."

"What are you talking about?" I cocked my head sideways and scowled.

"The Pill. You have to get off of it." He made no sense.

"Why?"

"I read an article that said the Pill could cause cancer. You have to stop taking it."

He had already refused to use condoms, but that didn't cross my mind. My seventeen-year-old gullibility brought me to the conclusion that he cared about my health.

Dace moved out of his parents' home and rented one of four apartments in an old house in a nearby town.

Being with Dace ignited the slow-burning rebellion I'd welcomed into my life as a child who dabbled with the supernatural. Our first date had been a lie. I could see that my parents didn't like him, but I determined to date him.

After yet another argument with my mother, I threw some clothes into two large garbage bags, scribbled a note that I was going to live with my boyfriend, and drove off.

Dace looked surprised when I showed up at his door. Within three hours, my dad arrived. "You don't have to come home, but you sure as heck aren't staying here."

"Then take me to Gramma and Grampa's." He did. That satisfied me, and I lived with them for a few months. During my stay there, Gramma filled my soul with love and my tummy with her apple butter.

My grandmother's apple butter represented an accepting smile and warm embrace, like an edible gift. It had the texture of applesauce and the color of red-brown cinnamon. The apples came from the trees in her yard. When it simmered on the stove, the house smelled sweet and spicy at once. She would make quarts of that love-in-a-jar and stock her pantry. More would be frozen in plastic containers. When I was little, for a couple days after each batch, I would run upstairs to the second floor in her house and inhale the lingering aroma of Gramma's unconditional love.

With my spirit calmed and feeling loved, I eventually returned to my parents' house for a continuation of the strife we called normal. I continued to visit Dace at his apartment.

"Guitars are like women," he had once observed. "Guys like the thin, sleek ones because they look sexy and cool. We like the thicker ones because they're good to hang onto. But with women, you don't know if the thicker ones will just get thicker, so we stick with the thin ones."

I heard him loud and clear. Although not overweight, my build was like an ironing board, sort of up and down. Gramma called me athletic. I may have been normal among my friends, but to him, I was thick.

I get what he's saying.

In response, I took diet pills I bought at the grocery store. They made me mean and short-tempered. We seemed to argue more than ever. Still I continued to take them. I was miserable, vacillating between hunger pains, bloating, heart palpitations, and burning stomachaches.

Why should I care what he thinks? He's a turkey. These pills are eating my gut. Still, his words had power over me. I wanted to please him.

That summer I worked part time in the meat department of a local grocery store. My direct manager was a five-foot-nine fat man in his early forties.

In the close quarters of the small meat department, he seemed to take advantage of every occasion to slide his big belly by me. "Oops—it's close in here." His obvious delight in the "oops" opportunities nauseated me.

He spoke of church and God, and quoted verses from the Bible. Yet he never missed the opportunity to laugh out sexual innuendos. After the initial awkwardness passed, I thought it somewhat funny. However, when I recognized the paradox of a so-called Christian, spewing dirty jokes, the humor drained.

With a childhood of Sunday school lessons under my belt, I knew enough to recognize hypocrisy when it rubbed up against me. I started hating my job. In my revolt, I stole packages of lunchmeat, steaks, and pork chops for my lover. It added a thrill to my days.

As I consumed diet pills, my attitude grew menacing. Reverting to an idea that had haunted me for years, I flirted with thoughts of suicide.

"You know, Dace, if I died, everyone would be better off."

"What? That's jive. Who are you talking about anyway?"

"Just everyone really. My parents are always ticked off at me. That jerk at work never lets up with his filthy comments. You think I'm fat. At least *I'd* be better off. There are plenty of knives at work." I left it at that. He didn't push.

Following the normal routine, I smoked pot on my way to work. I clocked in and shuffled to the back by the walk-in freezer to put an apron on. Flying high, I tottered, head down, and almost walked into a meat hook.

The manager grabbed me sideways and kept me from spearing myself. "Watch it, girl. You're gonna pierce your face." He seemed to hold on longer than necessary.

I blushed. "Ah, oh yeah. Thanks."

He slid his hands down my arms. "You'd better wake up, girl. Gotta look up when you walk around here."

I took a deep breath and nodded, grabbed an apron, threw it on, and entered the freezer to retrieve the long metal tray of Styrofoam plates full of ground beef. I groaned. The butcher had done it again. He took the old, brown ground beef and put fresh pink beef on the outside.

What a putz, I thought as I proceeded to wrap each foam tray of meat in plastic shrink-wrap, touching it onto the hot pad to seal the bottom. I added a price label with

20

the current date, making the whole thing look fresh. I hated being part of his duplicity.

Friday the store closed at nine. I anticipated the weekend, but had to work Saturday. Dace was mad, again.

"That's *our* time," he'd always whine.

"You know I have to work, Dace. I don't have a choice. I'm sorry." Working weekends was made worse anticipating the fight that would result later. It had become predictable.

Too much to worry about. I should blow tomorrow off. I just wanted to go to sleep.

Upon returning home from work that night, my parents stopped me in the kitchen. Dad tried to sound casual to avoid a nasty confrontation with me by using my family's nickname for me.

"K.J., what was Dace's mother talking about?"

I rolled my eyes. "When did you talk to his mother?" I didn't usually snap at my father, but he wasn't making sense.

"She called here today and upset your mother. What was she talking about?"

"How am I supposed to know? She's bananas anyway. What'd she say?"

"She called here and told your mother that you said you were going to kill yourself. She said that you were going to take a knife from the meat department at work and stab yourself."

Even though exhausted, my ability to lie well did not fail me. I let out an exasperated moan. "I have no idea what she's talking about, Dad. I told you she's crazy. Why would I do that? And why would I use a knife? She's nuts. Just don't listen to her. Can I go to bed now? I'm tired and I have to work in the morning."

"Yeah, go ahead. I told your mother she's just trying to cause trouble. We'll see you in the morning, babe."

Whew. I got through that confrontation quickly. I dragged my feet down the long hallway to my bedroom, closed the door, and turned my radio on. Getting ready for bed, I pondered the possible reasons Dace might have had for telling Janice that I had mentioned suicide. Did he tell her to call my parents? Did he think my parents would make me quit my job? *I guess he really cares about me.*

Early Saturday morning I stocked the meat case. Just before the store opened, my boss told me to come into the break room. My manager was there too. So was Dace.

"Dace, what are you doing here?"

Before he could answer, the owner proceeded, "Your boyfriend told me things you said your manager said—inappropriate things."

"He's an effin' dirty old man is what I said."

"Dace," I gasped, overwhelmed with the confrontation. My face smoldered with shame. I stared at the floor and refused to make eye contact with anyone.

"Gosh, Kelly. I'm sorry if I offended you. You're a young gal, and maybe you didn't understand me." The butcher sounded like Eddie Haskell from the *Leave It to Beaver Show.*

Although humiliated at the confrontation, I was furious that he would insinuate I misunderstood him.

"No, I'm not stupid. I understood you." My words were quiet but curt.

"So, Kelly, do you think you can still work here or not?" my boss quizzed me impatiently.

I paused. I needed the job. My boyfriend stood there shaking his head. "I don't think so," he chimed in.

"Kelly, what do you think?" my boss demanded. He wanted an answer immediately.

If I quit, my parents would be furious. If I stayed, Dace would be furious. Furthermore, staying would tell the filthy old geezer that I didn't mind his sexual wordplay. Frankly, I hated hearing about his wife's breasts and their intimate adventures.

"Nah. I can't stay here."

Dace smiled widely.

The storeowner sighed. "Give me your apron and clock out. I'll send your final paycheck to your house."

My lover walked me out of the store with his arm around my shoulders. I felt badly for letting the owner down and leaving the department shorthanded on a Saturday. While I feared facing my parents, I felt taken care of and loved. I liked it. He lit my cigarette.

That afternoon we hung out at the stone quarry at Nelson Ledges. Together we smoked pot under the trees beside the gigantic water-filled pit.

"I love it here at the Ledges," I whispered. He didn't answer. He seemed deep in thought.

He finally spoke. "I think it's time you learned how to meditate."

"Okay. Teach me." At least he spoke to me.

"Alright. Relax." He leaned against a rock, and I leaned against him. I took a deep breath and closed my eyes.

"Try to clear your mind of everything," he coached.

I concentrated. "That's hard. Just when I think I'm not thinking of anything, there I am in the back of my

23

mind saying, 'Am I thinking of anything?' I can't seem to shut my mind up."

"It's hard, I know. You'll have to practice. Tonight when you lie down to go to sleep, just picture the palm of your hand. Imagine every line and wrinkle. That'll help."

"That's it?"

"Yep. Just start with that. It's hard to stop all the conversation in your mind. This is a good place to start."

That night before I went to bed, I studied my hand. I shut the light off, crawled into bed, and turned the radio off. I pictured my palm, bringing each line into focus in my mind's eye. I tried to relax my mind and open up like he had suggested.

Dark dreams crept into my peaceful rest. I dreamed I was in my grandmother's attic, with the picture of my great-grandmother. The large oval frame with the convex glass held the image of a lovely woman who had died when my grandmother was just a child. Growing up, I had always wanted to look at the picture, but the eyes spooked me, as they seemed to follow me around the attic. Often I would turn the photo around so I didn't have to look at it, or so the woman couldn't look at me.

In my dream, I looked at the picture again. The woman's face morphed into a different woman, an older woman from a previous generation—a witch. *That* face was mine. Old and wrinkled, but I understood that I was a witch from a previous generation. I awoke with a start and shuddered with fear.

The next day I told Dace about my dream. He was very interested.

"You opened the door, Kelly. You saw that you were a witch many years ago. Do it again another night, but not tonight. Give yourself some time in between."

I agreed. I wanted him to be proud of me, and I seemed to have touched on something of importance to him.

The following weekend I told him I wanted to imagine my palm again and see what new information awaited me.

"You know, Kelly, I thought about it." He proceeded, choosing his words carefully, "You opened a door to the dark side—to the supernatural. When you open the door to go in, the door is open for things to come out too. I don't think you should ever do that again. You aren't ready for what might come out, and you're not really ready to go in. I don't think the door is *still* open just from that one experience, but you don't know what will happen next. Don't ever do it again, alright, Kelly?"

I didn't fully understand, but agreed. The experience had frightened me and made me question my lineage and my own soul's purity. Agreeing to not do it again was easy. Still, I couldn't help wonder why he didn't want me to pursue something that seemed so promising. Was he concerned about what might happen to me? Or afraid that something he wasn't ready to deal with would confront him?

I guess he just cares about me.

∞∞∞∞∞∞∞∞∞∞∞∞

While in my backyard smoking a joint one evening that summer, Dace was unusually quiet. After we ignited and snorted the last of the tiny roach, he stood in front of me.

"I think we should break up."

It was out of the blue, and I panicked. "Why? I thought you liked me."

"I do, but I think we should have some time apart."

I spent the night crying. A shadow of sadness engulfed me. I believed he'd broken up with me because I was fat.

"I won't eat anything but celery and drink only Tab until I lose fifteen pounds," I declared to Suzie.

"You're bananas. You can't live on that."

"Watch me."

I took every upper I could find. I bought diet pills from a friend at school whose doctor had her on a weight-loss plan.

Other friends said, "No, you want ludes," the drug de jour. But Quaaludes were depressants and I was down enough. No, I craved uppers.

I anxiously waited for Clark, a classmate, to bring some speed that Friday while my parents were at work. He had Christmas Trees, also called Green and Clears. We hadn't discussed price, but he supplied drugs for most of my friends, and I thought he'd be fair.

Clark's beat-up 1970 Pontiac Trans Am roared into the driveway. He ran to the back door. *He's in a rush. Good. Sell me the pills and split.*

"You alone?" he said at the back door.

"Yeah, my parents are at work."

"Lemme in." He pushed past me.

"Ah, okay. C'mon in."

He had a bad reputation, so I was unsure about letting him into our house. If my parents ever found out, they'd ground me for sure.

"You want some water?" I offered.

"Nah. Come in here." He hurried into the living room. "Come here." Clark grabbed me and drew me close to him. He kissed me roughly, straining my neck. "You want these Christmas Trees? Let's get it on." He pushed me onto the sofa.

26

Having only had two boyfriends, I had little experience saying no. Shame swallowed me up as I succumbed to Clark's full advances.

Within ten minutes, he was standing over me.

"You can have these Trees."

He tossed a sandwich bag tied into a knot, containing a couple dozen capsules, onto my bare midriff. I stood and put myself together.

"Ah, thanks." *Did I just thank him?*

"Gotta split. I've got more of those when you need 'em."

He ran out the back door and into his car. Sitting on the sofa in disbelief, I heard the Trans Am thunder down the road. I had sunk to a new low.

I just had sex for drugs. No effin' way. I didn't want to, but I didn't try to stop him.

I took a quick bath, gulped down four of the pills, and took my parents' car to the bridge in Parkman where Suzie and I used to hang out. I parked my car, walked under the road, and sat on the slanted cement. Occasionally a car rumbled overhead.

I think I'm going to live here. I'll just run away and live here.

Why not? I'd be out of the rain. I could steal food when I got hungry. I could do it. Surely, I could.

Hyper and yet depressed, I left the bridge and absentmindedly meandered along the sidewalk. I found myself walking along RT 422, a four-lane highway, to the Ledges. I craved pot and knew I would be able to find whatever drug I wanted once I got to the park that seemed to attract teenagers, pushers, and dope smokers.

A beautifully restored 1968 Ford Mustang pulled alongside me as I walked. The man behind the wheel leaned over toward the passenger window and beckoned me in.

"I'm not a crazy guy," he yelled. "You need a ride. You shouldn't be walking on this busy road. Why don't you just get in?"

"No, no thanks." I forced a slight smile and kept going. My stomach tightened. He followed slowly, checking in his rearview mirror at the traffic that whizzed by.

"Where you going?"

Tears stung my eyes. "I don't know."

"You shouldn't be alone here. Why don't you get in? I'm not gonna hurt you."

I hesitated. I knew better. Inside my head, I screamed no. But my apathy dragged me deeper into the canal of depression. I hopped in.

Gaining speed, he kept looking over at me. He wouldn't stop smiling. He was older, maybe in his mid-thirties. His thick, wavy brown hair came to the top of his shoulders. He was unshaven and dirty.

With the windows down, he had to shout. "What's your name?"

"Kelly," I yelled over the roar of the engine and the wind.

"I'm Leslie. Yeah, I know it's a chick's name. Hey, Kelly, what's a fine-looking young lady like you doing walking down this busy road?"

"I don't know."

"You don't know where you're going or why you're going there. I can take you." He laughed, punching the accelerator.

"Why don't you turn up here? It goes to the Ledges."

Leslie took a sharp turn right and we sped along the country road.

Memories of Elaine Zeigler flooded my mind. We were sophomores when Elaine disappeared. She had been vacationing with her family in Florida and had vanished from a KOA Campground in Brooksville. A shockwave had gone through our small high school as the news spread after Christmas break.

The year 1976 began, and America launched its yearlong Bicentennial celebration, but the disbelief and sorrow of our friend's kidnapping overshadowed any local jubilation.

Now here I was, being stupid and putting myself at risk. Would I meet whatever fate she had met? Would I end up dead at the Ledges among the numerous rocky crags? Would my body be weighted and thrown into the deep quarry with the many rusting cars scuba divers reported every year?

The parking lot came into view. "Wanna park here?" Leslie yelled.

I nodded and tensed. He shut the car off and twisted toward me.

"Now, Kelly, what's going on? What do you want?"

While having someone ask me what I wanted felt sublime, I felt uneasy about talking openly with a stranger. "I'm just here to score some weed." Surely, this guy wasn't a narc.

"I don't have any weed, but I can get us some beer, that's for sure."

Booze was my second favorite escape hatch—I'd been drinking since I was twelve.

"Sounds good to me." I smiled.

"I'll tell you what," he suggested. "Let's go out tonight. You got a car?"

"Yes, I can borrow my parents' car. Right now it's parked by the bridge. You can take me there."

"Well then, you meet me back here at seven tonight and we'll drink some beer. Sound good? Give me your number and I'll call if I'm delayed."

"That's fine." The thought of giving this stranger my address and phone number sent a flag flying high in my mind. I remembered when, at thirteen, I gave my address to Jesus-freak boys at a park in Pennsylvania.

A month later when they pulled into our driveway in their colorful van plastered with "Jesus Saves" and other such messages, my mother had been furious with me.

With the 1969 Manson Family murders of Sharon Tate and friends still fresh in my mother's mind, she had declared that those young men were there to kill us all.

But now, what did I have to lose? I'd been dumped. I wanted to party, and this guy offered me a free party. But would it be free? My speed hadn't been free that morning. What would he expect in return? *He* wasn't talking about Jesus. Mental red flags of warning popped up with everything Leslie said.

I chose to ignore the red flags, pushed the thought back, and gave him my information.

That night I told my parents I was meeting Suzie to go roller-skating with her nephews. They were just six and four, and we often babysat them while Suzie's oldest sister worked or went out with her husband. They were a handy excuse that worked every time.

Driving to Nelson Ledges, I worried about meeting with a man I'd just met that day. It was dusk, and the rocks, caves, and ravines at the Ledges were impossible to navigate in the dark.

Leslie arrived before me. "Where can we drink this beer?" he said. He looked better than when I'd met him earlier that day. He had shaved, showered, and changed clothes. That made me happy.

"Well, there's another part of this place up the road about a mile," I suggested. "We call that part Kennedy Ledges, although this whole place is actually Nelson-Kennedy Ledges. There's a dirt road off to the left. My friends have camped there before."

"Hop in. Let's go."

I got into his Mustang. He peeled out of the driveway and instructed me to pop open a beer for him and one for me. I pulled the tab off, threw it out the window, and handed him the can. I opened another for myself.

I guzzled the ice-cold beer. I hated the taste, but after the first can, the flavor disappeared into the chill. I just opened my throat and chug-a-lugged the way Suzie and I learned at parties her three older sisters brought us to. Two beers downed and we were parking the car in a small clearing among the trees.

"This is a great place," Leslie yelled.

"Yeah, my old boyfriend camped here. The cops never come up here."

Within minutes, conversation gave way to embracing, which advanced to fooling around on the hood of this beautiful, metallic-blue 1968 Mustang.

It was uncomfortable, but I only had to endure for a moment. An instant later, the worthless, hollow encounter morphed into another shameful memory.

We dressed and he took me back to my car. "I have to get going," he offered apologetically.

31

"Whatever," I responded. It wasn't the first time I'd been in this position. Wham, bam, thank you, ma'am. *It doesn't even matter.*

"I want to see you tomorrow." Leslie surprised me. Frankly, I didn't think I'd ever see him again. "I want you to meet my friend C.J. I'll call you."

As I watched him speed off, my mind reeled. I had to get home. Why did he want me to meet his friend? *I hope he doesn't tell him about tonight,* I worried.

∞∞∞∞∞∞∞∞∞∞∞∞∞∞

"Hello? Yes, she's here. May I tell her who's calling? Just a minute."

"Kelly, phone," Mom yelled toward my closed bedroom door at the end of the hallway. She didn't work on Saturday. She didn't have to yell. I could hear the whole conversation.

When I came into the kitchen, my mother covered the mouthpiece of the phone and whispered. "Who is Leslie? He sounds like a grown man."

I rolled my eyes and snatched the receiver out of her hand. "Hello? Hi there. Yeah. Yeah. Okay." I placed the handset back onto the wall phone and quickly headed toward the hall.

"Wait a minute," she snapped.

Stopping abruptly, I groaned, spun around, and snarled. "What?"

"Who's Leslie and where did you meet him?"

"And so the interrogation begins. He's just a dude I met at the Ledges. I'm going bowling with him and his brother tonight."

"When were you at the Ledges? You know I don't like you going there. Hippies and potheads hang out there."

"Whatever." I started to walk away.

"Get back here. Don't walk away from me." My mother seemed determined to win this round. "Why haven't you mentioned him to us before?"

"Maybe I wanted to avoid this," I retorted, waving back and forth, palms upward. "You want me to go back to Dace?"

"No, not really, we—"

Before she could finish her sentence, I snapped her off with another mean-spirited quip. Spinning on my heels, I shouted from the hall, "I'm getting ready. I don't want to be late."

"Is he picking you up?"

I muttered an annoyed, "Ah-huh," and closed my bedroom door.

Two hours later, I emerged with my makeup applied to perfection and a new shirt on. "Where'd you get that top?"

My heavy sigh and grimace told her I was ready for round two. I'd stolen the shirt at the mall and would conceal that information at all costs.

"Never mind. I want to meet him when he gets here."

"Are you serious?" I planted my feet firmly and glared at her, ready for a fight. "You just can't help but embarrass me, can you?"

"Look, Kelly. Your dad's working late tonight and I want to meet this Leslie guy. Just have him come in."

I waited on the back porch. The cool night air felt good and I inhaled deeply.

"I mean it, Kelly."

"I will. God, Mom."

"Don't say the Lord's name in vain or you won't go anywhere tonight, young lady."

My mother rarely backed down from my defiant attitude. The verbal jabs had become the defining point of this vicious dance we called a relationship. Mutual animosity kept the atmosphere in our house tense, and I felt certain that my mom couldn't wait until I turned eighteen and moved out. The feeling was mutual.

The crunch of tires on the dirt road announced Leslie's arrival and I went out to meet him. With the windows open, my mother could hear him come to a stop in the driveway. Muffled voices and snide laughter told her that had I informed my date of his required presence inside.

"That's cool," he said eagerly. He swung the car door shut. The grass rustled as we sauntered toward the back door.

"Mom, Leslie's here. You wanted to meet him, didn't you?"

She entered the kitchen and saw the man at the back door. "Hi. I'm Leslie. I'll have Kelly home by a decent hour tonight."

"Hello, Leslie. It's nice to meet you. Where will you be taking her tonight?"

"We're going bowling. My brother's in the car. Would you like to meet him?"

"No, that's not necessary. Have fun and bring her home safely . . . before eleven."

I rolled my eyes. *As if she even cares.*

"You didn't miss a beat," I whispered, mindful that the open windows afforded my keen-hearing mother audience to everything we said.

I got in the front seat and greeted C.J. in the back seat. Pulling out onto the main road, I lit a cigarette. "So, where are we really going?"

"We're going back to the Ledges to party."

34

My stomach flipped. He didn't expect me to have sex with this guy, too, did he? I didn't really know either of them. Again, thoughts of Elaine shot through my head.

At the Ledges, we stayed in the parking lot with other groups of people. I felt safe in the crowd. The sweet fragrance of marijuana hung in the air. WMMS, Cleveland's favorite hard-rock radio station, blared from cars in the lot. Occasional snorting could be heard. "Someone's got coke," Leslie said. "Kelly, want some cocaine?"

"No thanks."

I'd never seen the advantage of snorting coke. I had snorted it with no effect. I always felt a little guilty for wasting my friends' money.

"C.J., you want some?"

"Yeah. Think you can score?"

"I'll tool around and see what I can come up with." Leslie walked away and C.J. moved closer to me. I leaned against the back of the Mustang and lit up. I handed him the joint while holding in my toke.

"Leslie told me about you guys on the 'Stang hood. Hot."

Humiliated, I was grateful that the moon wasn't brighter. I gave C.J. a dirty look, snatched the joint from his hand, and took another deep drag. Holding my breath, I swallowed hard, choking back the smoke. Then I burst forth with a loud cough. C.J. laughed wildly.

"Shut the eff up, jackhole."

"Ooooh, a feisty one. Les told me you had a lip." Without missing a beat, he threw a verbal cross punch. "Hey, Kelly, did you know that Leslie is married?"

I froze. "He's what?"

"Yeah, he's married and his old lady's preggers. He didn't tell you *that* while you were doing the wild thing on the hood, did he?"

My gut wrenched and I thought I would throw up. I couldn't leave fast enough. Just then, Leslie walked up. "Couldn't score. Everyone's paranoid. Do I look like a narc? Crap."

From my expression, he could see something had happened. "C.J., what the heck did you do to her?"

"Just told her about Laura is all."

"Jackhole. I told you I would."

Leslie turned to me. "I planned to tell you tonight before I dropped you off, Kelly. Really." He reached for my elbows to draw me closer. I pulled away.

"When? After you tried to screw me again?"

C.J. snickered loudly.

"No. No, really. I was going to tell you tonight."

"Just take me home. I want to go right now."

"Suit yourself. C.J., hop in back."

I got in and we sped off into the darkness. I thought of what Leslie could do with a woman he wanted to keep secret. Fear overwhelmed me. He gained speed, and I imagined that he might wreck the car out of spite. I was never so glad to see the dirt road that led to my house.

Leslie walked me to the door. The light on the outside of the barn made a large, bright circle on the grass. He stepped just outside the circle and turned toward me.

"Can I have just one last kiss?"

"Why? You have a wife," I whispered.

"That's why—just one last kiss to remember you by."

I wanted him to go and to never see him again. Maybe giving him a kiss would speed his disappearance along. With my arms at my sides, I leaned forward at the waist and quickly kissed his mouth.

Spinning around, I headed toward the back door of the house.

"I'm really sorry, Kelly."

I strode inside without looking back.

Darkness filled the back room, and I climbed the two steps into the kitchen. I saw my mother's silhouette against the light from the living room.

"Kelly, I want to talk to you." She didn't sound angry. This piqued my interest. I stood before her in the dim kitchen. The barn light faintly illuminated her face, softening her expression. She was pretty.

"Kelly," she began with a controlled tone. Not just controlled, but kind.

I wonder who died.

"A woman named Laura called tonight."

Oh, crap.

"She said she's Leslie's wife. Did you know about her?"

"He just told me tonight."

"I didn't think you knew. You aren't going to see him again, are you?"

"No, of course not." I controlled the tone of my voice and swallowed hard. After all, Mom wasn't screaming at me.

Frankly, I couldn't figure her out. Then her words sank in. "I didn't think you knew." That was benevolent thinking toward me. Surprised, I didn't want to ruin the moment.

"He just told me, so I told him I wanted to come home right away."

"Did he also tell you she's pregnant?"

"Eventually he did. Creep."

"She called here tonight while you were gone. At first she was mad, and then she cried. I felt sorry for her. I don't know why she'd want to be married to a slimeball like him anyway, but she is pregnant with his baby."

"How'd she get our number?"

"She said she'd found our number on a slip of paper in his pants pocket. He'd rushed home to take a shower yesterday and left the paper in his dirty pants on the bathroom floor. Sounds like a real winner there, Kelly. I think you dodged a bullet."

"Yeah. I guess I did."

"But, Kelly, I saw you kiss him tonight. Why did you kiss him if you knew he was married?"

"He wouldn't get back into his car and go home. He wanted one last kiss before he'd leave. I figured I'd just kiss the creep to get him out of here."

"I understand. You'd better be careful from now on, Kelly. Well, it's late. Why don't you go to bed now?"

"I will. Thanks, Mom." I slowly turned around and began to leave. I stopped and looked back. The barn light shone through the window behind her, creating a halo. "Good night."

"Good night, K.J."

Shuffling toward my bedroom, my heart and head argued about my mother's motives.

She's setting you up. No, she actually understands. I wonder if something like that has happened to her before.

I went back and forth in my mind until I fell asleep.

By the next week, my broken heart had begun to mend. Then I heard a car come into the driveway. It was Dace.

38

Surprised, I met him in the yard. He got out of his car with purpose and approached me.

"I heard you were out with some dude named Leslie." He sounded accusatory.

Stupid Christine.

"Yep. You dumped me, so why not?"

"It was just a test, Kelly—a test to see if you'd wait for me or go out with some loser. You failed."

"Don't play head games with me, Dace. What was I supposed to do? Just wait around until you felt like coming back to me? Dream on."

"Actually, yes. That was the test. If you really loved me, you wouldn't have found someone else so fast. Where'd you meet this fool, anyway?"

"That's so bogus. How do you even know he's a fool? You're right, he was. But why do you assume I could only find a fool? I met him while walking to the Ledges."

"You were walking along 422?" His tone vacillated between anger and concern. "You got into a stranger's car? Were you trippin', Kelly?"

"I was looking to score some pot. You weren't around, and I just wanted to get wired."

As the blame game shifted from me to him and back again, his tone softened.

"You need to use your head, Kelly. He could've killed you and buried you in his backyard." He took me by the upper arms and drew me close to him. Holding me against his torso, he whispered, "I guess in your own screwed-up way, you passed the test."

Furious that he had tested my commitment to him, I wanted to pound his chest with my fists. Instead, I rested my head there and listened to his heartbeat. I felt so good wrapped in his arms again—secure and safe. I started to cry. He lifted my chin and kissed me deeply. His kiss was familiar and welcomed. I put my arms around him and held him tightly.

"Don't do it again, Dace. That was hard core. Don't ever do it again."

Chapter Four: Independence

It was senior year, and I drove a faded turquoise Rambler American. My grandparents bought me a light cocoa Ford Mustang with four hundred miles on it. I traded my Rambler to Dace for his extensive record album collection. Then he was mobile and I had some great tunes to enjoy.

The Who; Led Zeppelin; Crosby, Stills, and Nash; Crosby, Stills, Nash, *and Young*; Mott the Hoople; The Doors; Eddie Van Halen; Pink Floyd; Genesis; Rush; David Bowie; Bob Dylan; Aerosmith; The Eagles; John Lennon; Ted Nugent; Bruce Springsteen; Fleetwood Mac; The Rolling Stones; with over three hundred albums, I believed I got the better end of the trade.

Soon after the new school year started, I landed a job at a deli in a larger grocery store in Middlefield. I got it through a work program in school. DCT (Diversified Cooperative Training) was supposed to augment the lessons presented in the classroom—on-the-job training.

Christine tried to get me to join COE (Cooperative Office Education). "You'll dress up and work in an office," she cooed. She was barking up the wrong tree; I avoided all things prim and proper.

I had tried to enter OWE (Occupational Work Experience) because some of my party friends had. Although my personal no-homework rule—"If I don't get it done in study hall, it doesn't get done"—kept me at a steady C average, our principal said my grade average was still too high. He offered DCT instead, and I wanted out of school early each day and took him up on it.

A handful of students from Berkshire, our rival high school, came over for DCT class. The twenty-minute drive gave them the opportunity to smoke dope.

On Friday mornings, our instructor took us out to eat. I learned that some of my classmates struggled academically and others craved early dismissal like me. Most of us got high, and we soon became friends. That's where I met Melanie.

Mel got a job at the deli just before I did. We grew close through working in the tiny corner deli department beside the meat department in the store. Inside jokes about some of the regular customers, and stealing hot chocolate, whipped cream, Oreos, and Nutter Butter peanut butter cookies kept work fun for both of us.

She dated a younger guy from her school. Eric lived in a tiny dilapidated house outside of town. The lawn always needed mowing, and tall weeds had taken over the flowerbeds. He lived with his alcoholic father who used him as a punching bag. The abuse deflected to Melanie. This puzzled me since she was an intelligent, strong, independent woman. I couldn't understand why she tolerated his actions.

"He did it again last night," she reported one day at work.

"What?" Her scowl concerned me.

"Eric wouldn't let me leave his house. He put his stupid pistol against my head and played Russian roulette."

"Mel, you mean he pulled the trigger? Did he say there were bullets in the gun?"

"He said *he* knew, but I would never know."

"Why don't you just kick his can to the curb, Mel? Why do you stay with him? He scares me. He's a chump."

"He said if I ever leave him he'll come to my house and beat my old man up. I don't want my sweet dad to be concerned about this."

"Well maybe you should stop going to his house. You go every day, right?"

"Yep, almost every day. The sex is great, man. I just love him so much. He wouldn't be that way if his drunken, jackhole father didn't punch him all the time."

"Maybe *he* should leave then."

"I know, but he says he's all his father has. He feels he has to take care of him. Bananas, I know."

Dace hated my relationship with Melanie. Perhaps he sensed she could see through his facade.

Although he no longer cared to pretend with me, I still stayed with him. Maybe I stayed because I hated confrontation. Maybe because I had never learned how to say no. Maybe I still loved him; those sex hormones were powerful. It didn't make sense—but I stayed. I felt like a hypocrite telling Mel to leave Eric.

∞∞∞∞∞∞∞∞∞∞∞∞

It was senior prom. I planned to go whether Dace did nor not. With palpable reluctance, he agreed to join me, refusing to pay for anything.

Junior prom had been the opposite. He had asked if he could escort me. He'd learned my dress was robin-egg blue, and arrived in a pale Tiffany-blue shirt-and-tie ensemble. He'd given me a colorful wrist corsage, and I'd presented him with a matching boutonniere.

After he'd graciously posed for photographs, he complimented me on my dress and hair, calling me his "Helen of Troy."

He'd explained the mythological character. Daughter of Zeus, the most mighty Greek god, Helen's beauty was mesmerizing; she had a face that launched a thousand ships, starting the Trojan War. I'd been flattered, impressed by his knowledge, and loved his attention.

Now for senior prom, I bought his shirt-and-tie ensemble. I bought him a pale lemon shirt that matched the daisies on my bright cotton dress, and a boutonniere matching the corsage I bought for myself. I gave him his prom ticket. He agreed to meet me at the golf course hosting the event. I drove myself.

My period was late, and I fretted about being pregnant. The previous year's prom king couldn't be present because his girlfriend was in labor. I wondered if I would follow suit.

I danced with my friends and sat during the slow songs. Dace was absent for most of the evening, and loneliness engulfed me. If only I'd scored some speed.

He and some potheads from my class were out on the golf course getting stoned under the night sky. The few times he popped in, he refused to dance with me. When it was time to go, he snubbed the request to join the group for breakfast and then a day at Cedar Point, our favorite amusement park. "That's baby crap," he protested.

"But, Dace, it's my senior prom. It's the last chance I'll have to do this."

"I told you I didn't want to come to this thing. I agreed to come to this part only. You know I hate this crap."

I drove myself home and spent the following day sleeping. Thoughts of dumping him oscillated through my dreams.

∞∞∞∞∞∞∞∞∞∞∞∞

Years of fights with my parents made me believe they were pushing me out of their house. I had always anticipated moving out, but now I was afraid.

Dace came and went as his interest waned. I focused on completing the school year, keeping gas in my Mustang, and staying high—partying with friends.

Graduation day finally came. Dace didn't come to the commencement ceremony. Cardinal High School held graduation behind the school in the football stadium that year. We had ninety-three graduates, the largest class to that date.

As usual, I smoked pot on the way to the school. I lingered in the girls' restroom, took pictures, and talked with the girls a year younger than I, jealous that they'd return to the safety of school in the fall.

Surrounded by the crowd of people, loneliness swallowed me up. My sadness was complex. I'd fought with my parents that morning. My boyfriend wasn't there. Our relationship left me with few friends, as he demanded my time and attention. I couldn't wait to leave Cardinal, and yet, I knew I'd miss it somehow.

After everyone received their diplomas, we cheered in unison. "We are cool. We are great. We're the class of '78." A quick shadow of flying graduation caps tossed into the air, and everyone went his own way.

I sped home for my graduation party, smoking a joint along the way.

Dace didn't come to the open house my family had for me. Mine was a dry picnic at home, and he attended a classmate's party that offered plenty of beer. While it hurt my feelings, I didn't confront him because it wouldn't change anything. Besides, I looked forward to turning the page to the next chapter of my life.

Four days after graduation, I got an apartment with Pamela, a party friend from school. The building in Mesopotamia, a tiny Amish town in the adjacent county, had been a flour mill decades earlier and now housed three apartments. We called the town Mespo, Ohio.

Two blocks down, a park called the Commons included the only store in town. Swing sets, a gazebo, colorful flower gardens, and a hitching post for Amish buggies, combined to make four blocks of lush country charm. One-way roads bordering each side of the grassy park provided the way through town, north and south.

With the lease signed, I ran home to grab my sleeping bag, makeup case, and clock radio. Mom was home.

Announcing my arrival, I shouted, "I'm moving out." With arms full, I ran through the house. "I'll be back later for the rest of my stuff."

Gathering her wits, Mom called, "Wait a minute."

I stopped at the back door.

"You're moving out?"

I snapped my head around. "Yeah. It's what you've wanted all these years, isn't it?"

Mom plopped into a chair and stared at me.

I could be nice to anyone in the world, but I couldn't gather an ounce of sympathy for my mother. "She's an Irish, German, red-headed Scorpio," I'd spouted to my friends during my high school years. Now I shot her the best dirty look I could muster and left her sitting there, crying.

Slamming the car door, I spun out of the driveway and down the dirt road, Genesis blaring from my stereo. In a cloud of dust, life just changed forever—for everyone.

Pam and I had been smoking marijuana and drinking together daily for over a year before graduation. LSD, cocaine, crank (an amphetamine), and other drugs became part of our normal routine. Even so, alcohol remained my favorite. Not surprisingly, our apartment

46

soon became Party Central, with gatherings each night. New people came and went.

Independence was a fun adventure. Stoned, we found humor in the mundane. We wrapped a bathrobe belt around the Trimline phone and rolled on the floor in hysterics listening to it ring. "Sorry we can't come to the phone—it's all tied up." The phone wasn't answered for days.

Strangers came regularly for our nightly festivities. One evening a handsome man in his mid-thirties came in on a 1978 Harley-Davidson Sportster XR1200. After everyone smoked a couple of joints, he sauntered over to me. Looking down at me, just inches away, he purred, "Wanna go check out my new bike?" Nerves shivered my spine. I hadn't been on a motorcycle in years and never with a stranger, but something about this seemingly dangerous man intrigued me.

"Sure." I tried to sound nonchalant like I made this decision daily.

Outside, he gave me the statistics of his bike. I didn't hear him, nor did I care. My thoughts were spinning. He put his helmet on my head and tucked my hair into the sides. "Let's roll."

I gripped the seat beneath me.

"Hang on to me," he yelled over the roar of the bike. I squeezed him tightly.

We zipped around the park and down the road. Consumed with fearful thoughts, I watched the pavement whiz by in a blur. *What if I fall?* Within minutes, the thrill caught up with me—I loved it. All too soon, we arrived at the apartment.

"Did ya like it?"

"Yeah, I did."

"Maybe we can go again sometime."

"Maybe." I giggled and ran past him into the building. I didn't want to be alone with him; pretty sure I'd do things I'd be sorry for later. I hadn't had much practice with the word "no".

I had the opportunity to try the word out the following week when one of our former high school teachers showed up with a six-pack of beer. Pam and I had heard stories of him partying with students before. He was creepy and we didn't like him, but he did have free beer in his hands.

"I don't know what he wants here," Pam whispered. "We'll just drink his beer and then say we have to split."

We leaned on the kitchen counter.

"What have you been up to since graduation? I heard you girls have had some wild parties."

I lit a cigarette and popped open a beer. "People stop by. Sometimes we drink. Just whatever."

Pam finished her second can, and I chugged a second one.

Teacher Creepy moved onto the sofa. "Why don't you sit down for a while, Kelly?"

"No, we really have to go. They're waiting for us. Thanks for coming by though. Call next time so we can make sure we're going to be home longer."

Plan implemented.

"Yeah, we'll see." He left dejected.

We heard his car race away. "Yeah, and our phone will be all tied up!"

That Friday, Pam asked me if I wanted to join her on a run for some pot. "Sure. When are we leaving?"

"We'll leave in the morning. Let's take some 'Natural' tonight though." Pam brought out a sheet of acid.

Blotter acid is LSD-soaked paper covered with small pierced squares, each perforated into four tinier squares. Various pictures called blotter art decorated the sheets of paper. The "Keep on Truckin'" cartoon character, Mr. Natural, was our favorite way to take LSD. Pam laid several sheets of four-way hits on the kitchen counter.

"You selling these?"

"Yeah. There are twenty-five squares on each. I figure I'll sell a row of five tabs at a time."

"Cool." I had learned that, for me, eating just one quarter of a square didn't provide a heavy trip.

"We'll each eat a half," she suggested. I liked the portion option of four-way hits, learning how I reacted to each amount. I hadn't taken half before.

It wasn't like the purple mescaline Dace gave me once while we partied at the Ledges. The night I took the mescaline, I had a religious experience.

We had been driving the narrow road at night, and the realization of staying between the lines was overpowering to me. It was as if God Himself reached down and touched my soul implanting a deep understanding of the straight and narrow, granting a realization of how far off the path I'd come.

That night I became aware of God's unconditional love like never before. Holy warmth and godly love flooded over my consciousness. Still, I'd found it incomprehensible that any sort of epiphany could come whilst high. Maybe it was because I'd opened my mind to everything.

Dace had explained it as an intuitive awakening because mesc was natural—a member of the cactus family. I didn't know if this were true or not, but while enjoying my altered state of consciousness, I chose to believe him. However, when he added, "Jesus smoked mushrooms," I thought lightning would strike us at that moment.

But tonight it was Mr. Natural. The night was a blur with visitors, beer, pot, and surrendering to the Natural high.

At nearly nine o'clock in the morning, Pam's hoarse whisper into my bedroom woke me. "Kelly, we gotta go. I told Jeff I'd be there to get the pot at ten."

I hurriedly pulled my clothes on. Stepping over sleeping people on the living room floor, we crept into the kitchen, grabbed some dried-out cinnamon rolls from the counter, and ran out the door. At once I fell asleep in Pam's car. I awoke in front of a little trailer in the middle of a field on a dirt road . . . somewhere. "Where're we at?"

"Jeff's. I'm going in first to see if he's ready. You wait here."

I had no idea how long I slept in the car before Pam opened the door, almost spilling me out onto the grassless yard. "Jeff said he would give us some weed if I helped him bag it up. It's primo. Come on in."

Dragging myself out of the car, I stumbled up the trailer stairs. Once inside, I met Jeff, a handsome guy in his mid-twenties. Just five feet five inches tall, we stood eye-to-eye. His light brown curls fell around his ears, covered his forehead, and hung in his pale green eyes.

"Come back here, Kelly," Pam whispered. "You have to see this."

With Jeff leading the way, I followed them down the hall into the rear bedroom of the narrow, old trailer. I couldn't believe my eyes. The room hadn't a stick of furniture, but was full—literally full—of two-foot piles of dried and semi-dried marijuana. Several large black garbage bags stuffed full of the ganja lay here and there.

"Holy crap," I whispered. "Where did all this come from?"

"Don't start asking a lot of questions," Jeff snapped.

"Kelly, I'm going to help Jeff weigh and bag this stuff. You can wait in the living room."

"All of this? How long will that take?"

"Maybe not all of it, but if we want some free stuff I have to help him get it bagged."

I shuffled back and fell into a weathered leather La-Z-Boy recliner in the living room. The recliner, a floor lamp, a well-worn coffee table, and a dirty, torn sofa with faded orange and olive-green plaid were the only furniture in the room.

Bunch of garbage dump cast-offs. My head dropped backward and I fell asleep. Involuntary muscle spasms jerked me awake periodically. One such jerk threw my head forward. There sat an older man on the ugly sofa, staring at me. I tried to smile and slurred a "hello there." My eyes rolled back into my head and I fell asleep again.

Intermittently my jerking body woke me, always revealing the man staring at me. He remained expressionless and didn't speak. His narrow, dark eyes glared at me and made me worry. When did he come in? Who was he? A narc? Jeff's friend? Why wasn't he helping them bag the pot? I was embarrassed, aware of my spontaneous muscle contractions. As helpless as I was, I hoped he'd leave me alone.

"Where's Pamela?"

"Your friend's in the back room with Jeff. I think they're doin' the wild thing." The grim stranger had no facial expressions to read. *Friend or foe?*

The brilliance of the setting sun was visible through the dirty horizontal window panes when I awoke. I crept halfway down the hall and called for Pam.

"We're almost done," she said. I staggered back into the living room and fell into the recliner. Running my fingers through my hair, I tried to wake up. Soon they came out of the room, and Jeff shook the strange man's hand. *Friend,* I concluded.

Pam looked at me slouched in the chair. "You're finally awake, huh? Let's go." I stood and steadied myself. She hugged Jeff and took a large, clear zipper bag stuffed with pot, and we left.

I began to regain coherence on the way home. "Where did all that reefer come from?"

"He gets it from someone who expects him to weigh it and bag it up, and then sell it. They split the profits."

"Who grows it?"

"I'm not sure. I think it comes from Mexico." I wasn't sure if she didn't know, or just wouldn't say.

I lost the entire day. A quarter hit is best for me, I thought.

Returning home from my job at the deli later that week, I saw a girl sleeping in the corner of the hallway of our apartment.

"Who's that?"

"That's Pat. She ran away from home. She and her mom can't get along."

"Why's she here?"

"She needed a place to go. Of course, you understand about mothers. She'll be eighteen next month."

"We're harboring a runaway minor? You wanna get us in trouble?"

"Relax. I'll take care of her myself. You don't even need to know she's here."

"Well what about that dude that's been here for a week? When's he leaving?"

"Martin's just crashing here until he finds a place. It won't be long."

I was frustrated. All those people being there every day irritated me. They didn't pay rent or buy groceries, booze, or weed, but they lived there nonetheless.

During some of our parties, we played Chug-a-Lug, a board game that requires the loser to drink beer. The good-looking biker stopped by to play one night and asked if he could clean up since he'd just come from work. I hopped forward. "Sure."

Later I saw that he had used my loofah sponge. Black grease covered it, so I threw it away. Dirty, wet towels lay on the bathroom floor. It seemed that everyone took advantage of us and I hated it. Now *I* felt like the nagging mother.

∞∞∞∞∞∞∞∞∞∞∞∞∞

Dace lived miles away. The Rambler needed repair, and he didn't have the money to have it fixed. He didn't have a phone, so we seldom spoke. Our relationship waned. *If this is another stupid test to see if I'm going to go find him, he's in for a surprise. I'm too busy having fun.*

The phone rang.

"Hello?"

"Hi, Kelly. It's Bobbie. I'm glad I got a hold of you. Joe and I are getting married."

"Congratulations."

"Thanks. I'd like you to be one of my bridesmaids. Will you?"

"Sure. That'd be fun. What do I have to do?"

"Well, for now just come to the bridal shop at the Mentor Mall and get fitted for the dress."

"Okay. When?"

"Can you come next Saturday at two?"

"I'll be there."

Although flattered that Roberta asked me to be in her wedding, I didn't know what my duties were—I'd never been in one before.

Saturday morning, I took a quarter of one of Pam's Mr. Natural hits. She still sold it by the sheet, but in short time took more than she sold.

Today, just a quarter hit and I was mildly tripping, but was still pretty gone. "I can't go to the mall. This is potent junk. Maybe it's because I did so much last weekend."

"Then don't go," Pam said.

"I have to. I told Bobbie I'd be fitted today. I have to."

"Suit yourself." Pam had taken a whole four-way hit and didn't care. Her trip had already started.

Behind the wheel, I struggled to maintain control. I imagined that everything I thought about happened. *What if I cross the centerline and hit that car head-on?* I drifted left of center. *Stop it!*

What if I drive into the ditch? My car headed toward the right. *Stop! Maintain. Maintain.*

I slowed my car to help ensure safety. Cars whizzed past. I drove forty miles per hour. *I can't even enjoy this Natural. I should never have taken it this morning.*

Finally, I arrived, parked my car, and entered through the anchor store on the end.

Where is this bridal shop? Walking the length of the mall, paranoia set in. *Everyone's staring at me. I have to walk right. Everyone's looking.* My legs felt six feet long, and staying on my platform shoes was a balancing act.

Bobbie waited at the entrance to the store. "Kelly. You're here. Come on back; they're waiting for you."

Was I late?

"What are you on?" Bobbie whispered. "You trippin'?"

How does she know? "A quarter hit of Natural."

Bobbie clenched her jaw.

Why is she ticked off? She parties.

"Today? You had to take it today?"

"What? You party."

"Yeah, but today? You couldn't have waited until later?" Bobbie grabbed my arm. "C'mon. Just get back here, and don't say a word to my mom."

The fitting was a blur. Bobbie's anger bummed me out. Driving home, I fumed. *She wrecked my buzz.*

The wedding day soon arrived, and I went alone, smoking part of a doobie before arriving. Bobbie and her family greeted me at the church and directed me to the bridal room to join the other bridesmaids. Our long peach dresses had lace cap sleeves. The polyester fabric clung to our bodies and fell gracefully from the hips down. Each one looked beautiful. Bobbie had chosen well.

After the ceremony and photos, everyone piled into a white limo and went to a country club for the reception. I found my niche alone at the bar. *Ahh, an open bar. I love weddings.*

I removed my high heels, making my dress drag along the floor. I drank, ate, and drank some more, and relaxed, dancing every dance. In the middle of the crowd of people, I was lonely. *I want another drink.*

Intermittently throughout high school, I had taken afternoons off and gone into the woods at the Ledges and elsewhere, to drink wine. I had always preferred drinking alone. Now, being in a crowd, I felt more solitary than ever. Amidst smiles, laughter, and talking, a sphere of muffled isolation surrounded me like a dense fog.

Although a familiar boundary, I soon crossed the line between feeling good and being drunk. Not wanting to make Bobbie or her family angry, I tried to sober up.

I have to drink some coffee. I attempted to center my cup under the coffee urn spigot. Swaying back and forth, I struggled to stabilize my hand. "Steady, steady," I whispered. It poured to the wooden floor, splashing onto my dress—a perfect complement to the six inches of dirt from the dance floor.

Maybe some fresh air. I took my coffee cup out onto the front porch of the country club. Resting on the cement step, I leaned against the massive white pillar.

I couldn't wait to leave. How could I? I had to wait for a ride back to my car. I shouldn't drive feeling this drunk anyway. I drew my knees up and rested my head on them.

"Mind if I sit here?"

I looked up. I didn't recognize him, but he wore a tux, so he must've been in the wedding.

"Sure."

"Whatcha doin' out here?"

"Just getting some fresh air. I'm tired."

He leaned against me. "I'm tired too. Great party, isn't it?"

"Yeah. Bobbie's beautiful."

"A-huh. Where'd you meet her?"

"We went to school together. How do you know her?"

"Oh, I'm friends with Joe. I don't really know her. She seems like a nice girl."

"The best. Your loss."

He chuckled. The moon illuminated his face. I could tell he was in his late thirties. Not a bad-looking man, just weatherworn.

"You have a boyfriend here?"

"Nope, I came alone."

"I have a wife here. She's having fun. I'm not though. What's your name?"

I wanted him to go inside so I could compose myself. I had to drive later and needed to get sober. I remained silent.

"You're beautiful. The wind blowing your hair makes you even more striking. What's your name?"

"Kelly. Thank you." I forced a half-smile, unmoved by his attempt at smooth talk.

"Kelly, how about making an old married man happy and give me a kiss?"

I didn't have much strength to deal with this creep. I wanted him to go away.

"You're married. You should go kiss your wife."

"Oh, she's busy having fun. You'd make my day . . . you'd make my *life* if you'd give me a kiss."

"I don't think so." I looked away and put my head back on my bended knees.

He paused for a few seconds but wouldn't give up. "I'm going to go inside. But how about you just give me one little kiss before I go back in? That'd make me so happy. It's been lots of years since I've been kissed by a beautiful young girl like you."

Completely out of resolve, I sighed. "All right." I turned toward him. Putting his hand on my jaw, he lifted my mouth to his and kissed me. Backing away, he kept his hand on my cheek.

"Thank you," he whispered. "You've made an old man very, very happy."

"Hi, Stan. What are you doing out here?"

I could tell by how fast he pulled his hand away that his wife had come outside. I looked the other way. *Thank God. Maybe now he'll get away from me.*

The man stood and scurried inside with his wife. I heard her biting tone and his pathetic lies drift off into the building. I should have felt badly, but I didn't.

Serves the old perv right. He probably does that all the time. She should dump him.

"Hey, Kelly. Some of the ushers are going back to the church. Wanna go with them and get your car?"

"Yes." I jumped and went inside for my shoes and purse.

Two of the groomsmen and another bridesmaid hopped into a jeep, and I joined them. Stopping at the church to get our clothes, we found the door locked. The next thing I knew we were all at the apartment of one of the men. He disappeared into the bedroom and brought out a T-shirt for me to sleep in. He and the woman disappeared into the bedroom and left me and the other groomsman to sleep in the living room.

In the morning someone brought our clothes to us and took me to my car. Hangover drums pounded inside my head. I threw the soiled dress into the trunk and sped off to my apartment to prepare for work. *I should have that cleaned.*

The next weekend Pam and I dated two guys from the grocery store I worked in. I was with Brent, the manager of the dairy department, and his cousin Ricky escorted Pam.

When we got home, we found Dace on the long porch of our apartment building, leaning against the wall.

He'd hitchhiked there and waited throughout the evening. Situated under the porch light, he glared at us and took a slow drag on his cigarette.

Everyone exited Ricky's cherry-red Honda Civic, laughing and ignoring our annoyed visitor. I swung my sandals around, giggling, emphasizing disinterest in my old boyfriend.

We four strode the length of the porch toward the door. Dace towered over us, tall and thin, blonde and handsome. Suddenly, he stepped toward my date and with one violent kick to the face, sent Brent flying backward. For a couple seconds we stood motionless as Brent lay on the ground bleeding, two teeth on the dirt beside him.

"What the heck, Dace!" Pam screamed. Ricky helped Brent up and put him into his car.

Engulfed in fear, I did what came naturally—I ran. The streetlights lit my way to the park. Between my panting and the slap, slap, slap of my bare feet on the pavement, I heard Dace drawing closer behind. My eighteen-year-old adrenalin-powered physique nearly outran his twenty-two-year-old smoker's body.

As I reached the park, he tackled me to the ground. "Dang, girl, you can run!" Just then, the Civic approached. Dace threw me into a flowerbed and pushed my head into the tulips.

"Keep your head down and be quiet," he hissed. The Civic rolled by, the dim streetlights illuminating a pistol resting on the windowsill. We didn't move. We didn't even breathe.

Soon all was quiet and safe to go back to the apartment. In a state of confusion and shock, I sensed a fear of him that I'd not experienced before. Seeing his violent kick made me realize he still had issues controlling his temper.

We walked and he took my hand. I was afraid to pull it away. "You want me to stay with you tonight, don't you?" he purred.

"Why would you say that?" I desperately searched inside for that feisty girl who had run down the street earlier. But uncertainty hid her.

"Because that jerk could come back with his gun. You want me to stay and protect you, don't you?"

"I think we'll be alright."

"Well, are you going to take me all the way back to my apartment tonight?" His tone hardened. That alarmed me.

"No. Y-you're right. You can stay with us tonight. I'll take you home tomorrow."

"When you say, 'stay with us,' you don't mean sleep on the couch, do you?"

Uncomfortable, I was aware that my options were few. "I, I guess not."

"What do you mean, you guess not? Are you saying I can be with you?" he purred again.

"No" was a cobweb-covered word in my vocabulary. Fear didn't help release it either. With a nervous chuckle, I agreed.

His touch wasn't comfortable as in the past. Yet, he was gentle. By morning, I believed he truly loved me and, in his own twisted way, tried to take care of me.

Word spread quickly at the grocery store that a deli worker's boyfriend attacked the dairy manager.

"You'd better watch out, Kelly," co-workers warned. "The owner wants blood. Brent is his nephew. You knew that, didn't you? Your boyfriend had better get a gun, and you're getting canned."

"It's not my fault."

"Well, he's your boyfriend, isn't he?"

"He was. We hadn't seen each other in a while."

The owner called me upstairs to his office.

"Kelly, I understand there was some trouble at your apartment this past weekend."

I hung my head, fearing the ax. "Yeah. I, I mean, yes, there was."

"Your young man better find a lawyer, Kelly."

"Really?"

"Kicking someone's teeth out is serious business. Still, I don't think he's going to press charges. He's having his mouth fixed. He doesn't want trouble. And he doesn't want to talk to you anymore. Do you understand, Kelly?"

"Why not? It's not my fault." I found it hard to turn away from an argument with authority.

"You may not think it's your fault, young lady, but you will stay away from him if you want to keep your job. Do you understand me?" His stern tone left no doubt: if seen talking to Brent, I would be fired.

"Yes, I understand."

"All right. Now you go back to work."

Although relieved to have my job, I couldn't resist the temptation to approach my co-worker the following week when I saw him stocking the milk case.

"Hi there."

He glanced up but didn't answer. His face still had a green-blue hue.

"I'm so sorry. He's not my boyfriend anymore. I don't know why he did that."

He paused, looked around, and clenched his jaw. "It doesn't matter. I don't care. Don't talk to me or we'll both be canned. Just go away."

I hung my head and turned to go. I paused and looked back. "I'm sorry."

He exhaled noisily. "It's okay." He gave in, making me feel better. Better, except that I felt horrible for saying Dace wasn't my boyfriend. I believed that we should be together.

The following week he and I officially reunited. The thought that someone would fight for me was captivating. Talk at work died down and he was forgotten, thus securing my job.

∞∞∞∞∞∞∞∞∞∞∞

That summer, Pam and my other roommates planned to attend an annual smoke-in held in Washington, DC; a function of the Youth International Party—Yippies. I found it ridiculous that people who didn't care about anything political, suddenly fancied themselves Yippies. *They don't even know what it means.* I preferred to stay at home. Besides, I had to work.

The next month Dace bought tickets for the 1978 World Series of Rock at the stadium. We planned to spend the day enjoying Fleetwood Mac, Bob Welch, The Cars, Todd Rundgren and Utopia, and Eddie Money.

He drove my car. In the stadium parking lot we snorted coke and crank.

While sitting high in the stands smoking pot and enjoying the music, I watched a dude climb the girder and along the ceiling beam. Like watching a television program, I observed him. Then he let go and dropped. Without a sound, he disappeared down the opening to the next level.

A woman screamed, but the falling man was silent. I saw another woman lean over the railing to look. At once, she became ill. *What must he look like that she would be sick?* Dace hadn't seen it, and I tried to explain what I'd

62

seen. I struggled to talk because I was wasted. We got up, but I refused to look over the balcony to the lower level.

He took hold of my hand. "Let's go onto the field."

I heard an ambulance come and go. *I wonder if he died. Poor guy.* I remembered Sophia saying that people who die without Jesus in their hearts go to hell. *Please let him into heaven, God.* I couldn't think about God now—I was partying.

On the field, we grooved to the jams. Dreamlike, I stood facing my favorite bands and felt their music vibrate throughout my body. Stevie Nicks danced across the stage, costume flowing behind her. She was magical.

Most people had blankets spread out on the grass. Many slept, some were making out, and others just relaxed and enjoyed their buzz.

Suddenly a guy ran through, saying, "Excuse me. Excuse me. Excuse me." Another guy followed him heaving all along the way, soiling blankets, treading on people, and stumbling in his own vomit. A woman followed behind, apologizing to everyone. An interesting parade, they headed to the medical tent at the corner of the field.

Groans, shouts of obscenities, and others being sick followed. "Ah, let's move," Dace said. He grabbed my hand and we found another location.

The sky seemed unusually dark going home that night. As we sped along the narrow country roads into our remote county, Fleetwood Mac blasted from the stereo, and he slapped the steering wheel in time to the music like banging on bongo drums. His whole body rocked backward and forward, and he sang with gusto.

I saw a large black dog dart into the road ahead of us. We were speeding, and I feared if I screamed we would have an accident. With no time for him to miss the dog, I covered my eyes and lowered my head. Thud.

"Holy crap, I just hit an effin' dog."

"Should we stop, Dace?"

"No, it flew into the field. It's most likely already dead. I hit it hard."

"What if it isn't? Shouldn't we find the owners at least?"

"Kelly, it's three effing o'clock in the morning. If we go knocking on doors now, we'll get shot. No. We aren't stopping."

My chest tightened and my throat burned as I stifled my cries. *God, please let it die fast and let its owner find it in the morning.* Somehow, prayer came naturally to me. But was God listening? I wanted to trust that He was this time.

Chapter Five: Sowing and Reaping

I soon grew tired of Pam, our unwanted roommates, and their disrespectful habits. Besides, I had always been happier drinking alone, and missed my solitude.

By the end of the summer, I moved out of the mill apartment and into the little two-room apartment adjacent to my grandparents' garage. Built decades earlier for my great-grandparents, it had no bathroom. In bygone days, they used a "thunder-mug" potty. For me it was a chilly march through the garage and past the doorway to the greenhouse, to use my grandparents' facilities.

Dace wanted me to meet Calvin and Cathy. The couple had lived together for six years and had been his friends for even longer. They were eager to meet me.

He drove my Mustang, and we met at a café in a nearby town for lunch. They had stories of when the three of them traveled to New Mexico in Cathy's Honda Civic and the long-legged Dace rode cramped in the back seat. They'd experimented with psilocybin mushrooms on the trip, eating and smoking the psychedelic fungus.

After lunch we separated to shop in the stores along the plaza. I found a bookstore and got lost in the poetry section. Cathy browsed in a dress shop next door. The guys found a comic-book store.

I exited the bookstore and saw the guys opening my trunk. They were looking at my spare tire and whispering. The pile of peach polyester caught my eye. *The dress. I won't mention it. Maybe they won't notice.*

"I bought a book. I'll just throw it back here." I put the bag into the trunk and closed the lid. "What's next?"

They looked at each other. "We were arguing about what size spare tire your Mustang has. Dace won.

Um, I'll go get Cath and see what she wants to do,"
Calvin stammered. He dashed off to the dress shop.

Dace glared at me. "Is that the dress from that
wedding you were in?"

"Yeah. I have to have it cleaned." I lit a cigarette,
trying to look casual.

"No crap. What did you do in it? Looks like you
had a real good time."

"I was drunk and spilled coffee on it. No big deal."

Calvin meandered back. "Cathy wants to head
home now. It was nice meeting you, Kelly."

"Yeah, it was fun. Thanks for lunch. We'll see you
again later."

They got into their car and left. While we drove
back to Daces' house, he remained quiet. We got out and I
dashed around to the driver's-side door.

"I have to go home."

"Who invited you in? See ya." He slammed the
door hard, just as I approached to enter. I jumped back.

"Dace." I paused. He stormed up the driveway.

"You could've hit me with the door," I mumbled,
hoping he didn't hear me, still remembering his brutal
kick to Brent's mouth.

The next week while at work, I doubled over with
cramps. I stumbled to the restroom. Blood filled the toilet.

Asking a co-worker from the meat department to
replace me in the deli, I clocked out and drove myself to
the emergency room.

Leaning on the reception counter, I answered
questions while the room swirled around me. They
escorted me to an examination room. The antiseptic
smells added to my nausea.

Eventually a doctor came in. More questions and he left. A nurse came into the room. "Did he tell you what he's going to do?"

"No."

The nurse heaved a disgusted sigh. "You poor thing. He should've told you." She explained the tests that would ensue, and I signed papers that I didn't read.

Later, I waited in the room, recovering from the discomfort, shock, and embarrassment I'd just experienced. After what seemed like hours, the doctor returned with a clipboard in hand.

"Well, Kelly, it looks like your choices have caught up with you." I abhorred his judgmental tone. "You have some small stomach ulcers. You have an enflamed gallbladder. You have colitis—that explains the bleeding. Maladies such as these, found in a teenager, could be a result of excessive alcohol consumption."

How could he know all that just from those tests? I wasn't sure I believed him. It's true I had started drinking many years earlier. *Maybe it is possible.* Still, I had taken vitamins from A to zinc since age sixteen. Hadn't they helped at all?

The doctor handed me two pieces of paper. "Here's a prescription for Tagamet to calm your stomach, and stay on this bland diet for a while. You'll need to follow up with your family physician." (**Endnote 2**)

The doctor paused at the door and looked at my chart. He declared over his shoulder, "Oh and you *do* know you're pregnant, don't you?"

I couldn't move. "No." I forced the whispered response.

"See your doctor."

The door closed behind him and I sat in a daze, my mouth hanging open. No, I did not know I was pregnant.

At eighteen, I was already reaping the harvest of the seeds I'd sown in my life. The news of my pregnancy surprised me. But with no protection during sex, what did I expect?

As I drove home, my mind flashed between all the drugs I'd taken in the past month to the last time Dace and I had fooled around. I worried. *Will the coke and crank hurt the baby?*

∞∞∞∞∞∞∞∞∞∞∞∞

I settled into my new apartment. Living alone felt right. Being by myself, I'd be able to manage my intestinal issues and eat more healthfully. I had brief moments of reflection about God, but the tangible crowded them out.

I had to tell Dace. We were watching television at my place. There were only an old wicker rocking chair and an antique wooden stool in the apartment. He needed them both, so I sat on the linoleum floor.

Sitting in the rocking chair, he put a metal tray on the stool in front of him. Laying a magazine on the tray, he put the remnants from his bag of weed onto the unopened magazine. Stems and seeds mostly. He ripped the cover from a book of matches, held the magazine on an angle, and began to sift the weed with the matchbook cover with the precision and care that I used when picking the raisins from my raisin bran. Seeds spun down onto the tray. He rolled a joint from the pot left on the top of the magazine.

"I'd better get some more of this for the weekend."

He's in a good mood. Without talking, we smoked for a few minutes. I summoned my courage.

"I have to tell you something." How would the next few minutes play out? His biggest priority in life right now was scoring another bag. Would the news change his world like it had already changed my own?

68

He handed me the roach clip that held the tiny remnant of the joint we'd been smoking. "What?"

I took a quick drag and swallowed it. Trying to escape in the exhale, I croaked out the words, "You know when I saw the doctor the other day?"

"You mean at the hospital?"

"Yeah, then. Well, he said . . . that . . . I'm . . ." I sipped air between my pursed lips ". . . pr . . . egnant." I held my breath.

He paused, holding his toke in. His azure eyes glinted. He grinned. "Really?" Still holding the smoke in, he beamed.

"Yeah, I'm pregnant. I'm sorry."

He let the air burst out. "You shouldn't be. It's all right."

Since I didn't know what to expect, this was a puzzling but pleasant reaction.

"You tell your mom and dad yet?"

"No. I haven't told anyone."

He seemed pleased. "It's gonna be all right. I guess that means we should get married."

"If you want to."

"Well, of course I do. I felt we were heading in that direction anyway." More buoyant now, he moved quickly to scrape enough pot from the little pile of stems and seeds for another joint. He ground the pieces of stems with his fingertips. "Didn't you?"

"Didn't I what?"

"Didn't you think we were heading in that direction anyway?"

I hadn't thought much about it. I had spent the summer partying, being in a wedding, working—just experiencing life outside of my parents' house, enjoying independence.

"I guess so. Sure."

Two weeks later, responding to a knock on my door, I found Dace there with a duffle bag in his hand. He shoved past me. "I have more in the car. I'll be right back." I surveyed the bag he'd dropped on the floor.

"Dace, you can't move in here. My parents will be furious."

"Don't ask them." He leaned his guitar case against the wall.

"No, really. I don't think you should stay here."

"I'm staying." He glared, removed his guitar from the case, and got comfortable on the rocker.

That was it. He moved in and I couldn't stop him. My grandparents didn't mention it, but I assumed they weren't pleased.

Later that week we met with Janice for dinner at a local pizza place. Happy to spend time with us, she gladly paid for the meal.

Afterward, we returned to our apartment. He sat on the stool and gave his mother the rocker. I leaned against the counter beside the sink. He shared his pot with Janice and showed her how to make a homemade pipe out of a cardboard tube.

After we'd been high for a while, Janice burst out laughing. "We look like a bunch of simpletons here sucking on a toilet paper tube."

He gave me the look. It was time to tell her about the baby. Janice seemed unmoved. "Well, I wondered," she sneered. "I knew this happy horse crap couldn't go on forever."

Amazed, part of me rejoiced that Janice hadn't gotten angry, and part of me hurt that she didn't seem to care much.

The next morning my mother came to visit Gramma. When I saw her leaving, I ran out to her car. Mom rolled the window down. At once, I regretted all the pain I'd caused her. I had to do it one more time. Would my mother yell at me? Would she close her window in silence, drive away, and never talk to me again? I searched for a strength that I thought was inside somewhere. *Just do what you have to do.*

"Hey, Mom, how are you?"

"I'm fine, Kelly." Her tone sounded predictably cool. "What do you want?"

"I just wanted to tell you that I went to the hospital the other day. I had a weird attack at work." I hoped she would be so worried that she wouldn't get mad when I broke the news about the baby.

Her eyes narrowed. "Oh?"

"Yeah, the doctor said I have an ulcer and colitis."

"Really?"

"Yeah, he also said something about acids in my gallbladder."

"Are you going to have your gallbladder out?"

"No, no." I hesitated. "He also told me something you're probably not going to be very happy about."

Gripping the steering wheel, Mom tensed up again. "What?" Icicles dripped from her voice.

"He said I'm pregnant."

"You are, huh?"

Why doesn't she seem more surprised? "Yeah, I am."

"What are you going to do?" Oh, how I longed for her to offer some direction. However, having rejected guidance offered in the past, why would she propose any now?

"Dace wants to get married, I guess."

71

"So you're gonna get married?"

"Yeah, I guess so."

"Okay, Kelly. I have to go. I'll talk to you later."

Watching my mother's car back out of the driveway and head up the road, I fanaticized about the perfect scenario: I would have my parents over at our big house, with a picket fence and flowering bushes lining the driveway. My husband would come home from his job and we'd all have dinner together. My husband and I would cuddle, whisper, and act giddy. My parents would coyly ask what we were discussing. With deep love, we would look into each other's eyes and we would announce in unison, "We're having a baby." My parents would squeal with delight and we'd spend the evening discussing nursery colors and baby names.

But, no. I had made my choices and now had to live the consequences, the first being the total void of all joy in what should be one of the most joyous announcements in a person's life.

I stood motionless, staring at the road. Mom would tell Dad. They hated Dace. Would they ever be happy about this union?

I shuffled toward the apartment. I felt so small, so alone, so helpless. I didn't know what the future held, and quivered inside. I feared living with him. I was sorry that I would make Gramma cry and sorry I would disappoint Dad. I wondered what it would be like to grow bigger and bigger. Would Dace love me when I was huge? Would I be a good mother? I was horrified to shove a human being out of my vagina. Although it seemed surreal, my fear was very real.

In just three weeks, Gramma organized a charming outdoor wedding for Dace and me. The plans came together beautifully. I hadn't told my grandparents about the baby. They must have suspected it though. Perhaps Dad told them. We never discussed it.

My fiancé asked Leon, the only African-American in town, to be his best man, which surprised me. "Why don't you have Ryan be your best man, Dace? He's your little brother, after all."

"I don't want him."

"He's twelve. Don't you think you'll hurt his feelings? Why did you ask Leon?"

"Because I wanted to tick off the bigots in your family."

Leon had been a year ahead of me in school, in the grade between Sophia and me. Our dad had worked with Leon's mother. Dad liked her and never said anything negative about her family. Still, not wanting to fight, I didn't say another word.

I planned to wear the dress with sunny yellow daisies on it that I'd worn to my senior prom, with a ring of daisies on my head. Taking the dress out of the closet brought back prom memories. I had been a nervous wreck that night with my period being late and all. *Funny, it doesn't seem so earth-shattering now.*

My job to prepare for the wedding was to buy white shoes. Mom and Aunt Connie took me to a shoe store.

"Mom, stop here."

My urgency told Mom that she'd better be quick. I jumped out and vomited along the curb beside the shopping plaza.

How classy. How many brides-to-be have to stop to puke?

With wedding shoes in tow, I was eager to head home. My mom and aunt stopped at McDonald's for lunch. The thought of eating made me want to hurl again.

"I'll just wait in the car. I want to lie down here on the back seat."

"We're not going to hurry, Kelly."

"I know, Mom. It's okay. I'll just sleep anyway."

Lying in the car, with the windows down, I gazed into the sky and watched the tops of the trees sway in the Ohio autumn breeze. *I wish I were a bird in that tree.* Exhaustion won and I drifted off to sleep. I awoke with a start when the car doors slammed. "Buckle up, we're leaving."

I complied. "Okay, Mom."

Chapter Six: A Surprisingly Surprising Beginning

The wedding was charming. Held on a clear, unseasonably hot September day, it was outside on my grandparents' farm in Mesopotamia.

Now rented by an Amish family, the modest farm was located on a slight hill on a dirt road. It had been in our family for generations. An enormous brown stone stood in the front yard. My great-grandfather had engraved his initials—B.A.G.—on it and left instructions to use it for his tombstone. When he passed away, no one could move the mammoth rock. Instead, they bought a proper headstone. I'd always regretted that our family couldn't honor his wish.

Pear trees, apple trees, and peach trees flanked the yard beside the farmhouse. Grampa had graded a road beside them, making it wind down over the back hill.

Just behind the shallow rear lawn, a barn accommodated four horses. A bright white wooden fence, dotted with blueberry bushes, barricaded the pasture behind the barn.

I arrived early and, pausing at the top of the hill, examined the scene. *The backyard always seemed bigger to me.*

The steep hill had been the catalyst of fun snowy days. I joyfully reminisced about annual adventures with my dad, Sophie, and me sliding down in metal saucers, wooden sleds, a wooden toboggan, and eventually, long, turquoise plastic sheets made for zooming on the snow.

Springtime and summer memories were plentiful too. The hill cascaded into an area that resembled a beautiful park. A stream ran through the bottom of it. A shallow area afforded hours of collecting colorful pebbles and finding frogs.

Afternoons spent skipping stones over the deeper water made those seasons special. Trees and groomed grass made a fantastic picnic area. Our grandparents took excellent care of the site.

When Dad was a child, Gramma had found a Native American papoose board hanging from a tree. The wooden and leather cradleboard told of earlier times when Cherokee women lived or worked along the stream. For decades, my family found arrowheads throughout the property. Gramma had many displayed on sapphire-blue velvet in a glass and wooden box Grampa made.

The wedding was at the top of the marvelous hill, and the renters stayed away throughout the ceremony. My grandparents wove fresh-cut sunflowers up the sides of a vivid white trellis, draping the bright flowering heads across the top. Three short rows of folding chairs were for the few attendees. Only the immediate families were invited.

Christine, my maid of honor, wore her prom dress—a pale yellow prairie-style dress with white flowers on it, accentuated by a daisy in her hair.

The heat intensified my nausea. "I don't know why they call it morning sickness. It's more like twenty-four-hour queasiness."

"Oh, you'll be fine. You'll be fine. You look gorgeous." Sitting in the car, Chris moved the tiny compact mirror around to see the flower in her hair.

Groaning, I leaned back on the front seat in the car. I longed to lie down, but didn't want to wrinkle my cotton dress or mess my hair. I sat there with my eyes closed until just before I had to walk the grassy aisle.

A little boom box played a pre-recorded "Wedding March" I had captured the previous week. The church organist had been reluctant to help, but complied.

While walking, I tried to smile and hoped I wouldn't throw up. It couldn't end fast enough.

The words in the service sounded monotonous and were meaningless to me. The pastor from my parents' Congregational church officiated although he had never met Dace or me. He joined us afterward at my parents' house for cake and punch. Superficial chitchat consumed the two hours of eating and gift unwrapping. The humidity was overwhelming, and I ran to the bathroom twice to be sick. People pretended not to notice. Finally, everyone left.

My groom had reserved a room at a Holiday Inn about an hour away. He claimed he had asked for a suite, but there were none left.

After we left my parents' house, we drove to Leon's trailer in the woods. I was astonished. "We'll just stop by here and get a buzz on."

I sat in the dumpy twelve-foot-wide trailer in my wedding dress until after midnight. When I used the restroom, the filth appalled me. *Typical bachelors.*

Was Dace trying to show me who was in charge? Was he making a silent statement about the unimportance of this day? His insensitivity surprised me. I was sick and exhausted, but still too timid to complain. By the time we got to the hotel, he crashed, and I cried. *What a romantic wedding night. I can't believe he's treating me like this.*

The next day we bought groceries with the wedding gift money.

I loved the concept of being married. I got up each morning to prepare bacon and eggs for my husband. I was exuberant and hopeful.

Two weeks after the wedding, while talking with my parents, I learned that my new husband's grandmother had had an accident on the metal chair during the wedding. My mother wondered if the elderly woman was ill. I told Dace what Mom saw.

"Is there something wrong with her?" I said with the concern and innocence of a clueless teenage girl.

He was enraged. "You witch. You and your effin' gossipy family make me sick."

A strong slap punctuated his rant. My head spun to the right and hit the large window in the door behind me. The shock of the act joined the loud rattle of the wavy old glass pane, scaring me terribly. He stormed out of the apartment, leaving me alone and shaking.

I stood motionless, pondering the situation, and tried to calm down. Deciphering the incident, I concluded that I deserved a slap. I knew I had a smart mouth and my words may have come out wrong. Maybe I shouldn't have asked at all. Yep. No doubt, I deserved it, and it would never happen again. I was sure of it.

I'd better not mention his grandmother again. At that moment, a mental list of forbidden words began.

Despite his outburst, I had hope for a happy life. Working as a carpenter's helper, he made decent money and suggested I quit my job at the deli and relax for a while. That sounded heavenly. I didn't consider the long-term implications. Finding work as a pregnant teenager later proved impossible.

My not working gave Dace more power over me—another way he separated me from everyone. However, I thought his desire to care for me was romantic, and acquiesced. That week I gave notice at work.

I tried to find the rhythm of my new daily routine. I enjoyed taking care of my husband and loved the idea of being a wife and mother. However, soon my never-ending presence at home began to grate on his nerves. He became short with me.

He berated me for not having his shirts hung uniformly in the closet. "Hang my shirts with all the collars facing the same way. Button the top buttons. Can't you do anything right?"

I tried to fry pork chops. "You use Shake-N-Bake. Everybody knows that, stupid." Oh how I regretted not learning to cook while living at home.

Likewise, his behavior bothered me. He refused to go through the garage to use the bathroom. Instead, he urinated in the only sink in the little apartment—the kitchen sink.

He became impatient with my morning sickness. He didn't like it when I threw up in the snow-covered flowerbed beside the garage each morning. "Can't you stop that? Stay in here." However, I refused to vomit in the sink.

In the evenings, we watched *Sanford and Son* and *Laverne & Shirley* on television. They were loud shows and I didn't like them. My husband always took the padded wicker rocker and left the stool for me. As my tummy grew, sitting on the hard, slanted stool with no back support hurt. Still, I sat there night after night and watched the loud sitcoms.

Feeling cheerful one evening, I announced, "I have an idea. Why don't we ask Gramma and Grampa for another chair for in here? They have folding chairs."

"No, we're fine. I don't feel like bringing another chair in here."

"That's okay. I'll go get one. Be right back."

"Sit down. There isn't room for any more furniture in here."

"A folding chair, Dace. I can close it up when I go to bed."

"I said sit down. Just shut up and watch the show."

His attitude stunned me. But why? Why would I be surprised? I berated myself for expecting more of him. After all, he wasn't a giving person before we were married. Why expect him to become one now? Because I was pregnant? That didn't seem to matter to him.

We celebrated Thanksgiving with my new in-laws. Like several times before, his mother planned to leave Lino. This time they asked us to take Mr. Spots, their English bulldog.

I first met Spots when I was sixteen. While I sat at the bar at Christine's home in Parkman, he came snorting through the small, dark area by our feet. I screamed and pulled my legs up. "What's that?"

"That's my stepfather's ugly dog, Mr. Spots," she laughed.

He was the first English bulldog I'd seen in person. He sniffed and grunted, and waddled away with an indignant snort, spraying moisture everywhere.

I came to know him well. He was mostly white with brindle spots. With a thick head, broad shoulders, and widespread legs, he was bulldog perfection.

He patiently tolerated Chris dressing him in hats and scarves. Immediately upon outfit removal, he spun in a circle in elated independence and, with an unconditional love seldom found on earth, happily licked us, and ran down the hall in costume freedom.

Mr. Spots was sweet, and although we didn't ask my grandparents for their permission, we gladly welcomed him into our apartment. My grandparents said nothing.

My father-in-law declared we should feed our new pet the expensive frozen dog food he'd given him. He said it was the only food he could have. I foresaw it to be a financial hardship, but we agreed nonetheless.

In my mother-in-law's kitchen that evening, Chris fed Spots a bountiful Thanksgiving dinner. After our holiday feast, we took him home. The secret meal, combined with the upset of leaving his master, produced a pile of vomit during the night. Unaware of the dog's midnight hurl, the next morning Dace trod barefoot into Mr. Spot's putrid pool of illness.

Furious, he screamed and kicked Spots. I feared he would cause internal damage to our new pet or the dog would attack him and have to be killed. I lost my maternal head and, with my bulging belly, hung onto Dace's leg as he swung it to kick the dog, slowing each thrust.

"You can't kick the dog," I screamed, trying to make him stop.

"Maybe I should kick you then."

"Just stop kicking Spots." He did and left for work in a fury.

I soothed the shaking dog. When my head cleared, I realized how unwise I'd been and whispered an apology to my unborn baby.

The bond between Mr. Spots and me began that chilly morning. I sat on the floor and cried, and he put his front paw on my shoulder. He hung his massive head, then looked at me with teary eyes and groaned. Realizing he was crying with me, I hugged him. His enormous shoulders felt good in my arms. I'd found a new best friend.

Although Dace never struck Mr. Spots again, that marked the first of several times my best friend and I held each other and commiserated.

Chapter Seven: The Lights Go Out

December came, and with it, tragedy. Grampa was hospitalized with a mysterious illness. Gramma scoured her medical encyclopedia searching for an answer. She didn't drive, so someone took her to the hospital each day. She appeared tired, but always had time to chat with me in the evenings when Dace went out.

When he was out on rainy nights partying with his friends, I found myself praying to a God I learned about in childhood Sunday school classes but didn't know personally. Certain that God hated this abuser as much as I did, I'd pray, "It's raining and the roads are wet and slippery, Lord. Let him have a fatal car accident. Now's Your chance." It was like commanding an attack dog, "Sic 'em, God."

I enjoyed the evenings with Gramma, sitting in her living room and watching television. My husband had alienated me from my friends and most of my family. As long as we lived in that little apartment for free, he could not separate me from the most beloved person in my life. Although she hurt because her life partner wasn't there, our being together somehow brought consolation to both of us, and I treasured those times.

Gramma put her arm around me and told me she loved me, bringing me comfort when Dace's rude attitude became apparent. She had no idea about the terror I lived on the other side of the garage. I felt safe having her there. She was my rock, my closest friend—my reason to carry on.

To earn money, I agreed to babysit my cousin Linda's two-year-old daughter, Heather, while Linda worked in one of the factories in town. A single mother, she paid me a small wage. It reassured me to see a familiar and smiling face each day, and Heather was a fun diversion.

Throughout my childhood, my grandparents' house had always been a calm and magical place. Heather and I had great fun, as I showed the toddler my favorite things to play with there. We took the old cigar box full of marbles to the top of the carpeted stairs and released them, listening to them echo as they bounced down. Heather squealed with delight just as I had done as a child.

I showed Heather the clothes I had loved to dress in. Although far too large for her, I still put the hats, scarves, and gloves on the tiny girl.

Together we found containers of long-forgotten beads and dressed fancy for Gramma, whose quick smile accompanied a twinkle in her eye. She seemed to reminisce about Sophie's and my dress-up days.

One morning while I walked back to the apartment after using my grandparents' bathroom, Gramma called to me. "Kelly. Come look at this."

She sat on a small wooden stool in the greenhouse. She pulled an enormous headless chicken out of a five-gallon bucket, body half plucked. I gagged.

"Look at the size of this breast. Erma Miller brought this to me. Isn't this huge?"

"Oh, Gramma, that's so gross." I clasped my hand over my mouth and ran back into the bathroom, just in time. Later, I hurried toward our place on the other side of the garage and refused to peek into the greenhouse, shielding my eyes with my hand like a blinder on a horse.

"Look at this, Kelly."

"No, I can't."

Sweet and understanding, she chuckled.

Later that day, my grandmother came over crying. "Kelly, I just got a call from your dad. Sophia's mother-in-law has been killed in a car accident. Her car slid on the ice into a semitruck. She died instantly."

"Oh, Gramma. That's terrible. I'm so sorry. Poor Sophie."

"Deaths come in threes, Kelly. I wonder who the next will be." Her furrowed brow told me she thought my grandfather would be the second.

"No. That's just an old wives' tale. That's not true."

"It *does* come in threes. It *is* true."

"Don't talk like that." I hugged her. She appeared much smaller than normal. Since high school, I towered above my petite grandmother, but that day she seemed even tinier.

Grief dwarfs Gramma.

A couple weeks before Christmas my Uncle Steve from Utah came to visit Grampa in the hospital. The second morning of his visit, I had lain back down to sleep with Heather after Linda dropped her off. Dace had gone to work.

The sound of banging on the door that led into the garage woke me with a start. Half asleep, I opened it to find my uncle there with wild eyes. "Mother's dead. Mother's dead," he shouted.

"What do you mean?" I said impatiently.

"Mother's dead. I tried to wake her to ask where she keeps the coffee, and she's dead."

I followed him over to the house and . . . he was right. My Gramma had died in her bed.

The morning became a blur of outgoing phone calls and visits from the Amish neighbors who filed into her bedroom to keen over her body. The women's shrill wailing made my skin crawl. Soon Dad arrived.

The mortician came and took my grandmother away—her body wrapped in her bed linens and zipped into a gray plastic bag, wheeled out on a gurney.

In a haze of confusion, the morning faded into afternoon.

Gramma had suffered from asthma since youth. She'd told of an ailing childhood that included scarlet fever that turned into rheumatic fever. Those illnesses, coupled with chronic asthma, kept her on the porch for many years of her life. Thus, she learned about nature.

She appreciated the birds and flowers, identifying every living thing outside. Indirectly, her illness brought her a wealth of knowledge. If only I'd made the effort to learn more from her.

Dad had shared stories of his mother being at the mercy of doctors fumbling their way in cardiopulmonary medicine—a field undefined. When she was a young woman, the doctors told her to smoke cigarettes to loosen the mucus in her lungs. After severe coughing episodes, she put the suggestion aside. Also, she had traveled to Arizona on doctors' advice for respite, but relapsed upon returning home to Ohio.

She puffed on what she called her wheezer for most of her adult life. A little red peg full of white powdered medicine fit into the top of the clear plastic inhaler with a thick but wide opening for the mouth. She'd tap the peg and inhale deeply to help her breathe.

"Girls, get my wheezer."

Sophia and I grew up with this near-frantic request preceding a thankful sigh and a quick plop onto whatever was handy to sit on. We thought nothing of it, and the adults in our lives always had one nearby. There were wheezers in our house, in our grandparents' car glove compartment and trunk; wheezers in the greenhouse and on the patio. We were never without the little transparent lifesaver.

This morning Gramma's wheezer lay on the floor just under her bed, her arm stretched out toward the nightstand. It seemed she had reached for her wheezer and it fell to the floor. The doctor said her heart "gave out" and she passed away sometime during the night.

Caring for Heather that morning gave a tiny glimpse into what my future would be like as a mother in the midst of tragedy and torment. Linda came as soon possible to retrieve the child.

Other relatives arrived.

I was pregnant and miserable. I'd lost not only my grandmother, but also my best friend and neighbor—my reason to live. I sat on the edge of her bed, hung my head, and cried. What would I do now? Who would love me?

Sitting there crying alone in that bedroom with the doors closed, I felt someone beside me slip an arm around my shoulders and give me a soft hug. The warm reassurance felt familiar, and I looked up to see who was comforting me. I was still alone. I gasped, dropped my head again, and continued to weep.

The presence didn't feel like other uncomfortable, unseen specters I'd sensed before, but instead warm and calming. This was the first time I recognized the positive side of the spirit world. Was it Gramma? Perhaps an angel of the Lord was bringing me God's peace. Still, the loneliness was overwhelming.

While relatives continued to arrive, Dace insisted on taking me to Sears to buy a maternity dress. *Why is he concerned with what I wear? Maybe Dad told him to buy me clothes for the funeral.*

Until then I had worn my husband's jeans, unbuttoned and folded into a *V* at the top for my growing belly. His shirts worked fine too.

It was a depressing trip to the mall. His kindness and enthusiasm seemed misplaced as he bought me a maternity dress, a shirt, and a pair of pants. *If only he was this nice when I wasn't grieving. Dad must've given him money.*

Within hours, Angry Dace returned with a vengeance. He refused to come to the funeral, but went to work as usual. Work had never been that important to him. Having to explain his absence to everyone was more than I could bear. People directed their anger toward me, and inside I was a bloody mess, lost and alone. I hated leaving Gramma there in the snowy cemetery, and hated to leave without her comforting presence.

I wanted to die. The idea of killing myself couldn't be entertained now. I had a tiny person growing inside of me, and my conscience told me that would be wrong.

∞∞∞∞∞∞∞∞∞∞∞∞

The Saturday before Christmas, Dace was out with his friends. Grampa languished in the hospital, and I was alone in the house. My whole being ached for our loss. I needed to feel my best friend with me again.

I wanted to make her molasses cookies. I found her recipe and made batch after batch, trying unsuccessfully to replicate her delicious, soft, cut-out cookies. Scores of hard round molasses hockey pucks filled the piggy cookie jar. The glass pig in the periwinkle jacket had never held such failures. I just couldn't make them like she did.

Whenever alone, I would lie on my grandparents' bed, on Gramma's side, in the same position we found her, and plead with God. *Oh God, please just take me now.*

Take me. Take the baby. Waking an hour or so later, I'd realize He hadn't answered my prayer, and move on.

Time and again I begged God to help me out of my personal hell. I didn't hear Him or see Him working in any way. What I perceived as His rejection was too hard to handle, so I stopped thinking about God . . . until I begged Him once again to kill.

I celebrated New Year's Eve alone. Although grieving, I had no choice. I felt my parents didn't want me over there. I hadn't spoken to my friends in months. My grandfather was still in the hospital. As my husband drank at the bar with his friends, I sat at home, and the old prayers swirled around in my head.

Now's your chance, God. Everyone's drinking tonight. Lots of people have car accidents on New Year's Eve. Let someone hit him and kill him tonight. Please, please, please, I pleaded.

At 3 a.m., I discovered my prayers were unanswered. Mr. Spots dove toward the door as his master stumbled in, proclaiming his entrance.

"It's just me, Spots. Settle down. It's me." Still half asleep, I took pleasure in the fear I heard in his voice. *Someday, Spots. Someday,* I thought, rolling over and praying he would leave me alone.

On January first, while I was at my grandparents' rummaging through their refrigerator, the phone rang. "Hello?" It was Dad.

"Kelly, I just wanted to tell you Grampa died this morning in the hospital."

Three. My mind raced.

My heart sank. Still numb from losing Gramma, I didn't think I could endure another funeral so soon. The thought of the relatives converging on the place again was excruciating.

When I saw that my tormentor intended to go to the funeral, I assumed my father had demanded his presence. He sat in the funeral home chapel in his dirty blue jeans and tattered flannel shirt, slouching in middle-school style rebellion. He stretched his long legs out, crossed at the ankles, in silent defiance with his leather, mud-covered work boots in the aisle to trip anyone passing by. It was worse than not having him there, and I could feel the infuriated glares burn into the back of my head. Heartache upon heartache, I couldn't wait for it to end.

Relatives filled the house—relatives I barely remembered. Cousins last seen a decade earlier took over. Our dog stayed agitated by the noises he heard.

Aunt Margaret joined Uncle Steve from Utah. They strolled around the house looking at my grandparents' knickknacks.

"Oh, this will sell for a bundle," she commented. I saw them wander into the greenhouse, a sacred place to me. My aunt waved her fat little arm toward the shelves of flowerpots, planters, and various floral arrangement paraphernalia. "We can sell all this stuff. It should bring a lot at auction."

They're acting like vultures. I sought solace in my apartment. Digestive acids smoldered up into my throat.

The next evening the family told me to bring our pet over so they could see him. They had heard his Tasmanian-devil-like growls since their arrival, and they wanted to meet the English bulldog who sounded so vicious.

Excited to leave the cramped two-room apartment, he ran through the garage, through the back door, laundry room, hall, and kitchen, and into the dining room. He gained speed, and his enthusiasm propelled him into the living room and onto the closest person, who happened to be one of my cousins. As she sat in the large swivel rocker, Mr. Spots hurled himself onto her, knocking the chair backward into the bookshelves. She was pinned to the chair as the dog humped her neck and torso. She couldn't move for fear the leaning recliner would fall to the floor.

"SPOTS. Get down!" I leapt forward. My uncle pulled the dog's collar and brought the chair into place. The room roared with laughter, igniting Mr. Spots' enthusiasm again. He was poised to run to the next person in the room, but Dace grabbed his collar and brought him to the doorway. I guided Mr. Spots out of the room, calling over my shoulder, "I'm sorry. I'm so sorry."

Within minutes, my spouse joined me back in the apartment. He roared with laughter. "Way to go, boy. You got her."

"That wasn't funny, Dace. He could've hurt her. I've never seen him act like that before. I was afraid he'd bite someone."

"It's good," he retorted. "Now they're all afraid of him. They'll never come in this apartment for sure. Far out, Spots."

While I didn't understand his meaning at the time, I learned he planned to take whatever he wanted and hide it in the apartment.

In time, everyone left.

∞∞∞∞∞∞∞∞∞∞∞∞∞

The Amish neighbors had grown accustomed to entering my grandparents' house at will to use the phone or retrieve their ice cream from the freezer. The attorneys didn't feel it safe to have the house unoccupied and asked Dace and me to move in until the estate was settled. We brought some clothes over, hung them in the closet of the purple bedroom, and got comfortable.

That bedroom had always been magical to me. It was upstairs opposite the bedroom Sophie and I used during our wonderful childhood sleepovers.

The purple bedroom was in the front corner of the house, and one set of windows gave a view of the road. The windows on the other wall showed the driveway and apple trees.

Lilac flowers adorned the wallpaper. Arrangements of various artificial plum-colored flowers decorated the dresser and the antique ice cream parlor table by the driveway-side window.

I reminisced about being very young, sitting on the ice cream parlor chairs, having pretend tea with Gramma. She didn't venture upstairs often, but when she did, I loved to play tea party with her there.

A bright white chenille bedspread covered the full-sized bed. The throw pillows were white with purple pansies, with matching fringe and soft tassels on the corners.

The trinket boxes on the long dresser were amethyst glass, clear glass, and white milk glass. Stretched under these treasures there lay a white lace table runner. The lamps were milk glass, one with a faded floral shade and one with a white shade.

To the right just inside the room was a lengthy closet with sliding wooden doors. It housed dresses from Gramma's youth—perfect for dress-up.

In the corner toward the road was a small cedar closet Grampa had made for my grandmother's mink stole. The stole was the one bit of elegance she had owned. As a child, I needed permission to try it on, and then for just a short while and under the watchful eye of an adult. A shiny white rocking chair with worn lavender blossom cushions sat in the corner by the cedar closet.

I was comforted to sleep there and hoped my cherished memories would bring me peace.

∞∞∞∞∞∞∞∞∞∞

Sophia was home. She and I visited our parents. "Would you girls go to the store and buy some milk?" Mom said. "We're out."

I drove and Sophie joined me. We seldom talked since she lived in Columbus with her husband.

When in high school, Sophia asked Jesus to come into her heart and take over her life. As a teenager, she enjoyed going to see our cousins in Orwell, Ohio, and attended the youth group at the Nazarene church crosswise from their house. She and I never had much to discuss and had even less after she became a Jesus freak.

"I don't know if anyone told you this or not, Kelly, but I feel like someone should. You know you sinned, right?" It was a heavy conversation for a quick trip to the store.

"What do you mean?"

"I mean you got pregnant before you were married. The Bible says having sex before you're married is fornication—it's a sin. I just thought someone should tell you."

I began to cry. "I know. I think about that a lot. I'm so afraid God will punish me by making there be something wrong with the baby."

"He's not like that, Kelly. God won't punish a baby because of something you did."

"I do worry though. What if there's something wrong with it?" I didn't dare tell her I had snorted cocaine and crank the week before I found out I was pregnant. I believed this would be the perfect opportunity for God to punish me, and I worried constantly.

To me, smoking marijuana wasn't an issue. I'd stopped smoking cigarettes when I learned I was pregnant, but in my ignorance, thought pot was fine.

"Well, don't worry about that, Kelly. I just think you need to ask God to forgive you for sinning. Do that, okay?"

I agreed to ask for God's forgiveness later, when alone. But it didn't happen. If I was ever alone, I slept. If God tried to speak to me, I didn't listen. I spoke to Him when I begged Him to kill one of His creations—Dace.

The weeks rolled by and my belly grew. With no money for pregnancy underclothes, I rummaged through Gramma's dresser drawers for something—anything—to wear. For the remainder of my pregnancy, I relied on her bras and big granny panties for coverage. Wearing her underwear made me feel she was there with me.

∞∞∞∞∞∞∞∞∞∞∞∞

One Friday night when Dace was home, I saw him studying the calendar that hung on the wall in the kitchen. Again and again he flipped the pages, counting the weeks. *What is he doing?* We watched television and went to bed.

Having a nightmare, I awoke whimpering. Startled, I relaxed once I realized I was in my own bed. My breathing returned to normal. I lay still and tried to go back to sleep.

He got up, trying not to wake me. I heard him slide a magazine from the bottom of the pile of magazines on his nightstand. He disappeared into the bathroom. Several minutes later he tiptoed back into the bedroom, slid the magazine into place, and lay down. I felt nauseated.

Suddenly he jumped to his feet. "You lying witch. You slut!"

My protector barked. I jumped and blinked into the darkness. "What is it, Dace?"

"You lying, effing whore."

"What'd I do? What'd I do?"

"I'm not sleeping with you, slut." He stormed out of the bedroom and down the stairs, yelling all the way. I sat there, stunned, confused, and shaking. Mr. Spots grunted and dropped his head to sleep.

I reviewed the previous hour in my head. I'd had a nightmare and woken up crying. He disappeared into the bathroom with one of his filthy magazines. He came back and yelled at me. I couldn't figure it out, but thought it might have something to do with his persistent examination of the calendar earlier that day.

He's counting the weeks between my due date and the time we were together last summer. I'll bet he thinks I slept with someone else and this baby isn't his.

I ran into the bathroom and made it to the toilet just in time to vomit. Doing a quick turnaround, I had diarrhea. Depleted, I crawled back into bed and listened intently. Anxious, I tried not to fall asleep. I heard the rear door slam. *I think he's going out to sleep in the apartment.*

Was I safe? Would he return and kill me? I drifted off to sleep full of apprehension and fear. My pet lay dutifully at the foot of the bed.

The next morning I woke with a heavy sorrow resting on my chest. Intense loneliness engulfed my soul. What would happen to me? What was the monster thinking? It was Saturday. What would I have to endure today?

Although famished, I knew better than to eat his cereal. I rummaged through my grandparents' pantry for breakfast and found a pint jar of stewed tomatoes. They looked delicious, although I didn't know how my gut would react.

Warming the tomatoes in a pot on the stove, I mumbled, "Stupid colitis."

Enjoying the peace and quiet, I fed my bulldog and sat at the breakfast table. With a heavy sigh, I gazed out the window and ate in peace.

Gramma's collection of colorful glass vases lined the shelves Grampa had built across the window. The morning sun shone through, casting bright colors over the table and floor. Oh, how I loved mornings in the breakfast nook. I enjoyed warm memories of eating there with my grandparents.

Afterward, while I washed dishes at the sink, Dace came in. Although he seemed calm and smiled sweetly, I examined him out of the corner of my eye, unsure of what he planned to do. He leaned over and kissed me on the mouth.

"Good morning, tomato breath," he said softly.

I tried to smile and looked at the floor. His moods were making me crazy, and I lived in dread.

"I'm sorry about last night."

I couldn't believe my ears. He had never apologized for anything before. *He must feel bad.*

"That's all right, Dace."

Maybe it would be a good day after all.

Chapter Eight: Searching in the Darkness

The violence continued, but no one seemed aware. Dace worked during the day, allowing Mr. Spots and me to hang out, play, and nap, thus strengthening our bond. Together with Heather, we toddled around my grandparents' property.

The big, old, deep-red wooden sleigh still sat in the front yard, as Grampa had started decorating for Christmas. The happy memories were in stark contrast to the reality I presently lived.

I appreciated the rare occasions when my husband took me out with him. Even in happy, social times, he appeared ready for a fight.

At a party in the home of his married friends, a guy sat on my right while Dace sat on my left on a long sofa. My pregnant tummy bulged. We all smoked pot.

Although thoroughly stoned, I became aware that the man on the right had his hand resting on my knee. My gaze widened and I looked at my husband. He glanced at me, and my bulging green eyes glimpsed from him to my knee and back again. At last, he got it and stood quickly.

In one quick movement, he grabbed me by the arm and threw me behind him, grabbed the dude off the couch, and punched him in the face. The guy pushed back, and he threw him onto our hostess, who sat in a reclining chair. The host separated them and we left. Dace was furious, and we never returned—just one more friendship bridge burned, making his world even smaller.

His rage cost him many career opportunities as well. Punching his boss, getting into fistfights with co-workers, and telling his authorities off, all brought dismissals or caused him to leave jobs with great potential.

After losing his temper and being fired again, he took a job in a local plastic factory and hated every minute of it. He rotated working days and nights, and it cut into his party time. The responsibility of family did not suit him.

To my knowledge, we never had any money. Curious about why we struggled financially, I asked, "Dace, how much money do you make?"

"None of your business."

Stunned, I stared at him and then chuckled. "No, really. How much do you make?" I couldn't believe he was serious, and thought he'd say "psyche" and give me a figure. We were married, after all. Weren't we supposed to be a team?

"I told you—none of your effin' business. Don't ask again." I didn't. Another taboo topic for the List.

Thankful that Gramma had been a wise steward, we didn't go hungry that winter. There were Mason jars full of canned vegetables and fruits. The freezer stored bread, homemade applesauce, frozen vegetables, and fruits. And apple butter—the sweet, cinnamony goodness that triggered wonderful memories.

I often found myself inhaling deeply when upstairs, subconsciously searching for the aroma of apple butter—longing for my grandmother's love.

The food lasted for many weeks, but when it ran out, I didn't know what to do.

One Saturday morning Leon stopped by. He and Dace were going out. I knew better than to ask where they were going.

"Can you take me to the grocery store when you get home later?"

"I don't know when I'll be home."

"Well, we don't really have any food around," I timidly said. "I have to go to the store to get some."

"What about the pantry?"

"There isn't enough left to make a meal."

"Freezer?"

"It's pretty empty too. I mean besides Spots' food. Anyway, we need your cereal. The store closes at six tonight."

"We'll see."

They came home in the late afternoon and plopped on the couch.

"Hi, guys. Have a good day?"

"Yeah. What do you want?" He avoided the "what did you do today" question.

"I need to go to the grocery store, remember?" I reminded him quietly.

He pulled out his stash and Zig-Zag rolling papers. "We'll go after we smoke a doobie."

I watched the clock. Although afraid we'd be late, the fear of him embarrassing me in front of our friend won out, and I kept my mouth shut. My gut burned with hunger.

Dace stood. "Let's hit it." We all got into his car, with me in the back seat.

We arrived at the grocery store just as they were about to close. "Can I have some money?" I said.

"I'll go in with you to pay."

The lights shut off toward the rear of the store when the three of us entered. "I'll be quick." I rushed toward the cereal aisle. I didn't see my husband's brand of cereal right away and instead grabbed a box of Cheerios. More lights turned off, and I hurried toward the front.

"Is this it?" his voice thundered. "We came all the way down here for this?"

Leon laughed as my face burned crimson.

"That's all there's time for. They're turning the lights off."

"Go get what you need," Dace's voice boomed in the empty store. I waddled off into the darkness; laughter echoed after me.

I bent over the now darkened meat case, my belly pushing against the glass. Delirious with humiliation, I grabbed a small package of pork chops.

In the front of the store, Dace grabbed it from me. "We're not coming back here again tomorrow. I'm not taking you to the store every effin' day."

I forced the corners of my mouth up. "That's okay. It'll be all right."

"If you didn't need food, why did you make me bring you here?"

By now, the owner and one cashier were left and stared at me.

"The store's closing, Dace. Let's just go."

The owner looked at me with compassion. "That's okay. You get what you need. We'll wait."

Yearning to be invisible, leaving was the next best thing. "It's okay," I whispered. "I'll wait outside."

"Stay right here," my tormentor yelled. He loved his power over me, and delighted in disgracing me publicly.

I waited by the door while he paid for the food. My upper body ached, and I thought my heart would burst through my chest. I swallowed hard and blinked back the tears. Stifled cries burned my throat.

Oh God, get me out of here. Let me just drop dead right now. Overwhelming isolation engulfed me.

At home, the guys smoked another joint while I cooked the pork chops. A tough lesson about not frying the chops remained filed away in my memory bank. I took some freezer-burnt hot dog buns I'd found earlier, crumbled them, and added salt and pepper. I moistened the pork chops with water and pushed the seasoned breadcrumbs into the sides. I put them onto a broiler pan and put them on the top shelf in the oven.

I'm not going to have enough to feed Leon too. Dace will really let me have it now. Why doesn't Leon say anything to him?

"G'bye, dude. Thanks for the dope."

The door slammed. I heard him drive away.

I peeked my head into the living room. "Leon gone?"

"Yeah. He gave me a spiff for later. Maybe we'll smoke it after dinner."

I wondered if leaving the joint was our friend's way of making me feel better. He must've realized I was mortified at the store.

After I washed the dishes, I joined him in the living room. "Wanna smoke this with me now?" I was surprised he'd waited for me. Maybe he felt sorry after all.

I found it odd we always had money for new guitar strings and marijuana. Guitar strings, marijuana, and we always managed to purchase the expensive frozen dog food Lino warned us to feed our pet. With vivid memories of his introductory hurl incident, we weren't ready to oppose that mandate.

Winter drew to a close and I entered my third trimester. Mr. Spots and I were inseparable. When the heating oil for my grandparents' furnace depleted, we had no heat. As we blanketed off the living room, our world condensed to one room. We kept the wood-burning stove ablaze during the evenings with Gramma's magazines, and twigs gathered from the woods beyond the field behind the house.

One evening Dace cleaned out the stove and put the cinders into a paper shopping bag. He put the bag onto the back patio and the next morning there was only pile of cinders. Apparently, hot embers in the ashes burned through the bag. Realizing the potential for a fire was frightening. That day, I pondered God.

Our lazy pet spent his days curled up at the end of the sofa. I kept one of Gramma's crocheted blankets spread over him to keep him comfortable.

∞∞∞∞∞∞∞∞∞∞∞∞

I welcomed spring with hopes of warmer days.

My four-legged best friend and I wandered around Gramma's enormous round flower garden. I reminisced about a lifetime of beloved moments with her there. In time, I cut some early spring blossoms for indoor bouquets. They weren't beautiful like the ones Gramma could put together.

The greenhouse, so expertly built with Grampa's loving hands, no longer brought life. The baby's breath that once filled in the spaces between the decorative cement stepping stones, turned brown. The growing shelves that had held numerous pots of seeds, sprouts, buds, and blooms were just dust-covered shelves with empty containers of soil.

The wall shelves of extra pots, colorful character pots, traditional clay pots, and a plethora of vases, swiftly became the breeding ground for spiders.

The dirt-sifting screen lay motionless in the dirt bin. No one cared about "clean" dirt. No one knew how to perpetuate the flowering life that was the norm throughout my childhood. The deteriorating structure reflected my frame of mind.

Standing in the greenhouse, I stared through the dirty windows in the back and my thoughts returned to my early childhood.

Grampa often parked his tractor behind the building. Sophia and I played on it, and we loved to bounce up and down on the round clutch pedal. I remembered a time I played alone, singing and bouncing behind the house. It had been chilly—autumn, maybe. At once, I heard a shot in the woods behind me and something brushed the top of my head. I stopped bouncing and looked around. I spied a hole in the wood between the glass panels of the greenhouse.

I remembered running to tell my daddy something went through the top of my hair and into the wood. He didn't pay attention to me at first, but in my typical hyperactive fashion, I repeated myself until he joined me so I could act out my story.

"I was bouncing on this thing here, and—"

"You shouldn't bounce on that, Kelly. That's the clutch."

"Grampa always lets us bounce on it. You saw me bounce on it before, Daddy. Listen."

"I'm sorry, K.J. Go on. You were bouncing and what happened next?" His expression emanated love.

Bouncing as I told the story, my voice bounced too. "I was singing, and then I heard a shot and something touched the top of my head."

"It did?" he humored me.

"Yes, it did. Then I saw this little hole here." I jumped down and climbed up on a discarded cement block to reach, wiggling my index finger inside the hole.

"What was that, Daddy? Can a bee go into the wood like that?"

My father leaned closer to examine the hole. I climbed back up onto the tractor. His countenance changed and he looked at me. He gently bowed my head to examine the top of it. "You said you felt it touch the top of your head?"

"Yeah. It went through my hair. Was it a bee, Daddy?"

"Probably, Kelly. Let's go inside." He helped me down from the tractor and gave me a firm sideways hug against his leg.

"I don't want you playing back here anymore, Kelly Jean. And don't bounce on that clutch anymore."

"But Grampa said we—"

"I don't care what Grampa told you. No more bouncing on the clutch, and stay in the front or side yards."

I remembered hearing him tell Grampa something about "those darned Amish shooting toward the house again." Apparently, when I was on a down bounce, a bullet had skimmed over the top of my head. It entrenched in the wood between the glass panes.

Reminiscing, I wondered why God spared me then. Wouldn't everything be much better now if I'd been killed that day? I wouldn't have to endure the ongoing torture of my husband's wild emotions now.

"Why didn't you just take me then, God?" I whispered.

Together with Spots, I rambled through the spacious rectangular vegetable garden in the side yard, wishing for something to sprout for dinner. The one thing Dace grew was marijuana. It grew behind the garage next to my great-grandmother's mint plants.

"Mentholated joints," he exclaimed with ignorant exuberance.

The Amish often helped themselves to the mint that grew behind the garage. They used it in their tea. We teased about the real possibility of them accidentally snipping some marijuana in their mint harvest.

"That'll be a cup of tea they'll never forget," we chuckled.

I was grateful for my grandparents' diligence in paying for the daily newspaper in advance and looked forward to its arrival each day. I often sat on the living room floor, leaned forward with my abdomen lying on the carpet, and poured over the want ads, hoping for a job a pregnant girl could do at home. My furry best friend, with arrogant head up, would traipse across it, twisting his foot with each step, tearing the paper. This always garnered the attention he sought, refusing to be ignored. He made me smile, and I loved him for it.

The abuse escalated, as did my desperation. Always walking on eggshells, I never knew what would set Dace off. I tried to find a pattern. Certain words and phrases incited instant rage. I began to add to the List in my mind of things never to say. Trial and error was a painful process.

I pondered the two times my husband seemed genuinely loving. When we lived in the apartment beside the garage, he brought flowers home to me one day. No occasion or explanation, just beautiful flowers.

The other time, we had just moved into my grandparents' house. As I fell asleep one night, I heard him whisper, "You are my little blossoming flower." Those memories made me feel loved. As my belly grew, I clung to those thoughts with anticipation of a brighter future.

In my naiveté, I hoped having our baby would change things between us.

The happy day in April came. Two weeks past my due date, I had an obstetrician appointment Friday afternoon. After my morning shower, I stood nude in front of the long dresser mirror in our bedroom. I was huge.

I knew nothing about stretch marks, and when I'd initially spied pale purple lines on my body, I panicked. I'd called my mother, who told me what they were and that they'd never go away. "They're unavoidable unless you use special lotions while you're pregnant."

Why didn't anyone tell me this? I was irritated. Now I had matching ones on other parts of my body. My navel stuck out like a large nose.

This morning as I surveyed my enormity, something looked different.

"Hey. My boobs aren't lying on my belly." I wanted to tell somebody the baby dropped, but who would I tell? Dace was at work. I'd been alienated from my friends, and my mother was in Columbus visiting Sophia.

"Hmm. I'll ask the doctor about it." I learned my doctor was on vacation and one of his two colleagues would deliver the baby if I went into labor during the weekend.

Another doctor in the practice performed an internal exam. It hurt. Afterward I sat with my legs hanging over the side of the table.

"You get dressed and I'll be right back in," he advised.

When I stood to dress, I saw blood on the paper cover where I'd been sitting. I dressed and waited for the doctor to return.

"There was blood on the table." My voice quivered. "Why?"

"Oh, don't worry. I stretched your cervix." He demonstrated by parting his index finger and middle finger into a *V*.

"But why?"

"Oh, we just do that to help you along a little. It's okay. You don't want to be pregnant forever, do you?" He flashed a fake smile and left.

That concerned me because I hadn't heard of it before. At home, I scoured Gramma's medical books, but found no reference to helping a pregnancy along by stretching a cervix.

I was nauseous throughout the evening. By the morning, I couldn't shake the pain in my lower back.

My father came that morning to fix the washing machine. I wanted to chat with him, but felt uncomfortable. I craved his company, so I opened a folding chair in the laundry room and stayed with him for almost an hour.

"I'm sorry, Dad, but I have to go lie down. I went to the doctor yesterday and I don't feel very good right now."

"No problem, K.J. You go lie down. I'll tell you before I go." I vaguely remembered him announce his departure.

My husband came home around noon and found me dozing on the sofa. He woke me.

"Dace, I'm really sick." I told him what the doctor did and that I believed labor had started. "The pains come and go."

"Have you timed them?"

"No. I'm just trying to sleep."

"Well, let's time them." His excitement seemed genuine.

Within a few hours, it was time to go to the hospital. I called my doctor. As promised, one of the other two physicians in the practice would meet me there.

My baby's father was bursting with pride while driving to the hospital. He slowed to yell out the car window to a friend, "Hey, my wife's having a baby." Again, I felt loved. *Maybe this baby will make him happy and he'll change.*

He stayed by my side throughout the labor and delivery, and appeared to enjoy the time in the labor room with me.

Between contractions, I regaled him with a tale of gossip about the doctor on call. He had a reputation of being a ladies' man and having relationships with his nurses while being married to others. I'd pause the story while my coach timed my contractions, and then I'd continue.

"Maybe my doctor wanted him to deliver this baby to help him make his alimony payments," I joked.

I brought a daffodil from Gramma's garden to be my focal point, following what I'd learned in a Lamaze lesson.

Ah yes, Lamaze class. My thoughts returned to the time he promised to go with me. The birthing coach's attendance was mandatory. I needed to go to prepare for this very day, but after the second class he refused to return. We'd watched a video that first time. A new one the instructor promised would show less blood. I remembered shaking with fear.

"I don't think I can do that," I had whispered to Dace.

He'd laughed. "You don't have a choice at this point, now do you?"

There was no turning back, but I thought more classes would help prepare me and ease my mind.

I had pleaded with him to go with me the evening of the second class. "Would you rather I ask Melanie or my mom to be my birthing coach?"

Enraged, he punched a hole in the bedroom door. A Led Zeppelin poster hung in an odd place told anyone who ventured upstairs all was not well in the beautiful purple room.

He had gone to class that night with a vow he'd never go again. He was sullen and rude to everyone. An invitation to join another couple for ice cream afterward was met with a snort and quick exit. I apologized and followed behind in a blur of shame.

Now, with just two Lamaze classes under my belt and whatever knowledge I had gleaned from my grandmother's medical books, I would deliver.

Turning my head toward the flower in the vase hurt my neck. I couldn't have the table across the bed because it would interfere with the routine exams the nurses performed. Consequently, I looked straight ahead at a picture that hung on the bathroom door at the foot of the labor bed. The photo showed a cute baby boy with a blanket over his head. Not what I planned, but it was something to focus on to take my mind off the overpowering pain.

"This is all Eve's fault," I screamed, remembering the Bible story of Eve offering Adam the forbidden fruit, and God's declaration that women would have painful labor henceforth.

The nurse gave me a shot of Demerol for the pain. While it didn't completely relieve it, my mind disassociated from it, causing me to care less.

Dace even enjoyed that part of the day. He chatted with the nurses who came in and out, giving them his perceived update.

Finally, they said to push. By that time, I hated that photo of the baby. "Look at your focal point," my husband coached. Even in my drugged delirium, I knew better than to tell him to take a hike like I desperately wanted to.

"I don't want to look at it anymore," I snapped.

At 7:02 p.m., just five hours from the time I arrived at the hospital, our baby was born. The nurses positioned a large mirror for me to view her birth.

Dace had always called my tummy "Demetrius," hoping for a boy. When they announced it was a girl, I turned to him and gasped, "It's a girl. Is that all right?"

"You never question the sex, young lady," the doctor retorted. "You just thank God it's healthy." The nursing staff fell silent. The doctor did his minimum requirements and left.

A nurse bent toward my ear and whispered, "Doctor has a Down syndrome sister, honey. That's why he's so sensitive about questioning the sex of a baby. Just be happy she's healthy." She smiled sweetly to comfort me.

Moved onto a bed, I waited in a recovery room. The nurses soon handed little, swaddled Star Aries to me. "You nurse her now, honey. Just call if you need anything." I hesitantly took the tiny cocoon.

The new father stood beside the bed.

"Dace come here. I can't do this." I was uncertain because I still felt the effects of the Demerol. "I'm afraid I'm gonna drop her. Help me."

He reached toward the baby to catch her in case I couldn't hold on to her. With no guidance, she wouldn't latch on.

I suppose that's something they taught in the Lamaze classes I missed, I silently groused.

About fifteen minutes later, the nurse returned. "How ya doing? Oh, she needs help." She positioned the baby's mouth properly. "There you go. She's latching now. You feed her and I'll be back."

"I still feel sorta drugged. I'm afraid I'll drop her. Will the Demerol hurt her?"

"No, you won't drop her," the nurse assured. "The Demerol will wear off. Don't worry about it."

Soon they came to take tiny Star to the nursery, and Dace left. The next day my mother came to the hospital to see the baby.

"She's not in the nursery," she observed. I couldn't understand and inquired at the nurses' station.

"Where's my baby?"

"Oh, they took her down the hall for tests. It's routine."

It didn't feel right to me. *Why would they take her away during visiting hours?* That afternoon the pediatrician came in to speak with me.

Dr. Burgos was from the Philippines and spoke with such a heavy accent I had a hard time comprehending her English. She tried to explain something about Star's fontanel. They had taken X-rays of her head.

By the time the doctor left, all I absorbed was "water on the brain" and "surgery by age two or permanent brain damage." I sat alone, shaking and feeling as if I'd be sick.

I wished Dace were with me. Then again, I was glad he wasn't. I wanted someone to be with me, but whom? Something inside me told me I would find comfort in the Bible in the nightstand. I got it out and searched through the book. It made no sense to me and I didn't know where to read.

A nurse came in and I asked her to explain what the doctor meant. After two explanations, I still was unclear on what was wrong with Star.

I scoured the Bible for some comfort, something that would make me feel everything would be all right. I pleaded for God to make my baby well.

I'm so sorry I had sex before being married. Please don't let my baby have water on her brain. Oh God, I beg You. I wept until I could cry no more.

By the time Dace arrived after work, my face was puffy from crying. I tried to explain what the doctor and nurses had said. He flippantly told me not to worry about it. "Star looks all right to me," he concluded. Still, I was frightened.

"Maybe this is God's punishment for us fooling around before we were married."

"That's bull crap. She's fine." He curtailed the conversation and left. I sat on the bed suspecting eighteen wasn't old enough to handle water-on-the-brain problems in an infant. I trembled, feeling deserted and inadequate.

The next morning, the staff swept Star away for further study. Later that day, as I prepared to take the baby home, all joy left me. The nurse came in.

"Mrs. Easton, Dr. Burgos wanted me to tell you that what we felt when we pushed on the top of your infant's head was just an unusually large soft spot. It wasn't water as she first suspected. We were feeling her brain."

I gasped. I'd always heard you shouldn't touch, certainly not push, the baby's fontanel. "Well, you didn't hurt her, did you?"

"Oh, no. She's fine. Babies are a lot more resilient than you might think."

I gladly swaddled my newborn to go home. Dace pulled the car to the front of the hospital, and the nurse brought the baby and me out in a wheelchair.

The ride home seemed extra bumpy. *I guess he's just in a hurry to bring us home.*

Eager to have our baby home, anxious about what life would be like with a newborn, and afraid of my husband becoming jealous of the time an infant takes, combined to make an emotional cocktail that burned my gut and made me tremble all over.

Chapter Nine: The List Grows

Bringing our daughter home to my grandparents' house seemed perfect. I perceived Gramma's spirit with me and never doubted my ability to care for my newborn.

Dace appeared proud and content at first. Yet when he hit me while I held our child in my arms just days later, I couldn't deny he had an anger problem and wouldn't—or couldn't—control his temper.

Well aware of change, Mr. Spots was ready to accept his "sister." He sniffed her bald little scalp, snorted snot, and shook his head, pelting everyone with his long strands of drool. With this, his seal of approval, Star was welcome.

She slept in a tiny yellow antique crib beside our bed. Her father replaced the light bulb in the lamp on the nightstand with a transparent blue bulb, making it possible for me to care for her in the night without a blaring light illuminating the room.

At first I thought him loving and thoughtful to do this. *A gift for the baby. This way it won't hurt her eyes.* Then I learned his intent; he wouldn't be awakened by the light. He did not intend to help—ever.

Doctor's orders said no stairs, so each morning I threw everything I thought I'd need for the day, to the bottom of the stairway. With great care, I carried Star while my beloved pet led the way in our morning parade.

I had a brand-new, full-size crib upstairs in the nursery, the miniature crib in our room, and an heirloom baby basket from Germany downstairs on the dining room floor for her naps. I'd often forget something in her room and would have to climb slowly back up.

Two weeks after the arrival of our precious daughter, I learned of an additional phrase for the List. A phrase from days past, used by his abusive stepfather; a trigger phrase to be avoided forever thereafter.

Following an exhausting day of caring for our infant in a two-story house, I stood halfway up the stairs and asked my husband to bring me the clock radio I'd forgotten in the kitchen. I would need to set the alarm for him for work the following morning.

"Get it yourself," he muttered from the kitchen.

"You're so lazy you disgust me," was my lamentable response.

"Lazy" and "you disgust me" were new line items on the List of dangerous terms.

"Get back down here," he seethed. When I entered the kitchen, he slapped the side of my head, knocking me to the floor. I tried to get up, but he slapped me down and choked me against the metal cupboards.

Those vintage buttercup-yellow cabinets I had always loved as an integral part of my Gramma's charming kitchen were now just painful walls of affliction, unyielding to my skull as I fought for breath. That began a brutal three-hour tirade.

"Put the baby in the other room," were the only words spoken once we were upstairs. I was terrorized and exhausted. With the wounds of childbirth still fresh, the blood flowed as I succumbed to my tormentor's sadistic demands.

Later, still in shock, I deliberated. *Can your husband rape you? Yes, I guess he can.*

Chapter Ten: Maybe God Does Care

With an already demolished self-esteem, I surveyed my post-baby body in the mirror. I sagged. "I'm just eighteen and everything droops, Mr. Spots."

Dace had an ever-growing supply of porn magazines. From tasteful to trashy, he loved them all. I studied them.

"What do these women have that I don't? Well, they don't have stretch marks and they don't look wilted, that's for sure." My best friend just snorted. I needed an exercise regimen.

Remembering old ads for sauna belts that promised quick weight loss, I wrapped plastic wrap around my waist. I thought I could spot reduce as I sweated.

Next, I found a Jack LaLanne exercise program on television. Every morning I cinched my middle with cling wrap and put Star in the playpen in the living room. I made weights out of two Mason jars full of water.

With the jars and a broomstick, I exercised with Jack. Living in a two-story house with a newborn, not having much food to eat, and exercising, worked together to help reduce and tone my body.

Even so, it became more difficult to please my husband. I examined the women in his magazines and determined I required a sexy garter belt and nylons.

I rummaged through my grandmother's panty drawer. "Nylons. Now I need a garter. I'm sure these weren't meant for what I have in mind, Gramma." I found large girdles with garters. Poverty breeds creativity. "I can do this." I cut a big white girdle down to bikini height, hemmed it, and tie-dyed it with burgundy dye I'd found in the laundry room.

While he enjoyed that, it was short-lived. I soon learned it's impossible for a woman to compete with the fantasies promoted in pornographic magazines.

∞∞∞∞∞∞∞∞∞∞∞∞

The weather got warmer and I wanted to tan over my stretch marks.

One Saturday, with Dace out with his friends, I put Star in her basket to sleep on the table in the covered back patio while I lay on a beach towel on the grassy corner of the greenhouse.

The sun felt good. I let my mind wander, enjoying memories of lying in the sun at the quarry with my friends the summer before. *I can't doze off. I have to remember Star.* I pondered how life had changed in just twelve short months.

The hot sun made me thirsty. I hopped up and into the patio. Gently lifting the wicker structure from the table, I headed inside. "Come on, sweetheart. Let's go inside for a few minutes." I placed the basket on the kitchen table and poured a glass of cold water from the faucet.

Without warning, a thunderous sound filled the yard. I gasped. Eight cows from a neighboring farm tore around the corner and stampeded through the yard, trampling my beach towel. My jaw dropped. *I would've been stomped to death. What would've happened to Star outside in the heat? Who knows when Dace will be home? Maybe God is looking out for us after all.*

∞∞∞∞∞∞∞∞∞∞∞∞

Another blessing in my life came in the stocky shape of my best friend, Mr. Spots.

I continued to babysit Heather throughout the week, and Mr. Spots seemed to feel somewhat displaced with her around. His huge chest dwarfed the little girl. As he wandered by her, he often bumped into her with his shoulders, knocking her over. He kept on walking, eyes forward, looking strangely satisfied. It always made Heather giggle.

One sunny day, Linda came early to pick her up. When she knocked on the storm door, our bulldog ran to the back room, lunged forward, making his Tasmanian devil sound, and broke the window in the door. My cousin panicked and ran to her car. She honked her horn and waited for me to come out.

I ran out to the car with my dog at my heels.

"Oh my gosh, Linda. Did you see what he did to the door?"

"Yeah, that's why I'm out here. He scared the crap out of me."

"Well, come on in. He's all right as long as I'm with you."

I brought her into the house. "She's our friend, Spots." He saw I welcomed her, and relaxed.

"He's just guarding the house and protecting you both," she said. "I know I don't have to worry about you guys here alone."

Such was the protective nature of Mr. Spots, my best friend. Many nights, Dace staggered home after a late night of drinking with his friends and slinked into our bedroom. Spots, sleeping at the foot of the bed, always jumped into attack position, growling as he tried to focus in on the intruder in the doorway. Dace's panicky plea, "It's just me, Spots. It's me," always made me grin, secretly hoping my guardian would attack him and make me a young widow.

Living in my grandparents' house, surrounded by their things, didn't bring the comfort it once had. Frightening, violent happenings eclipsed the warm

118

magnificent memories of a happy childhood with my loving grandparents. I was grateful to have Mr. Spots to love and protect me.

The solitude I experienced was often hard to bear. I ached for my grandmother while I sat in the living room at night. The stark reality of my tormentor's presence and my existing nightmare obscured my recollections of fun evenings watching *The Lawrence Welk Show* with my grandparents and eating homemade cookies.

On two separate occasions our pet growled and chased something the entire length of the living room. The first time he did, my husband and I both saw twinkling lights or sparkles in front of him as he jumped and barked, biting into the air. Was it Gramma? Was it God or an angel? Was it the evil force that drove Dace's every move? Whatever it was, Spots saw it and chased it, no doubt protecting us.

Our beloved English bulldog appeared to feel my emotions. When I laughed, he ran in circles, smiling with his wide mouth open. With joy, he whipped his large head around, flinging his strings of slimy slobber east and west, north and south, in classic *Turner & Hooch* fashion.

Likewise, my pain was his pain, and when I cried, he cried. I wept often as my life unfolded into a daily challenge of avoiding slaps and being choked. As I sat on the floor and sobbed, Spots would lower his head, put his enormous paw on my shoulder, and cry. With sorrowful groans, tears streamed down his wrinkled face, staining his fur. We often wept together. He was wonderful to hug. He laid his head on me, and I wrapped my arms around his massive shoulders, clinging to him as jointly we grieved over our lives with Dace, our wicked master. "Mr. Spots, without you I'd lose my mind."

I think Spots hadn't forgotten our initial night of bonding and repaid the gesture one evening. Star slept in her nursery, and we were downstairs. In a rage, our master began to assault me. He held me upside down, smashing my head again and again into the bottom of the wicker baby basket. With unnerving cries and whines, my protector jumped on him repeatedly, distracting him, allowing me to fall and run free. Perhaps he was saying, "You can't hit my best friend." Maybe he thought me being dumped into the baby's basket was unsafe for her. Whatever was going through his beloved canine mind, he saved me from another beating.

∞∞∞∞∞∞∞∞∞∞∞∞∞

I still hadn't told my parents about my husband's abusive ways. The birth of baby Star had changed our relationship. We'd forgiven each other for the fights we'd had when I lived at home, and we finally got along. They didn't acknowledge a problem, and I thought mentioning it would jeopardize our bond.

One hot summer Saturday, I took Star and Spots to visit my parents. I laid the baby on a blanket on the dining room floor while I got fresh diapers out of the dryer in the basement.

"Kelly, come quick." My mother sounded frantic. "Get up here."

I ran up the stairs two by two. Rounding the top of the stairs, I saw my mother fearfully leaning over our pet, who stood over Star.

"Spots won't let me pick her up," she called out. There stood the enormous bulldog with his massive paw resting gently on Star's tiny torso, protecting her. My baby had found her first best friend. He moved aside when I approached. "Good dog, Spots. Good dog."

Chapter Eleven: Leaving the House

Somehow Dace found the money for another World Series of Rock concert at the Cleveland Lakefront Stadium, featuring Aerosmith, Ted Nugent, Journey, Thin Lizzy, AC/DC, and the Scorpions. I hated to be away from Star and because I breast-fed her, I couldn't drink, pop pills, or snort anything. I still smoked pot.

We got a local Amish girl to come over to babysit. In typical Amish fashion, she didn't come alone. She brought two of her sisters and a girl cousin.

For me, this concert felt different. Aerosmith's songs made my heart hurt. Journey's songs made me cry. "Red Ted" Nugent didn't energize me like usual. AC/DC just creeped me out. Having a baby changed how I looked at life. *This will be the last one of these things I go to.* I couldn't wait to go home.

∞∞∞∞∞∞∞∞∞∞∞∞

Our child was just three months old when my husband said I had to find a job—caring for my cousin's daughter didn't bring in enough money. I didn't want to leave Star, and wept. After I gathered myself together, I agreed to look for employment on Monday. I'd babysit until the end of the month.

With a new week, I tried to have a new attitude. *Gotta carry on,* I thought as I dressed in my best clothes and went to Ohio Job Service. My skills were limited, but the job counselor found a position that would be a good fit. I'd taken two years of typing in high school. The job for the County Auditor's Office required basic office skills. To qualify, I had to take a test and interview with the auditor.

As soon as he saw I might have a job, Dace quit his job at the plastic factory. He wanted to stay home. With

121

my little cousin still in our care, he agreed to watch her and Star while I tested and interviewed. I was a nervous wreck that morning.

"Do you think you could run the vacuum while I'm gone?"

"I'll do better than that," he chirped. "I'll clean the whole house and make dinner."

"You won't have time to do all that and play with Heather and take care of the baby. I'll be home as soon as I can."

I came home to find the entire house cleaned, our infant sleeping, and Heather watching *Sesame Street* on television. He was in the kitchen cooking chicken.

"This place looks great. How did you have time to do everything? And where did you find that chicken?"

He dripped with arrogance. "Oh, it's easy. I don't see why you can't do it. You just let me handle everything and you work. The chicken was in the freezer." It was an unexplainable Dace mystery.

Mrs. Byler, an Amish neighbor who lived on a farm about a mile away, said she and her daughters would babysit for us. I agreed so Dace could look for a job. The family had several daughters, and they loved my baby. Her husband seemed crass and angry. He worked the dayshift in a local factory. Sometimes I saw him come home when I picked up Star. He never spoke, and only grunted in response when I greeted him.

I worked part time. The women in the auditor's office were kind and loving. I kept a framed photo of my daughter on my worktable. I often had to excuse myself to the restroom to pump breast milk with a little manual pump. I made the connection between seeing the photo and my milk coming down and took the picture home.

As my grandparents' estate settlement progressed, we had to get out of the way. While we tried to pack our possessions, the predator-like relatives swooped in from Utah and Oregon.

We moved our belongings back into the apartment. When I went back to the house to grab my afghan off the bed, it was gone. My grandmother had crocheted it for me as a graduation gift. It was in the Utah U-Haul trailer hitched to a van and when my father asked for it, the relatives got tense. They were there to collect all they could to sell. Boxes of flowerpots, planters, dishes, blankets, and glassware were moved into the trailer.

The family from the Pacific Northwest viewed everything with antique collector eyes. They searched in the attic for old picture frames, tin photographs, antique doilies, and such. They tagged pieces of furniture and moved them into their large moving truck as fast as possible.

The beautiful glass display box of arrowheads disappeared from its place. Throughout my childhood, the box sat on the bookshelf in my grandparents' home. In those days, only the adults could open it to examine the beautiful arrowheads. They handed them to me one at a time. I had to stand right beside them while I touched the smooth sides and sharp points of each. Black ones, white ones, brown ones, and mottled ones, large ones, small ones, and a few tiny ones. *Memories will be all I have after these vultures leave.*

With the crowd of people scurrying around grabbing what they could, I felt overwhelmed. It was daunting to take care of my family amidst the questions and directions of what was where. My frustration and anger remained inside. Fortunately, the bones were picked bare and the scavengers would soon go home.

One evening my husband raced into the apartment, breathless with excitement. "Look what I got. I pulled it out of the back of your uncle's van. They'll never find it in here. They're afraid to come in here because of Spots." His evil laugh disquieted me even more.

He held a beautiful antique mirror. It belonged to my grandmother's mother. The frame was ornate plaster painted gold. Age tinted the glass, but that added to the vintage charm.

"What else do you want me to take? I can get anything and put it in here."

"Thank you, Dace, but, no. Don't take anything else. I have all the stuff that was already in this apartment—my great-gramma's stuff."

"But don't you want more of your grandmother's things?"

"I have enough. I just want them to leave. I don't want any trouble. They're leaving in the morning. Thanks for the mirror, but that's enough."

Later that night after I had gone to bed, he went to the bar. When I awoke the next morning, the photo of my grandmother's mother in the beautiful oval frame with the convex glass leaned against the wall behind the bed. Not sure who had it first, I said nothing.

At daybreak, I heard a commotion in the driveway—angry voices. Afraid to go out, I strained to listen. I stayed in the little apartment and cried. I heard my uncle's voice. I thought they'd already left. This fiasco couldn't end soon enough.

Someone persistently knocked on the door leading into the garage. I didn't open it. "Kelly, it's me—Dad." I opened the door and my father stepped in. "Uncle Steve says Dace loosened the nuts on the wheels of his van."

"What? He's at work."

124

"He thinks he did it during the night. He noticed it when he drove the van into town to gas it up."

"I don't think so, Dad. I mean, he went out with his friends last night, but why would he care to do that? He wants them gone as much as we do."

The flicker of a mischievous grin flashed across my sweet father's face. "Steve thinks Dace tried to kill him. Well, don't worry about it. He caught it in time and they didn't have an accident. I think they just have too much weight in there."

The conversion van was full from top to bottom. There were boxes strapped to the roof. The trailer hitched to the van also had boxes packed from top to bottom, front to back. It sounded logical.

"Here, babe." Dad handed me a silver ring topped with a white pearl in a simple setting. "This was Gramma's wedding ring. She wore through a couple others, and this was the last one she owned. The funeral director gave it to me before they buried her. I think you should have it."

I took it and put it on my thumb. "Gramma had big hands," Dad chuckled, "from working hard." He began to cry. We both did. Together we hugged for comfort and strength. "Well, I'd better get out there. You stay in here, K.J. They'll be gone soon."

"Thanks, Dad." I sat on the old wicker rocker and examined the ring. It was unpretentious and beautiful — just like Gramma had been. My heart warmed with love.

With everyone gone now, I moved some things back into the house, soon to be listed on the real estate market. Most of the dishes were gone. There were very few cooking utensils. It was a good time to relocate.

Chapter Twelve: Same Show, Different Stage

Dace, Star, Mr. Spots, and I moved into a little rental house with beautiful hardwood floors and a stone fireplace. With two small bedrooms, one bathroom, and a basement, it sat in the woods beside the owners' house. This was the first house the Willis family built. As their family expanded, they built the large house next door where they currently lived.

Just after we moved, Mrs. Byler, the babysitter, mentioned a wound on my baby's palm. Star kept her hands in fists, and I hadn't noticed it when I collected her the previous day. *I need to bathe her better. I guess I didn't open her fist.*

"My daughter Sarah heated Star's bottle up on the stove in a stainless steel bowl," the babysitter explained. "She had Star on her lap, and my other daughter, Ruth, put the hot bowl in front of her. The baby reached out and grabbed the rim. She has a blister on the palm of her little hand."

Mrs. Byler gently opened the tiny fist, exposing a soft blister that covered half of her palm. I winced. "Aw, poor baby. I honestly didn't even notice it. It must not have bothered her last night."

"Well, we put burn ointment on it. When I told my husband about the burn, he got angry." The woman's gaze fell. "He said we can't babysit her anymore."

"Why? I know it was just an accident. She's fine."

"He said we can't risk being sued."

"I'm not going to sue you."

"My husband said you are poor and will sue if Star gets hurt. I'm sorry, but today is our last day. He didn't even want us to watch her today, but I told him you had to go to work."

I was speechless. I'd been uncomfortable with how this sweet woman and her daughters appeared to fear her husband. *Maybe this will make their lives easier.*

It was Friday. I had the weekend to find a replacement. I bought a newspaper and made a couple of phone calls from the gas station. "Babysitting Provided"—the address was close to our rental house on Nelson Ledge Road. I called.

The advertiser was Yankee, not Amish. She had an infant of her own and babysat a toddler. Although pregnant with another baby, due in five months, she would do for now. We agreed on the fee, and our child started on Monday.

New house notwithstanding, the violence escalated. Although I'd learned to live with Dace's rages, his misogynistic behaviors grew more disturbing.

One Saturday he looked forward to going out with friends. We didn't have a clothes washer or dryer, and earlier that day he hand-washed his blue jeans. He gathered wood from behind the house to build a fire in the fireplace and hung his jeans over the fireplace screen to dry, humming all the while. He left happy and ready to party.

Late that night he came home in a rage. His entrance startled me. He grabbed his porn magazines from the nightstand. With adrenaline-powered strength, he tore them in half and burned them in the fireplace. "Burn, witches, burn," he seethed. I peeked into the living room and saw sweat pour onto his brow.

Afraid, I snuck back into bed, being sure to stay out of his way, not daring to ask any questions. I never found out what instigated his performance. Perhaps someone denied his advances at the bar. Some woman somewhere infuriated him, and I thanked God I hadn't received his anger for a change. Although happy he burned his magazines, I knew in time he'd spend more money to replace them. Money we apparently didn't have, despite my husband's new job.

The following weekend he partied again. Late Sunday morning, he remained in bed from having stumbled home drunk the previous night. I played quietly with Star in the living room. Suddenly, a loud knock on the door echoed in the little house. There stood one of his old friends.

"He's sleeping right now. Do you want me to wake him up?"

"Yeah, if you could."

"Um, all right. Have a seat and I'll try to wake him."

As a rule, I wouldn't wake Dace, but Jim lived forty miles away, so I thought I should. I knew the routine by now. Situated beyond the foot of the bed, I called his name—twice. I wiggled his foot and jumped back. He often woke up swinging, and I knew better than to be too close.

He rose to his elbow.

"Dace, you have a visitor in the living room."

"Who is it?"

"It's Jim."

"Tell him I'll be right out."

I sighed; relieved he wasn't angry with me for waking him.

He sat upright. I hid my surprise when I saw his face. He had a huge black eye. He offered no explanation, and I didn't dare ask. *Maybe he'll tell Jim.*

Shuffling into the living room, he carefully rubbed the sleep from his eyes. "Hey, Jim. Whatcha doin' this morning?"

128

"Dude, you got quite a shiner there. You get that last night?"

"Yeah," he chuckled. I thought I heard him shush Jim. "Just a little misunderstanding."

When Jim didn't pursue it further, I gave up ever learning who punched him or why. Just another Dace mystery.

Seeing that shiner gave me a hint that maybe he wasn't invincible after all. I often fanaticized about hitting him in the head with a large frying pan or baseball bat while he slept after a night of partying. I always feared I wouldn't hit him hard enough or fast enough and he'd jump up and kill me. *If someone could give him a black eye, maybe I could kill him after all.*

∞∞∞∞∞∞∞∞∞∞∞∞

Subsequent to losing another job, Dace studied to be an electrician via a correspondence course. He became nocturnal.

As he studied, silence was mandatory. As usual, so was sex.

If, in my new-mother exhaustion, I voiced that I wasn't up to it, my tormentor would put his feet squarely on my back and with one quick kick, land me on the floor beside the bed. "Get out of here. I don't want to see your face."

I spent several nights shivering on the sofa without pillow or blanket. I found some warmth beneath the seat cushions. The cold Ohio nights with no heating oil in the furnace and no wood for the fireplace taught me to acquiesce whether I felt like it or not. Just one more chore before I could finally fall asleep.

While studying to take a test, he said my voice grated on his nerves. "I can't stand the sound of your voice. Don't say a word."

There are times when a wife must communicate with her husband. "Is this shirt dirty?" "You got a letter today." "Dinner's ready." For the few times I spoke, I tried to change my voice and use different inflections. Sometimes it worked, sometimes it didn't. I wasn't to talk to our baby either. Striving to remain silent in his presence intensified my loneliness. After he passed his test, he relaxed and engaged me in conversation.

We had no food in the house, so there was no way to create meals. However, I still had an old tin container of cinnamon from Gramma's house. The apple butter was just a memory, but the smell of cinnamon delighted my heart and cheered my spirit.

Twice when my husband wanted milk in his coffee, I snuck the cup into the pantry and creamed it with breast milk—a secret act of insolence I relished for years to come.

Buying nursing pads was out of the question. There were a few disposable diapers left from the hospital gift bag. My baby had an allergic reaction, so I didn't use them. I cut them into squares and put them in my bra. When the diapers were gone, I took one of Gramma's white cotton bed sheets and cut it into strips. I folded the strips into squares as nursing pads. They were no more absorbent than when I used the same cotton strips as feminine pads in my underwear, months later.

For a couple weeks, we had only flour, instant milk, and Dace's cereal. When the cereal ran out, I made pancakes for his breakfast. While we did have the pure maple syrup my father gave us, we had no butter. He threw his fork across the room, narrowly missing me. "How am I supposed to eat this crap with no butter?" With no money to buy food, he still expected food to be available.

My baby had become quite plump with only breast milk. In time, she began to pull away while nursing. Her contorted expression indicated the milk didn't taste good, and I fought feelings of rejection. Within two weeks of this new behavior, she weaned, and I had to find food to feed her.

Instant milk in the bottle, and for breakfast what I called "paste cakes"—flour and water with (maybe) a little powdered milk. For three days, she gobbled this tasteless fare. On the fourth day, as I scooted my chair to the highchair, she looked at the plate, scrunched up her face, and softly cried the saddest and most pathetic cry. "I know, baby," I cried along with her. "I know." At that, I began to steal food from my parents' pantry while they were at work.

Our daughter was a joy but sometimes babies cry for no apparent reason. Dry diaper, full tummy, all things seemed in proper order, but still, Star cried. "Go get her," her father barked into the night.

Many nights I begged God to make the baby stop crying. I walked, bounced, and shushed her. Putting a bottle of milk in her mouth worked for just a few minutes. Sensitive babies can discern tension and fear in the home. Nights held little rest for me.

Exhausted one evening, I left the dinner dishes in the sink to wash in the morning. After getting her to sleep, I fell into bed myself, weary.

At 2 a.m., I heard, "Get your lazy arse out here and wash these dishes." His voice boomed throughout the little house with the hardwood floors, waking us both. Panicked shrieks came from the nursery.

"I have to get the baby."

"No, I'll get her. You get in here and wash these effin' dishes."

He retrieved the screaming, frightened infant. She squirmed and arched her back in an attempt to pull away from him. He held her tightly.

Smart child. She can sense danger. I envisioned myself prying the child from his arms. Within seconds, several scenarios flashed through my mind, all of which ended badly. *I just have to hurry.*

I cleaned the dishes in record time. I had to dry them and put them away before he would give our now hysterical baby to me.

"May I have her now?" My hair clung to my cheeks wet with tears, and I struggled to regain my composure.

I sobbed in silence, holding little Star securely against me. Returning to the nursery, I whispered to her. Pacing the floor, I quietly sang, "You are my sunshine, my only sunshine. You make me happy when skies are gray." I choked the sobs back not wanting him to come in and make me put her into the crib before she calmed down.

Chapter Thirteen: The Clouds Are Moving

On a sunny weekend in September, Dace worked at his new job as an electrician's apprentice. Saturdays were mandatory, and I loved having him gone part of the weekend—one less day to deal with his volatile temperament.

My small hometown celebrated the annual Homecoming Festival. I'd enjoyed the festivity during my childhood with Suzie, and longed to return. I put Star into her car seat in my Mustang and headed for town.

I parked in the parking lot beside the gas station and took her out.

Thomas Wolfe's book title *You Can't Go Home Again* rang true for me as I held my precious five-month-old. I surveyed the village Suzie and I ran around in as kids: a tiny post office, wooden gazebo, and a two-pump gas station. Across the street stood a closet-sized grocery store and the quaint bicycle shop and hardware store. One square—that was Parkman, Ohio.

We always considered the town ours; ruling from our bicycles in the summer and on foot when it snowed. Now it moved on to the next generation without us. The cloud of lonesomeness hung closer than usual.

Children tried to climb the greased pole for the five-dollar bill taped to the top. That had been me just a few years earlier. A photo of me halfway up the pole made the newspaper. I'd been such a feisty girl. It seemed a world away. I ached for yesterday.

We drove to the old wooden Community House and parked in the gravel parking lot. I talked softly to my baby as I got her out of her seat, and she squealed with delight. I cuddled the chubby girl and walked with a bounce in my step toward the white, two-story building.

Signs hanging on the porch pillars announced homemade crafts and baked goods for sale and a Beautiful Baby Contest. I didn't think her father would approve if I entered Star into the contest, but then, how would he find out? I signed her up.

In the building, my mind flooded with memories of my adolescence full of fun times with Suzie, serving at pancake breakfasts and checking coats on many a New Year's Eve. Giggles echoed in my head, and hundreds of scenarios flashed by.

Holding my happy baby, I meandered along the perimeter of the large dining area and studied once again the aging framed pictures of graduates from a high school long gone. The thought of time marching on made my chest ache. I remembered laughing at the yellowed pictures and making fun of the hairdos. *What I wouldn't give now for a good laugh with Suzie—about anything.*

A familiar face—Dan, my friend Ruth's brother, was there. He was four years older than us. His high school girlfriend had been in the grade ahead of us. She'd gotten pregnant in her junior year, and they got married. After the birth of a second daughter, they divorced. He and his daughters lived with his parents since then. Now here he was with his two-year-old entered into the contest. A quick once over, a shy grin, and we greeted one another quietly.

We sat beside each other on a bench in the foyer and waited for the contest to begin. The door was open. An occasional breeze brought welcomed relief from the stifling heat. With each short puff of air, the discerning eye could see everyone lean forward, chin upward, taking it in. A deep breath and disappointed sigh sat them back into place and looked like an unsuccessful wave at a football game.

Dan remembered me as a skinny little brat who used to hang out with his sister. I remembered him as a popular football player who played the drums. His drum set stayed in their basement. He'd often warned us to never touch it, but we'd play them when he wasn't home, banging like the rock stars we saw on album covers. Now here we were, sitting together, our childhood problems miles behind us, holding our baby girls.

We briefly chatted about how silly it was to have our kids in the contest. "It's just for fun," we rationalized.

My baby's age category came next. The judge was a girl of about eight.

Kids are impartial. That's sweet. The child's eyes danced when Star waved her arms and batted her big, round, baby-blue eyes. Slight beads of sweat glistened on her bald little head. The young judge surveyed the other two babies too. At the far end of the foyer, the girl's mother sat at a table covered with ribbons and trophies.

The girl took a blue ribbon from the table and handed it to me. I smiled and thanked her. I kissed my sweet baby on the cheek and savored the momentary ray of sunshine that warmed my spirit. For that instant, I didn't worry about Dace, his abusive ways, or how I would explain the prize.

Then the woman at the table called the girl over and whispered in her ear. The child meandered back to me, cocked her head to the side, and with an awkward expression, took the ribbon from me. She handed it to another woman, looked at her mother, who nodded, and then relinquished the award.

My gaze met Dan's. He rolled his eyes and whispered, "Politics." I wished him luck and left, determined to get home before my husband got there.

Crossing the parking lot to my car, I hummed and lightly bounced Star on my hip. Determined to remain happy for the sunny day and time out with her, I ignored the voices in my head.

Now people are rejecting your daughter too. People will discard her because of you. You fail at everything you attempt. As I buckled my infant into her car seat, I shook my head, casting off the negativity that threatened to pull me under. With a huge forced smile, I cooed, "You are a winner and Mommy's little princess." I gave her a gentle smooch on the forehead and closed the car door.

Heading home, I stopped at the gas station outside of town where Chris worked. Her boyfriend owned the tiny attached bait and sandwich shop. She often gave us free food. This time I stocked up on napkins because we were out of toilet paper at home. That would be my excuse for not being home if my tormentor got there ahead of me. Thankfully, I made it home first and he never found out about the Beautiful Baby Contest.

Several times throughout the next few years, I allowed myself a stolen moment here and there to think about Ruth's brother. I fantasized about the two of us married with a family. Even though just a silly daydream, it brought me momentary comfort and hope, albeit false hope.

Chapter Fourteen: Another Word

It was Thanksgiving eve and we planned to be with my family for a big meal the next day. Dace hated relatives and family gatherings. Above all, he hated my family.

"You know, we're never going to celebrate the holidays when Star grows up. And we sure as heck won't be with your family."

I was determined not to fight. *He won't get a rise out of me tonight.*

He wouldn't stop his verbal attack. "We're never gonna tell her about Santa Claus and other bull crap like that."

I couldn't hold my tongue. "Those holiday fantasies are an important part of childhood, Dace. You can't say that."

This fueled his fire. "You gonna tell me what to do? I'll tell you how we're gonna raise this kid, and we aren't going to lie to her about stupid childhood fantasies. They're lies that cost money and make you be with family. You know how I hate that."

In my misdirected maternal battle stance, I mumbled, "Then maybe we should get a divorce."

Divorce—another word for the List.

Within seconds, I was on my back. He knelt over me, choking my neck until I saw stars. I struggled to breathe. He loosened his grip and slapped my face.

"I'm sorry. I'm sorry. I'm sorry," I screamed, and with primal instincts, flung my head from side to side to avoid his strikes. Blood vessels broke on my left jaw— reminders for the rest of my days of my marriage to a violent right-handed man. His strong palm fell across my eye several times.

He got up. Panting from his fit of rage, he flopped backward into a chair and lit a cigarette. I stumbled to the bathroom. I knew this attack wasn't finished, and needed to escape my reality. *Maybe if he thinks I've passed out he'll leave me alone.* I fell to the floor.

He ran into the bathroom. "Get up, dumb-arse."

Please go away. I concentrated on not moving my facial muscles. He left the room.

Thank God. I assumed it over.

Splash! Cold, dirty water poured on my head—sticky Piña Colada water from the blender—remnants of his afternoon binge.

"Get up, dumb-arse. You could've hit your stupid head on the bathtub."

He dragged me out to the living room, banging me along the walls. He knelt with his hands clenched around my throat. I gasped for air and pleaded through broken sobs, "Why don't you just kill me and get it over with?"

"Yeah, you'd like that, wouldn't you?" he hissed into my face. "Well I'm not going to kill you. I'm just going to make you wish you were dead." And he did— consistently.

The next day at my aunt and uncle's house, I tried to hide a black eye behind my stringy blonde hair. Stress and lack of nutrition made my hair thin. My eyebrows were falling out and I weighed less than one hundred pounds.

My cousin stared at me. "What happened to your eye?"

My mother, aunts, and cousins watched me for an answer. I wanted to scream, "What do you think happened? Haven't you people figured it out by now? He beats me, and you act like you don't know."

138

Instead, I blushed. "Oh, I fell in the bathroom last night. Pretty stupid, I know."

Whether or not anyone believed me, no one said another word about it.

I didn't realize it at the time, but I was pregnant with Baby Number Two. Star was just eight months old.

∞∞∞∞∞∞∞∞∞∞∞

Although he still bought Mr. Spots the expensive food, the dog had to eat less of it. Not a very active English bulldog, he didn't seem to notice his reduced food intake.

How did Dace think food came into the house when he wouldn't give me money to shop? Stealing my parents' food became a regular event. While at their house, I did laundry in their basement, on the sly. They must have figured it out because they bought me a used washing machine. I couldn't buy laundry detergent, so I washed clothes in the hottest water possible. They dried well on the line in the backyard.

I loved the clothesline. It stood high, and I reached to hang the clothes on it. Outside, looking heavenward, I loved inhaling the fresh air, and the way the sun warmed my skin. The crisp winter air made me feel alive and free.

A government check came in the mail one day. I learned we received a sizable income tax refund.

"All I want out of this check is a fuzzy toilet seat cover," I said.

"Frills," he retorted. "That's frivolous and unnecessary."

I had no idea where the money went.

I also wondered what happened to my husband's paychecks, although I suspected he spent them at the local bar. I imagined Mr. Big Spender enjoyed his short time in the spotlight each week, buying his friends drinks.

One morning when I stepped out of the shower, I felt a familiar tingling sensation in my breasts. It reminded me of being pregnant or when I lactated. I tried to ignore the feeling and left for work.

The Ohio winter was in full force. I still worked at the County Auditor's Office which was in the opposite corner of the county. Travel became more precarious as the roads got worse. We talked about the fact that the cost of a tow, if I slid off the road, would take almost an entire paycheck.

Just at that time, I observed bumps on our little girl. I asked her babysitter about it. "They may be flea bites," she said. I also saw small bruises on our sweet baby's upper arms.

"She's pregnant, you know," I told Dace about the caregiver. "I think she's just so huge that she can't bend over to pick Star up. I think she picks her up by her shoulders and is bruising her."

"You aren't taking her back there."

We concluded I should quit my job.

"Okay. I'll give them my two weeks' notification Monday."

"No. You aren't taking her back to that sitter, and you don't have time to find another one for just two weeks. Call them in the morning and tell them you quit."

Therefore, I quit my job, on the phone, without notice. Making the call from my landlady's phone doubled my embarrassment.

Soon, I felt the strange feeling in my breasts again. When Dace headed to work, I drove to Birth Right for a free pregnancy test. The receptionist directed me into the restroom. A few minutes later, I gave the tiny paper cup to a different employee, who took the specimen away to test it.

Several minutes passed before she came back into the room. "You're pregnant," she said matter-of-factly.

I stood there holding my eight-month-old baby on my hip, and in my nineteen-year-old shock and naiveté, said, "But, I already have a baby."

She chuckled. "Well, you're going to have another one."

I stood motionless, staring. "What am I going to do?" I whispered. "I used birth control."

I explained I'd used a diaphragm and conceptive jelly. The mornings after we had sex, I'd douched with baking soda before going to work.

"It must be a boy sperm to have survived that long." Her cut-and-dry manner lacked the emotion I needed at that moment. "You must've douched him right up into an egg. We can help you with clothes for the newborn. Why don't you go in the clothes closet here and get something now?"

Numb, I walked into the room and glanced around. Nothing registered. I desired to leave immediately but didn't want to appear ungrateful. I didn't require anything—I'd just had a baby. I took one infant sleeper. "Thank you." I slowly headed toward the door.

"Is that all you're taking? Here." The worker ran into the closet and grabbed another sleeper. "Take another one."

"Good-bye. Good luck," they called after me.

I put my little one into her car seat and crawled in behind the steering wheel. I didn't start the car. I sat motionless.

Good luck? I wanted to run back inside and beg for help. I wanted to scream, "I don't know how to do this. He hits me. I'm scared. How can I protect *three* of us?" No. I just sat in the driver's seat, with my hands on the wheel at the nine and three o'clock positions, and stared. The sob I stifled in the clinic found its way up and burst out in a loud groan and gasp. Still stationary, I dropped my head and cried, clenching the wheel. I dared not let go.

I pulled myself together enough to head home. While driving, I wept because I was on square one again. My secret plan was to stay home with our child until she started kindergarten, find a full-time job, and leave my tormentor. Now I had to start the five years over.

At home, I read my grandmother's medical book. I learned that douching with baking soda enhances the vagina's alkalinity, making the swimming environment better for the Y sperm to reach the egg.

My husband came home that night and, with excitement, skimmed through a guitar magazine. He talked about what guitar he wanted to buy next. Jim came over with a Gibson Les Paul 25/50 anniversary guitar, autographed by Les Paul himself. Jim had ordered the expensive guitar and was thrilled to have it in his grasp.

"It's like God signing the Bible," Dace exclaimed. He talked about playing in a band with Jim and how the first album cover would look. He planned to buy another guitar.

Pregnancy made me feel sad and guilty, believing I was taking his money.

A few days later at home, I told him. I kept repeating, "I'm sorry." His reaction surprised me. He seemed genuinely excited about another baby. When I said the woman at Birth Right suggested it might be a boy due to the circumstances surrounding the conception, he became even more excited. I, however, wasn't thrilled. I longed to leave him, but felt I couldn't now.

My sour attitude brought a routine retort of, "No, because I'm *pregnant*." I sounded like I was spitting poison. After hearing me say it a few times, he slapped me and said he never wanted to hear it again.

Bitterness toward Dace aside, within a couple of weeks, maternal love welled up in my heart. Although full of fear, I anticipated a little brother or sister for Star and contemplated the changes the new arrival would bring.

Chapter Fifteen: Refuge for a While

The transmission in the Mustang broke. The car was only a couple of years old and worth fixing. However, with no repair money, and impatient landlords living next door who wanted the car out of the driveway, I put an ad in the newspaper to sell it. Newer model, low mileage, broken transmission, I asked just $300—a great price even for 1980.

A sixteen-year-old came with his parents. The exuberant boy bounced all over, inspecting the car, his enthusiasm palpable. The adults tried to reel him in and spoke nonchalantly to me. "Will you take less for the car?"

I was large with child and needed money. It hurt that they asked me when the price was already unbelievable. I had to have it out of the driveway and, frankly, had no fight left in me to haggle over the price. "I guess so." They twisted the knife when they required change for three $100s.

"I have no money. That's why I'm selling the car," I said in bewilderment. They dug through their pockets and found change for the third $100, giving me $250. They chained the car to the bumper of their truck and pulled it the length of the dirt driveway.

The Mustang was a gift from my grandparents. Seeing it disappear in a dust cloud brought down a haze of gloom. I dropped my head and shuffled toward the house, dejected. *No one cares. Gramma's gone, and there's no one left to care.* Suddenly I remembered I was wearing Gramma's underwear and bra. Somehow, it made me feel better—loved.

My landlady slid her kitchen window open. "You finally got rid of that broken-down car?"

"Yes, Mrs. Willis, it's gone."

"Good. Looks much nicer around here now."

I closed the door behind me and stared into the little house with the detailed stone fireplace and wooden floors. The beauty escaped me. It all looked ugly; I despised everything. I paused and, for a moment, let my mind wander. *I wonder what Dan's doing these days?*

Star whimpered as she began to wake. "And *that's* why I breathe, Mr. Spots. Gotta carry on." I hurried into the nursery to retrieve my precious reason for living.

∞∞∞∞∞∞∞∞∞∞∞

With the summer upon us, my husband became restless once more. He got mad at work, punched a co-worker, and got fired—again. We heard rumors of numerous jobs available in Dallas, TX, so he decided to find out. We gave the Mrs. Willis one-month notice and planned to move in with my parents.

While packing to move, I tackled a chore I'd put off for a year—cleaning out the drawers in a tall dresser. In the top drawer, I found our wedding cards. While reading each of them, I found a $50 bill. My pulse raced. Should I tell him or hide it? If he found it, he'd punish me for keeping it a secret.

Maybe God gave me the $50 those people screwed me out of when they bought the Mustang.

Afraid to hide it, I told him.

I showed him the bill that evening. "Hey, look what I found in a wedding card today." He snatched it away from me. "Let's buy some groceries for staying with my folks, okay?"

"Are you stupid? This is going for some primo dope." That was the last I saw of the money.

We moved while he prepared to travel to Texas.

Living in my childhood home brought calmness and made me feel safer. I remained in awe at the food options in the refrigerator and appreciated the ability to grab a piece of fruit at will. I rummaged through the upper cupboards taking mental inventory of the baking ingredients, cereals, crackers, and cookies. I loved kneeling in front of the lower cupboards and rearranging the cans of soup, vegetables, tuna, beans, and various sodas. I was more excited than a child on Christmas morning.

The only downside was at first my mother wouldn't allow our pet in the house. He stayed in the Rambler with the windows open—a terrible life for a loyal dog who had a family to protect. Surely, he must have thought I'd betrayed him.

Within days, though, my mother softened. "Oh, he can live in the basement." Great news because it was cool down there.

A week later, Christine took Spots to live with her and her boyfriend, the gas station owner. Although relieved he could live in a cool house and relax, I missed my best friend terribly.

Two weeks passed and my parents asked me to find out when their son-in-law planned to leave. I resented them putting me in the middle. *Why can't they ask him themselves? Can't they see I don't need this?*

I approached him during a quiet evening outside. He calmly smoked pot. "Um, my parents wondered when you planned to go to Dallas. Do you have any idea when that might be?"

He was infuriated. "Okay. I'll leave right now." Mumbling expletives, he threw his belongings into the Rambler and left that night.

My mom and dad were full of questions, and I was embarrassed. I tried not to cry. "Oh, he just wanted to get a jump on the trip," I lied. "It's cooler to travel at night."

For two weeks, we didn't hear from him. At last, he called one evening, from Phoenix, AZ. He was staying with his mother and Lino, with whom she had once again reunited.

"Hi, Kelly. Guess where I am right now." He sounded peaceful and happy. Not the same man who left in a fury two weeks earlier. "I'm lying out beside my mom's pool, smokin' a doobie."

"They're in Phoenix, aren't they? What happened to Dallas?"

"I had no choice, Kelly. I was sleeping at a rest stop and someone robbed me. I had no cash. I had to come here. God knows your stingy parents wouldn't help me."

The verbal knife hit its target in just under two minutes. A new record? Not hardly. Keeping me on the defensive ensured I wouldn't object.

With Dace gone, I no longer had to worry about upsetting him in front of my parents. The tenseness left when he did, and I felt safe in the presence of my family.

A hot, humid summer, I spent much time in my parents' basement.

To help me earn money, my father brought boxes of parts home from the rubber factory he managed. I sat in the coolness downstairs and trimmed flash from the edges of the parts. He paid me by the box.

While Star and I waited in Ohio for Dace to send for us, the abuse continued via the telephone for months. "I'm getting on a plane to come there and kick your arse," became a familiar valediction.

I poured my feelings out to him in a letter. I wrote about how the violence made me feel unloved,

147

unappreciated, and unsafe, and how I believed it would hurt the children. I begged him not to be so angry and cruel once we reunited. Writing the letter was risky, but cathartic.

That summer Lino chose to have Mr. Spots move to Arizona with them. They had acquired a female English bulldog and were eager to breed the two. My father-in-law flew to Ohio to retrieve him, but promised we could have him when we joined up in Arizona, after Baby Number Two arrived.

Because of the unusually hot weather, the airlines warned about the danger of shipping larger animals. Still, Lino insisted, and Christine met him at the gas station to give him the dog.

Prior to leaving town, my father-in-law stopped by to see my daughter and me. I gave him my written plea for relationship stability, in a sealed envelope. "Would you please give this to Dace for me?"

He assured me he would. I later learned he read it and talked with his step-son about being abusive. Still, no one stepped in to do anything.

Unfortunately, our beloved pet didn't survive the flight, and a necropsy showed he died a Jimi Hendrix death—asphyxiated vomit. Ice cream was in his lungs—a going-away cone, compliments of Christine.

No one told me of his passing until just before we moved to Arizona. Throughout the summer, I was regaled with stories of Mr. and Mrs. Spots and their fun antics together, elaborate stories that made the news of our pet's death more difficult to accept than if they'd been honest with me from the start. Wanting to "spare [me] the pain" had to be Janice and Lino's bad idea; my tormentor hadn't cared about my level of comfort in the past.

∞∞∞∞∞∞∞∞∞∞∞∞

Mom was out of town when I went into labor. My father was in the barn polishing antiques on a buffing wheel, a side job he had enjoyed for years.

I waddled out to the massive pole barn they used for a workshop and garage. "Dad, I'm not sure, but I think I'm in labor."

"Oh! Let's get you to the hospital, babe." He shut the motor off, jumped over the electric cord, and ran toward the house.

"Don't hurry, Dad. I may be just having Braxton Hicks contractions; I don't know."

"Better to be safe, K.J. I don't want to deliver this baby right here at home. Grab your stuff. Let's go." I could understand why he felt the need to rush: I used a different obstetrician this time and would deliver in the adjoining county.

Dad didn't take time to clean up. Although still smudged with black soot, he drove my toddler to a friend's house, and we continued to the hospital. The forty-five-minute ride in the pickup truck felt extra bumpy. I concentrated on not showing my pain through the contractions.

"I'm sorry this darned truck's so bumpy, K.J."

"Oh, it's okay, Dad. Don't worry. Like I said, I may not even be in labor." The pains increased, but I determined I wouldn't show my discomfort.

At the hospital, they wheeled me away. "We'll let you know her condition as soon as we can, Mr. Newsome."

The emergency room doctor checked me and confirmed my advanced condition. In the labor room, I kept thinking, *this is probably the last baby I'll ever have. I should enjoy this—experience this.*

There were no other people in the room. Throughout labor, a deep loneliness pervaded my consciousness. The progress intensified, and I recognized the signs of transition.

"I have to push now," I told the nurse.

"No you don't. It's too soon."

"Will you check me? I have to push."

"We can't check you every five minutes," she barked. "It increases the risk of infection."

"Then give me some Demerol!"

Within five minutes of receiving the shot, the baby crowned.

"She's crowning. Find the doctor."

Smug satisfaction vied with drug-induced apathy and I smirked at the nurse. "I told you so."

Just a few hard pushes, a quick readjustment of the mirror for me to watch, and he was out.

"It's a boy," was the shout within the delivery room.

The nurses whisked me on the bed to the nurses' station and handed me the phone. Much to my surprise, I was able to dial my children's father in Phoenix. "It's a boy," I whispered.

I heard cheers and shouts on the other side of the call. "Sam is here."

"I'm going to go now." I gave the phone to the nurse, who answered a couple of questions and hung up.

"Did he sound mad?" I asked the nurse.

"Mad? Why?"

"Because I didn't talk to him. I gave you the phone."

"Of course he's not mad. That's just silly."

Not in my world.

Still not sure if I was in labor, my father waited, ready to drive me home if necessary.

A nurse entered the waiting room and tried to give him the brand-new baby, still covered with vernix caseosa.

"I'm a little dirty to hold a newborn, don't you think?" My indignant father told the nurse to wait. He dashed to the restroom to wash up to his elbows and returned to take Samuel Stone in his arms.

After a few moments, the nurse took the little one back to finish cleaning him.

Two days later we came home. He was the infant, and now Star was the big girl—too much for a tot of just sixteen months. In short time, though, they became best friends for life.

The months passed fast. Their daddy worked in Phoenix as a burglar alarm technician and lived with his parents. He saved enough money to fly us out to join him.

My parents threw a going-away party for the babies and me. All of our local relatives came for the event. While I basked in the warmth of my family's love, I couldn't cast out my sadness.

They were so happy. They laughed and hugged me, wishing me well. Didn't they know? Did they truly think I was off to a wonderful life in the West with a husband who loved me? Did they really not know? The emotions of the day overwhelmed me, but I soaked in every minute, every touch, every smile, and every hug from the precious people I'd grown up with. Not having them around would feel weird.

I dreaded new life without my safety net. Who would I turn to if I needed help? The thought of God being with me never entered my mind. I felt alone.

Dad secured a shipping crate from his factory. It would ship with other containers going out West. I crammed it full of household items, small appliances, clothes, personal files, the highchair, and the car seat. When packing our suitcases, I realized I'd put the airplane tickets in the container necessitating a trip to the factory where it had already been taken.

At the factory parking lot, a forklift brought a wooden pallet out of the semi truck. The workers opened the lid to my container. I climbed onto it while my dad and other men watched. I was embarrassed by my stupidity. I thought hard about where it might be, reached in, and grabbed a file.

"I found it," I sung out, waving it in the air. *Thank you, God.* The thought of more public humiliation was unbearable.

"Good thing, young lady," one of the men called out. "We were just about to leave. You caught us just in time."

Thank God. Maybe this will be a blessed reunion after all. I hope my husband will be patient and kind like these men have been. He read my letter. I'm sure things are going to be better for us.

Chapter Sixteen: A New World

Preparing to leave Ohio was stressful. I didn't know what I'd get in to, and I wouldn't have my parents there to help. I vacillated between confidence in a brighter future and hopelessness, continually aware of the ever-present loneliness that hung like a cloud over me.

Four-month-old Samuel and twenty-month-old Star were about to be ripped from the peace and security of their grandparents' home. My mother couldn't eat and wouldn't talk. While she tried to contain herself, it intensified my isolation.

Flying with two babies presented a challenge. My daughter hated the seatbelt and cried when I insisted she keep it on. She and her Gramma were close, and when the plane touched down at our interim stop, the fidgety toddler was happy when I unfastened the restraint. She stretched to peer out the window and sighed heavily. "Ahh, Gramma."

"No, baby. No Gramma." I quietly cried.

They didn't make us disembark while refueling. I changed the baby's diaper and tried to settle his sister. The flight attendants gathered near, chatted with me, and admired my children.

Arriving at the Phoenix Sky Harbor International Airport on a November evening was surreal. Outside, the well-lit parking lot felt like being indoors. The temperature difference from Ohio was dreamlike.

I had saved for months to buy an ounce of marijuana to surprise Dace, and took the risk to smuggle the lid of weed in my underwear.

That night I gave it to him beside my in-laws' pool. For that moment, he was head over heels in love with me.

His kindness made me hopeful about our future together. *Maybe the letter made a difference after all.*

He furthered that hope when he took me to a Suns basketball game. He also took the kids and me to the Phoenix Zoo. His joy of our reunion was short-lived, however.

We stayed with Janice and Lino for a few weeks. The responsibility of caring for his own family replaced the carefree lifestyle he'd become accustomed to.

He got an apartment for us in a nice complex in northern Phoenix. Ours was an end apartment in one of the many long one-story brick buildings of the ten-year-old site.

His parents loaned us a few pieces of furniture—a turquoise imitation leather couch, two black bar stools so we could eat at the peninsula countertop, a mattress we put on the floor, and a small television set. They bought cribs for our babies.

A woman who lived in the apartment opposite ours came to welcome us. When she saw we had two babies and one high chair, she offered use of her highchair. Her son had outgrown it.

We had no curtains for the windows. I hung a sheet on nails over the living room window in the evenings. We didn't cover the high bedroom window with anything.

As usual, we didn't have any money, but had new guitar strings and marijuana. I still didn't know how much my husband made. "It's none of your business," he continued to say.

One of his co-workers, Max, lived in the same apartment complex. Dace occasionally rode to work him. He and his wife, Sally, had a little girl a few months older than Sammy.

I could drive to the grocery store and home, when I had the Rambler. Camelback Mountain was visible from our apartment, but we never got there. The babies and I enjoyed a nice park within walking distance until it got too hot to be outside.

Sally became a casual friend. I didn't have opportunities to meet other people, and the unfamiliar surroundings increased my lonesomeness.

Everything was foreign to me. Rock gardens replaced green yards. My in-laws forced grass to grow beside their pool, but the sharp vegetation cut my baby's knee. Christmas lights adorned Saguaro cacti. "Do not pick the jojoba beans" signs peppered the outer roadways.

We didn't have a telephone, and I used the coin-operated public phone in the laundry room of the apartment complex to call my parents. I used the system Sophie and I used with the pay phone at our high school.

In those days, we would call home without inserting coins. Mom would say, "Do you want me to pick you up after majorette practice?" Clicking the receiver down and up once meant "no," and twice meant "yes." We narrowed the details by this yes-and-no system.

Now, they said, "Kelly, if that's you, click twice." I did and they called right back. I'd sent the phone number to them in a letter. Our conversations and hope of seeing them again kept me going. They were my lifeline.

Lyrics to Pink Floyd's "Wish You Were Here" inundated my thoughts. Hearing Dace's voice singing the song intensified my homesickness.

During this time, Christine also moved to Phoenix and lived with her parents. She had run from her boyfriend in Ohio, having stolen much of his property and money. She thought she could skip out on her car loan too, but found her car repossessed one morning. She and I didn't have much in common anymore. She worked days and we rarely saw one another.

Just before Christmas, while in the apartment's laundry room, I saw something run behind a washing machine. I had read a notice on the bulletin board about a missing ferret. The owners offered a ten-dollar reward for finding it. I went to the apartment listed on the sign and told them where they could find their pet. They followed me and captured it. I reminded them about the reward, and they reluctantly gave me ten dollars.

I used the money to buy ingredients to make Christmas cookies and banana nut bread for my parents' presents. I waited for Dace to give me cash to mail them, but he never did. The holidays passed and the treats stayed in the freezer.

My husband ate his big meal during the day. There was baby food and the occasional pork chop for dinner, but seldom anything for lunch. In my hunger, I often stared at the pictures in the red gingham Better Homes & Gardens cookbook Janice had given me. With eyes closed, I licked the pages and imagined what the food tasted like.

My daytime hunger got the best of me, and in time, I ate the Christmas goodies for lunch and sometimes for dinner.

The days ticked by and temperatures elevated. Despite the heat, my tormentor wouldn't allow me to use the air-conditioning in the apartment until he arrived home from work. "Don't waste it," he'd warn.

One day Lino came over. It was 102 degrees Fahrenheit outside.

"Why is this door open?" he demanded.

"It's hot in here."

"Turn the darned AC on."

"Oh no. Dace said we can't use it until he comes home."

He shut the door, walked to the thermostat on the living room wall, and lowered it to 79 degrees. He pivoted toward me. His jaw grated forward and backward. He said in controlled, perfect enunciation, "If he says anything, tell him I did it." Then he left.

His step-son constantly told me I couldn't make smart choices. He advised whenever I had a decision to make, I should ask myself, "What would Dace do in this situation?" and do that. I'd lived by that decree since our wedding.

The babies and I enjoyed the cool for forty-five minutes. However, Dace wouldn't be happy and I'd pay for agreeing to this breach of the rules, so I soon shut it off again. When he came home, I told him what had happened, and he praised me for obeying him. Twisted satisfaction surfaced in my heart. While a quiet sadness lurked in the back of my mind, I was pleased he approved of my action.

Shortly after moving into the apartment, with the door open, I sat my baby son on one of the stools. While I talked to him, making him laugh, his sister played with her toys behind me in the living room. I turned around and she was gone. Panic clenched my throat.

I put Samuel into his crib and ran outside calling for Star. I looked on the side of the building to the left, along the wooden fence. I ran the length of the sidewalk to the right while calling her name. Neighbors heard the anxious tone in my voice and came out to help. She wasn't quite two and had disappeared so quickly.

The lady from two apartments down asked where my other baby was. "He's in the apartment," I said. She got him out and held him while helping to search. I ran to Sally's and told her I couldn't find my daughter.

Stories of abductions flooded my thoughts. *Look in the Dumpster* came into my mind. I squeezed through a hole in the fence to climb the huge bin at the neighboring apartment complex. *No Star, thank God.* A fence surrounded the communal pool—*not there, thank God.*

Neighbors called me to Sally's apartment to give a description over the phone to the Child Find representative. While describing my blonde cherub, I heard shouts of, "They found her." Someone ran to me and gave me the news. I blacked out and slid down the wall. The next thing I knew they brought my daughter to me. The toddler held a pen and had ink on her arms.

In questioning her, they learned she had followed a kitty. She dashed to the left side of the building. She must have stooped to pet the cat behind the large air-conditioning box when I looked on that side.

She followed the cat to the other side of the building into a unit with an opened door. The couple who lived there didn't have children. They'd left the door open while at the laundry room. When they returned to their apartment, they saw a little blonde head on the other side of the couch. She'd found a pen and paper and had drawn on the paper and her arms.

Though I was happy she was safe, my relief quickly left, overcast with fear about what her father would do when he found out, and rightly so. In his fury, I felt the ramification of my "stupidity" and "terrible mothering" that night.

Through that incident I met two families on our side of the apartment complex. One man called himself Wild James from Mississippi. Raised in a religious orphanage, he called me "sis."

158

"Where I come from, we call the girls, sister, and the boys, brother." He and his wife, Beth, had a little boy. She worked in an office, and he collected disability due to hip problems. She was the one who carried Sammy during our search, and appeared to have the colorful remnants of a black eye.

Another family, Lance and Ginger, were their neighbors. Although they collected disability, they looked able-bodied. Both worked as prostitutes. She had two kids. Seven-year-old Della had severe asthma. Dwayne, the three-year-old, hardly spoke a word. The elder took care of the younger. Their mom bragged about warning Della if she had a breathing attack in the night, she had to get her own medicine and shouldn't, under any circumstances, wake her or Lance.

One day when the bigger kids were at school, I heard rustling in the bushes in front of the apartments on the other side of the sidewalk. I investigated and found Dwayne crouched amidst the foliage and covered with blood. Crying, he held his head. I took his hand and encouraged him to come out. He said he'd hit his head on a brick. I led him to his apartment. His mother wasn't home. No one answered my knocking. I opened the door and heard the shower running.

"Lance!"

"Yeah, I'm takin' a shower."

"I know. Listen, Dwayne is bleeding really badly. Can you come out here?"

"I'll be right out."

He came out of the bathroom with a towel around his waist. He dressed and took Dwayne to the hospital. They came home a few hours later. The child was all smiles as he ate an ice cream cone. He had several stitches in his head.

I pondered that for days. Why was this little boy afraid to tell his dad he hurt himself? What was life like with parents who were prostitutes? How did it feel to be low on their priority list?

Lance and Ginger often accompanied Wild James to Mexico. They said they bought DMSO—a medicine they claimed helped with their physical problems. They always came home with bags of marijuana and uproarious anecdotes of their trip. They entertained me with stories of crazy rides in their convertible. She mooned truck drivers and flashed her breasts at them. Whichever guy was not driving mooned elderly lady drivers on the freeway. They laughed nonstop about their Mexico trip antics.

∞∞∞∞∞∞∞∞∞∞∞∞

Working for a burglar alarm company, Dace often received calls to investigate a business when the alarm sounded. He sometimes arrived at the site ahead of the police. I found myself praying again.

Now's your chance, God. My husband's going out on an alarm call. You could have a burglar just shoot him right now. Or maybe the police could think he's the burglar and kill him. Please, God. Please have him killed.

I couldn't understand why God wouldn't answer my prayers. Surely, He hated this beast as much as I did.

My husband liked to party after work with his co-workers, so I never knew if he was alive or dead, as we didn't have a telephone. Often my last thought before drifting off to sleep was, *if he's dead, the police will come here and tell me.*

Late one night he burst through the door, gasping from running. The babies were asleep in their cribs, and I slept on the mattress on our bedroom floor. He fell beside me and held my head down.

160

"Don't move," he directed. Just then, a helicopter hovered above our building and a searchlight shone in the bedroom window, onto us on the mattress.

"Close your eyes," he snapped. Through my eyelids, I saw the bright light from the helicopter. The spotlight lingered on us in our bed before it moved on. *God, please don't let them shoot me.* Within two minutes, the helicopter moved on and he fell asleep. I never learned what that was about. I dared not ask—just another Dace mystery.

Another night he came home late and burst through the door, winded. He was stoned and furious because a policeman had given him a ticket. Standing in the middle of the living room, his arms hung down and away from his sides like the Incredible Hulk's. His hands poised in claw formation. He surveyed the room with wild eyes, his curly blonde hair tossing back and forth.

Grabbing his acoustic guitar, the nearest thing available, he smashed it into the counter, the stools, the floor, and the wall. Strings sprang and bits of wood flew in all directions like toothpicks, filling the room with its echo and twang. Hatred seethed from every pore of his body. He breathed venomous prayers to Satan, asking him to do horrible things to the officer.

I thought about my sleeping babies in the next room; chills danced along my spine. *Oh God, please don't let them wake up. Please.*

I sat in silence, listening to his rant, careful to not make direct eye contact or draw attention to myself. Miraculously the children didn't wake up and he eventually stumbled into bed exhausted and fell asleep.

Calling on God during terrifying or lonesome times was the sum total of my prayers. It didn't occur to me to look for blessings from day to day or to listen for

God's response. I focused on survival and keeping my babies safe. *Why doesn't God just take this monster out of our world?*

Our relationship grew more and more volatile, and I strived to lessen the stress and be more compliant. Although I filtered every thought through the "What Would Dace Do?" mindset, it seemed I could do nothing right. At times, my fear got the better of me in a confrontation and I reverted to my old ways and ran.

One day during a fight, I ran around the left side of the building down the narrow grass strip between the brick structure and the fence. He caught me and we struggled against the bricks. Realizing I couldn't get away, I rolled into a ball with my arms curled over my head.

He snarled, "Crap. Get inside."

I peeked out from behind my arms and saw my tormentor a foot away.

"I said get inside. Eff!"

I jumped up and ran into the apartment. I waited in the kitchen, barely breathing, unsure of what would happen next.

He entered holding his right hand with his left. Spewing expletives, he ran into the bathroom and slammed the door.

Still unsure of what happened, I stood outside the door to listen.

"Dace? W-what's wrong?"

"I hit my effin' hand." He opened the door and returned to the sink. His blood swirled down the drain with the cold running water. His knuckles turned purple, swelling rapidly.

I thought through the past few minutes. He had slapped me, chased me, and pushed me, but he hadn't punched me.

"What'd you hit?"

"I hit the effin' wall."

"You mean the brick?"

"Yeah. It hurts like heck."

Things were getting worse. He had never hit me with a closed fist. Somehow, that had made it seem not as bad. Was it actually wife beating if a fist wasn't involved?

The next morning, a Thursday, after he left for work, I made a call from Sally's phone to a hotline for battered women. Sally called a taxi, and by 4 p.m., the babies and I were in south Phoenix at the Pilgrimage House, a shelter for victims of domestic violence. The organization paid for the cab.

The intake interview was quick. The man-hating counselor sat back in her chair. Her greasy hair was pulled slick into a ponytail—the perfect topping to her self-righteous, judgmental expression.

She shook her head. "You should have come sooner. He won't change," she jeered. "Everybody thinks they'll change, but they don't. Someday he'll hit your kids."

I jumped to his defense. "Oh no! He'd never do that. He loves his children. He's a good father. He'd never hit them."

She just shook her head, assigned me a room, and gave me some money to buy food for Samuel.

"I'll have a playpen put in your room for the baby. You and your daughter can share the bed. There's food for you both here. Go buy the baby some food at the store on the corner a couple blocks down. Lights out at eleven."

I hesitated, but knew if I didn't go, he would have no food. Out of my safe, middle-class suburban neighborhood, I was nervous. Nonetheless, I walked to the convenient store with Star on one hand and Samuel in his umbrella stroller.

All stares were on us when we entered the little shop. I bought six jars of baby food, which the expressionless cashier stacked into a tiny, thin paper bag. Going back, while we crossed an intersection, the stroller collapsed. The bag ripped, and jars rolled on the pavement in all directions. I couldn't let go of Star, and the buckled stroller squished the poor little guy. I put the torn bag down, opened the stroller, and locked it in place. Gathering the tiny ripped bag and runaway jars took time. I got everything together and hurried to the curb while cars waited. Everyone saw, but no one did anything.

At the shelter, the food choices were refried beans, white bread, and peanut butter. Cockroaches infested the facility. They scurried out from under the toaster, from in between cans of beans, and across the countertops. My daughter and I ate peanut butter toast for dinner, and her brother had strained chicken and peas.

I put my son in the playpen, and his sister slept with me in a twin bed. I spent the night propped up on one elbow, flicking cockroaches off her while she slept. The thought of roaches on him in the playpen was too much to bear. I couldn't bring him into the twin bed too. If he woke, he wouldn't go back to sleep, and besides, there just wasn't room for three of us. *He'll be safe because he's off the floor in that playpen. God, please don't let bugs hurt him. Please.*

The next morning I examined him carefully. *No bites, thank God.* I took my babies to the Crisis Nursery, as suggested.

The Crisis Nursery was a shelter for children in at-risk homes. The immaculate facility stood behind the hospital, and a doctor visited each day to check the kids over. All children had to have a delousing. A bath and hair washing with medicated shampoo were mandatory before they were dressed in clean clothes and free to play.

Star hated to have her hair washed. Throughout her young life I had tried everything—cradling her in my arm, getting myself wet; tilting her head backward, not allowing even a single drop on her face; having her hold a dry washcloth over her eyes. Still she screamed because she just hated to have her hair washed. Unfortunately, to stay there, a shampoo was unavoidable.

I tried to help while they washed her hair. Even while she screamed, they were kind and patient with her. The workers moved quickly and soon were done. My happy babies played with the clean toys and munched on healthy snacks.

I was relieved to leave them there. I didn't have to explain myself to anyone—no one asked questions. It warmed my soul that they just seemed to understand and care. I wished I were a child so I could have someone care for me that way too.

At the shelter, they assigned me to a different room. I shared a small bathroom with another bedroom. It had a toilet, sink, and a shower. With backed-up plumbing, I had to have my feet in two inches of stagnant water to use the toilet. Showering the next morning, I stood with my feet on the side of the stall and leaned in to avoid standing in the foul water.

That day, I joined other women from the shelter, going from agency to agency. At the job service bureau, I learned they had one job to offer me—a night desk clerk at a "no-tell motel" in a dangerous part of town. Nighttime babysitting would be a problem, so I didn't qualify. *Thank God. I'd be jumping from the frying pan into the fire if I worked there.*

The welfare office proved hopeless. With no address of my own, they couldn't help me.

We stopped to eat lunch at a church that fed the homeless. A long line of men waited to go inside. The pastor from the church announced the women would go first. Moving toward the front of the line, I spotted one of the homeless men with a shopping cart. Apparently he had traded his pants for something since he wore only a shirt and coat and nothing on the bottom. I must have beamed with Midwestern girl shock because they roared with laughter when I hurried by.

We ate our lunches as fast as we could, then left.

The thought of finding a job and a place to live overwhelmed me. The next day, I resolved I'd rather take my chances in my nice north Phoenix apartment with a spouse who left for work every day, than to live like that. I called Sally and asked to have Dace come to the phone. While Max ran to get him, Sally told me my husband cried when he learned we were gone. I found that hard to believe—I hadn't ever seen him cry.

"Dace, I . . . I want to come home."

Silence. Then his icy tone sent a chill up my spine. "Where are you? I'll come get you."

He didn't sound sorry or even nice on the phone. I feared what he would do once I got home. Still, I gave him the address, hung up, and waited.

He picked me up at the Pilgrimage House and we drove to the Crisis Nursery to retrieve the babies. He seemed anything but repentant or pleasant, angry that I left the children at the nursery. Back home, nothing changed.

By now, the neighbors knew what was going on. Beth mentioned it to me one day. I said my husband had a foul temper. She said James did too.

"Did you have a black eye the day you helped look for Star?"

She nodded. "I just feel so sorry for him." Her sweet Southern drawl made her likeable. "He can't support his family because of his hip problems. The poor man's frustration makes him violent sometimes."

"Why do you stay with him, Beth?"

"Oh, Kelly, I love him and he's a good father to our son."

I never mentioned it again. Clearly she wasn't someone to help me if my tormentor became more violent. She wouldn't even help herself. Making excuses for a man's vicious behavior seemed like such a cop-out.

I know my husband is a dirtbag. There's no excuse for him. It's me who needs help. I only wish I wasn't so scared. I'd just like to get rid of him — forever.

Chapter Seventeen: Exploitation

Wild James was always friendly to everyone. No one outside his immediate family witnessed his violent side. He and Beth invited me to bring the babies over during the day to watch television in their air-conditioned apartment.

Trying to acclimate to living in the desert was a challenge for us. My baby had been fussy for days. One day at their house, I mentioned it while Sammy sat on my lap crying. "He's been so cranky—ever since we moved into this apartment, actually."

James went into their kitchen where they had a large water cooler, and poured cold water into a copper mug. He sat beside me on the sofa and held the cup to the baby's lips. Sam's chubby hands grabbed the cool cup. Holding it tightly, he slurped and gulped until he had to come up for air. Cold water splashed onto his bare chest. He gasped and guzzled some more. I laughed, "He looks like a little old man in the desert."

"He *is*, sis." James's Southern drawl wasn't as endearing as his wife's. "He *is* in the desert, and he's thirsty. Just look at him."

Although thrilled my son was getting what he needed, I was distressed he was dangerously thirsty. "Poor little guy." I made a concerted effort to give the children water throughout the day from then on.

Late one afternoon the babies and I were enjoying the cool air in Beth and James's apartment. Beth had just come home from work. She, Lance, Ginger, James, and I smoked pot in the living room while the kids played with toys on the floor in front of us. Their kids played outside. As my arm rested on the arm of the sofa, I felt something crawl on my right elbow—a huge praying mantis.

Without thinking, I swatted it with the back of my left hand, sending it flying toward the front window.

"There was just something on my arm," I announced in a quiet voice. "It was a big bug. I smacked it across the room."

"Treasure!" Beth cried. She and her husband jumped up.

"Was it a praying mantis?"

"Yeah, it was."

"Oh no. Treasure! Where did you hit him to?"

"I hit it toward the window, why?"

They ran to the window and gently pulled the curtains back.

"Do you see him?"

"No, be careful where you walk."

"Here he is."

"Is he okay?"

I watched them in amazement. They appeared to want the bug to be all right. "What are you doing?"

"That's our pet praying mantis." Beth sounded exasperated. "That's Treasure. I think you hurt him."

"I'm sorry. I didn't know he was your pet."

"You should've asked," her husband snapped. "You don't just swat insects across the room."

Really? "I'm sorry. The kids and I better go now. Dace will be home soon. I'm sorry. I hope he's okay."

"I do too. Bye, Kelly."

Treasure didn't make it, but they forgave me. They excused my impulsive violence because I was stoned. "I would've killed it quicker if I wasn't stoned," I grumbled.

One weekend they were planning a party and invited us. Dace glanced toward me. "She has to stay home with the kids. I'll be over later." At home I pleaded, "I feel left out. Can't we take turns going?"

"No, Kelly. But I'll tell you what. I'll give you some bucks and you can go buy a bottle of booze for yourself. I'll leave you a couple joints and you can have your own party here."

That sounded great to me. I'd always preferred to drink alone anyway. I took his money, hopped in the car, and drove to the liquor store. I chose a pint of my favorite gin and grabbed a bottle of tonic water.

"Tanqueray? You have good taste. May I see your ID?"

I hadn't brought my wallet. "Oh shoot. I didn't bring it. Don't I look twenty-one?"

"Nope. You have to show us your ID before we can sell you this gin. You can have the tonic though."

I dug in my purse and found the laminated miniature copy of my high school diploma. "Here. This is a copy of my high school diploma. See? It says I graduated in 1978. That makes me twenty-one."

"You could've graduated at sixteen or seventeen." Clearly, they were flirting.

"Oh, c'mon now. Do I look that smart to you?" I flashed a toothy smile.

"Well, you look pretty good to us. Sorry though. We can't sell you the Tanqueray."

Flattered, annoyed, and afraid my husband wouldn't allow me to return, I grinned and left the store. "I'll be back."

At home I parked the car and ran to our apartment on the end. Skipping through the door, I announced, "I have to get my ID. They won't sell it to me." I grabbed my driver's license and ran out before he could stop me.

At the store, the men behind the counter seemed surprised—their mouths dropped open. "We didn't think you'd be back."

I smiled and gave them my license. "Here I am," I taunted, pointing to the photograph. "I'm a bit heavier in that picture since I was pregnant with my *second* baby."

"We never would've guessed it. Here's your gin. Enjoy."

I embraced the momentary happiness that gripped me. Strangers flattered me, I had my favorite gin, and I would be by myself to party hardy. I was thrilled.

At eleven thirty that night the doorbell rang. I was drunk and in my bathrobe. Through the peephole I saw James. I opened the door a crack.

"Everything okay, James?"

"Oh yeah. Dace is passed out at our house. I just wanted to come over to see how you're doing." He came in and closed the door.

"Oh, I'm fine. I prefer to drink alone anyway."

"I notice I caught you in your housecoat."

I pulled my robe together at the top. "I'm getting ready for bed."

"You know, sis, if you were at my orphanage when we were kids, the boys would've eaten you up."

My face burned red. Uncertainty gripped my gut. *Where's Dace?*

"You guys have been having some problems, haven't you?"

I was embarrassed, but too drunk to care. "Yeah. A little. Is he all right?"

"Yeah, he's just passed out. I can go wake him up and tell him you want him home, if you'd like."

That would surely enrage him. "No, just let him sleep it off, I guess. He'll come home when he's ready. Is he okay being there?"

"Yeah. Well, sis, I can pray for you if you'd like."

I was taken aback. *Pray for me?* "Uh, well, sure. Thanks."

He stood beside me and put his arm around my shoulders. "Dear Lord, please help my sister here. Help her know that you're with her." He reached into my clothes. I jumped. "It's all right, sis. I'm here for you," he whispered then continued to pray.

My head spun. How could he be praying and feeling me up at the same time? What if Dace saw him? Petrified, I couldn't stop him. *God help me!*

James whispered into my ear, "Let's go to the bedroom, okay?" I remembered Beth's shiner. My tormentor hadn't ever given me a full-on black eye from a fist. My neighbor was even more dangerous. Amid my drunkenness, I was terrified. Guiding me, he turned me around, and I stumbled along toward the bedroom.

As we lay on the mattress, he touched me and I cringed. He whispered, "If you aren't ready, sis, just tell me and I'll stop."

That was the out I'd prayed for. My heart pounding, I nodded.

"You want me to stop?"

"Yes, I do. I'm sorry."

He sat up. "I won't force you to do anything you're not ready to do, sis."

We got up. I quickly cinched my robe while we went to the living room.

"I'll send Dace home when he wakes up."

"Okay. Thanks. Good-bye."

He left and I locked the door. I leaned against the door, clutching my bathrobe at my throat. My heartbeat thundered in my ears and I wasn't breathing. What had just happened? He had stopped. Still, had I just committed adultery? What if my husband ever found

172

out? He'd kill our neighbor and then kill me. *Oh God, please forgive me. Please don't let Wild James tell Dace. Oh God, I'm so sorry.*

Chapter Eighteen: Grateful for Life

It was spring in Phoenix and Star turned two. My parents sent money to buy her a new pair of shoes. I bought her rust-colored suede shoes with rubber soles. The next day we watched television in James and Beth's air-conditioned apartment. The toddler wasn't used to the rubber soles yet and she stumbled forward, hitting her face on the bottom of their console television set. She bled from a small horizontal cut by her the bridge of her nose just below her right eyebrow.   We got the bleeding stopped, and by the time her father got home, she was fine. Furious because he knew it would leave a scar, he cussed my parents for buying her shoes and me for choosing a pair with rubber soles.

I had enough cash left over after buying the shoes to buy a cake mix, frosting, and Kool-Aid for a birthday party. Since we left the apartment door open all day, the neighborhood kids came and celebrated with us.

Christine came to the party with her mother. "We just came from the abortion clinic," she announced in typical Christine-Attention-Getter fashion.

I gasped. "What?"

"Yeah, Mom took me for an abortion this morning."

Janice nodded in agreement. "You probably didn't have to tell her that now," she said sheepishly.

I stood there astounded. It wasn't so much Chris's decision, although it grieved me, as it was her indifferent attitude. I was in the midst of celebrating the birth of an unexpected child, while holding another unexpected child in my arms, reveling in our little party, and knowing those babies were the only reason I got up in the morning. Her apathy was incomprehensible.

These two crass women had nonchalantly come to a party thrown to celebrate life, having just ended a life, and proudly announced their choice, putting a damper on this rare day of happiness. I squelched my loathing and put on a smile.

"Have some cake," I suggested and walked away.

Thank you, God, for Star and Sammy. They are my reason to carry on.

Chapter Nineteen: Eager to Please

One evening while I prepared dinner in the kitchen, baby Sammy sat against the cupboards at my feet. I browned ground beef in an electric skillet on the countertop. Mad that his meal wasn't ready when he got home, Dace screamed and threw a glass ashtray at me. It hit the upper cupboard beside me, shattering tiny pieces of glass into the ground beef and onto Sam's bald head. He wasn't cut and hardly noticed. "Someday he'll hit your kids." The counselor's words came back to me.

The following week, in a fit of anger he threw a full glass of water at me. It smashed into the wall above the baby, in his swing. He swung, wide-eyed, back and forth, showered with water droplets and bits of broken glass. Alarmed and sensing the violent tension, he burst into tears.

"Someday he'll hit your kids." Again, the angry, man-hating counselor echoed in my head. I hadn't believed her, but he seemed to be more careless with their safety.

Star stayed in the bedroom playing. I breathed a sigh of relief. *Thank God she didn't come out.*

"Now clean it up," he snarled through clenched teeth.

"I will as soon as I get him out of here, okay?"

"Just hurry up."

I rushed my son into the bedroom. I checked him over to make sure he wasn't hurt and hugged his trembling, chubby little body against my shaky stick frame. I quietly closed the bedroom door behind us. My daughter stopped playing for a minute to see what I was doing. I bounced the baby gently trying to calm him—to calm us both.

"You are my sunshine, my only sunshine. You make me happy when skies are gray. You'll never know dear, how much I love you . . ."

"Get out here and clean this up!"

Samuel relaxed and I put him into his crib with a few toys. "Good boy, Sammy. Star, you stay in here and play like a good girl," I whispered and shut the door.

∞∞∞∞∞∞∞∞∞∞∞∞

A single mother named Shannon moved in on the other side of the sidewalk. Her daughter, Joey, was just under two years old and didn't talk. The woman had long, strawberry-blonde hair cut into the popular Farrah Fawcett haircut. She wore tight clothes and was flirtatious.

I liked not being the newbie on the block and invited her to come for coffee one evening. Star played with Joey while we visited. Dace seemed taken with our neighbor, and she loved his attention. Her conversation kept returning to her sexual dissatisfaction.

"It's hard when you don't have a husband." She purred, "I mean you *wish* it was hard."

About a month after she moved in, he said to me one evening, "You know, Kelly, we should call Shannon's bluff."

"What do you mean?"

"She's always talking about not being satisfied, right?"

I knew where this was going. I wanted to disagree but enjoyed his calm demeanor and playful conversation.

"Yeah. What are you getting at?"

"Well, let's call her bluff. Let's ask her to come to bed with us."

"Ahh, I don't know, Dace."

"Oh, come on. She'll probably say no. It'll make her shut up. Put up or shut up, ya know?"

"You really want to?"

"Yeah. Just try it. I don't think she'll say yes, but she'll have to show her cards. Come on."

He was happy and excited. I loved seeing him content and calm. "All right, I'll ask her tomorrow."

"Far out."

That night we enjoyed a relaxing evening smoking pot and not fighting. He played his guitar and talked about being in a band someday and what their album cover would look like. I craved more pleasant nights like that. Maybe this was the answer.

The next day Shannon and I talked while the kids played.

"You know, you're always complaining about not having anyone to have sex with. Well, why be so frustrated when we have good old Dace around?"

"What are you saying, Kelly?"

"We talked, and I'm just saying you don't need to be frustrated when he's right here."

"All right, but you have to be there too."

"Why?"

"Cause I don't want you saying I'm stealing your man. You have to be there, too."

"Okay."

"Okay. Then how about tomorrow night?"

"I'll tell Dace. I'm sure that'll be all right."

My spirit sank and I thought I might throw up. My gut quivered all day. That afternoon he rushed through the door. "Did you ask her? What'd she say?"

"Yes, I did ask her, and she said as long as I'm there too. She'll come over tomorrow night."

"Groovy. The two prettiest girls on the block with *me*."

The next night Shannon came after she'd put Joey to bed. My kids were asleep when she got there.

My husband gently touched her face and whispered breathlessly, "Why don't we all go into the bedroom?" I thought I'd be sick.

Her eyes flashed. "Sounds good to me. C'mon, Kelly."

Resentment flooded my soul—I couldn't remember the last time he touched *me* tenderly.

The three of us moved into the bedroom and closed the door. They kissed and I struggled with intense jealousy. *This makes him happy*, I reminded myself.

I envisioned grabbing her by the hair and flinging her into the closet. I clearly pictured it and it looked easy. Did I dare do it?

The very real possibility of my tormentor hitting me in front of her, making a choice against me, kept me from striking out. I felt powerless. I felt violated.

After she left, I quietly cried in the bathroom, and when I came out, he was sleeping.

The next day he hurried off to work. Shannon went to work, and I sat at home feeling dirty and unworthy to be the mother of two precious, innocent babies.

A few days after this encounter, Wild James approached me on my way to the laundry room. "Dace is a lucky man."

"What do you mean?"

"He had the two most beautiful women on the block. You think we don't all know about it? He's a lucky man."

Humiliated, I worried about his tone of voice. He seemed to be teasing, yet a bit angry. Perhaps he was upset because I wouldn't fool around with him, but allowed someone else in my bed. Whatever the cause, for the second time, I felt afraid of him.

"That was a mistake, James."

"Oh, I know how it is. We had a friend of mine join Beth and me once in Mississippi. She enjoyed him more than she enjoyed me. We had a *big* fight that time. Broke her nose. I know all about those mistakes."

I swallowed hard. "I'd better get this laundry in before the kids wake up." I jogged around the corner to the laundry room.

"Stupid Dace," I mumbled. "Stupid, fat-mouthed arse."

One day the next week my husband came home from work with his foot bandaged. He had crutches and wore a walking boot. Max helped him into the apartment. They were laughing.

"Oh my gosh. What happened to your foot?"

"He's a little clumsy," Max joked. "He'll tell you all about it."

Dace thanked him for helping him home, flung the door shut, and plopped onto the sofa.

"What happened?"

"Just something at work. Don't worry about it. Turn the air on." He lit a cigarette.

"Is it broken?"

"You don't see a cast on it, do you? It'll be fine. I have lots of pain meds here. I have the whole week off. It's gonna be great."

I got the message—no more questions.

He enjoyed his pain medication all week, but never told me what happened. Just another Dace mystery. The next week he returned to work.

I was washing Star's hair when he came home. I didn't hear him because of her normal hair-washing cries. In the blink of an eye, he picked me up and threw me behind him. He dropped to his knees and backhanded my child's face, screaming for her to shut up. His big turquoise ring cut her.

A feeling came over me I hadn't experienced before. With untold strength and vehemence, I jumped on his back. "You can't hit the babies. You can't hit the babies." I screamed until my throat hurt.

He fell backward then turned to me. Instincts took over and I got up and ran out the door and down the sidewalk. I came to my senses, realizing he could lock me out and further hurt the children. I saw him hobbling in his walking boot, screaming obscenities at me.

I sprinted back and passed him. I ran into the apartment and got the tiny screaming toddler out of the tub. I wrapped her in a towel and held her close to my own trembling body. Samuel was swinging in his swing.

Dace slammed the apartment door, huffing and puffing, and sat on the turquoise sofa to have a cigarette.

He stood and looked at me in the hallway, and in a controlled rage, whispered, "You get those babies to bed and come out here and get yours."

Although still daylight, I put Sam in his crib and got Star into her pajamas. She was quiet now, staring as if in shock, the cut beside her eye swelling. I kissed her and put her into her crib. With a quivering voice, I whispered, "I love you. Be a good girl. Be quiet now and go to sleep."

I desperately wanted to crawl into her crib with her. I imagined there would be safety in there. I visualized myself crawling in and it collapsing, inciting added fury from her father and horror for them. No, I knew better.

I looked at my daughter. Our gaze locked and I froze. I believed she knew her mommy was about to receive the worst beating of her life. "I love you," I whispered.

In the few seconds it took to walk into the living room, my thoughts whirled. Would I ever see my babies again? Would Star remember me telling her I loved her? Would that monster hurt them or run away after he killed me? How long would it be before anyone got in to help the children? Who would raise them?

Just as I entered the living room, he grabbed me, tipped me upside down, and dumped me headfirst into the baby swing, which collapsed.

Minutes turned into hours.

I have flashes of memories of that night. I was in our bedroom closet being held up by his thumbs in my eye sockets. I felt my toes touching a cold metal toolbox on the floor. Clothes hangers tore into my head. I heard my voice say, "I'm sorry, I'm sorry, I'm sorry."

"I'll let you down when you stop."

"What?" I cried in a brief moment of lucidity.

"Don't you see what your hands are doing?"

I became aware that I was trying to push him away—first my right hand then my left, in rapid rhythm like a choreographed dance. Against all human instincts, I let my arms fall to my sides. *I'm going blind*. He pulled back, and hangers gouged deep into my scalp as I fell onto the toolbox.

The next thing I knew, the sun shone and my attacker was leaving for work. I was breathing and I could see. I leaned over the counter into the large horizontal mirror in the hallway outside the bathroom and examined myself. My front bottom tooth was chipped, bruises covered me, the hair on the back of my head was bloody,

182

but I was alive. He peeked in at me. My quiet shock rivaled my pain.

"You chipped my tooth," I mumbled. He pivoted and left.

The morning progressed normally. I wanted to leave him, but had become timid and fragile. I sat on the sofa, smoked a cigarette, and watched my toddler play. I stared at her bruised eye. *Now you've gone too far. Now you've hurt our baby.*

I sought help from Lance. He had connections, and I asked him to have my tormentor killed. Ginger wasn't home.

"He has a $7,000 life insurance policy through work. I'll use $2,000 to bury him and you can have the rest."

"No, no," he warned. "The neighbors know you fight. Everyone can hear you. It *will* get back to you. You will go to prison and you won't be with your babies. You need to go to Ohio where you belong. Can you call your dad?"

I used his telephone to call my father at work in Ohio. "Dad, it's a matter of life and death. The babies and I need to come home right now."

"I'll call the airport right away, K.J. Give me your number. Stay by the phone until I call back."

Twenty minutes later the airplane tickets were at the airport. But the plane was leaving soon.

Fear competed with the will to survive as I rushed to leave. Bruce Springsteen sang in my head while I took a quick shower and packed two suitcases and a box of cloth diapers. Lyrics to "Born to Run" punctuated my every move.

I took the two highchairs to the neighbor who lent us hers. I laid them down behind the two-foot cement wall that bordered the patio in front of her apartment, so Dace wouldn't see them when he came home.

I took some of my things to Lance and Ginger's apartment. Lance called a cab and gave me a pack of cigarettes, twenty dollars, and a kiss on the cheek. He promised to send my stuff to me when I gave him postage money. I never saw my stuff again. Unfortunately, Gramma's wedding ring was among those possessions.

We almost missed the flight. The airline personnel rushed our bags and us onto the tarmac to board the plane. One stopover and we'd be home.

Although in a dreamlike fog, I became aware of the stares. I couldn't understand why people gawked at us at the airports. Later I pictured the scene in my mind. There we were—my two-year-old running around with a black eye, saying, "Where's Daddy? Where's Daddy?" I sat with my fat baby boy on my lap while I chain-smoked cigarettes. Wearing my high school graduation gauze halter sundress, I had unwittingly exposed countless bruises on my back, arms, and neck. In my haste, I hadn't washed my hair well enough and it was matted with dark blood on the back of my head. Yes, people stared—and no one said anything.

At Cleveland Hopkins Airport, my father's mouth dropped open when he saw the kids and me. He fought tears as he asked just a few questions and drove us home. During the hour-long ride into the country, I fell asleep. Once at home, my mother helped us prepare for bed. She saw we were exhausted. Seeing her precious first grandchild bruised broke her heart, but we were home—and safe.

The next few days were a blur of shame, contrition, and physical healing. My parents both worked in factories, and the kids and I stayed alone during the day.

Fear rose inside me. To help ease my mind and his own, Dad showed me where he kept his guns and ammunition. He took me into the backyard by an open field and taught me to use one of his guns. It was loud and had a kick, but I got the hang of it.

"Now you know where I keep the guns and where I keep the ammo," he instructed. "If you ever see Dace coming up the lawn and I'm not here, you take these and shoot him. Don't let him in the house. Just shoot him before he gets here. Drop him, Kelly."

It sounded scary to me. Part of me didn't think I could shoot another human being, and part of me burst with hope that he would arrive so I could eliminate him from my life and my nightmares.

The familiarity of my parents' house was comforting, and their abundant food supply overwhelming. I weighed less than one hundred pounds, and my hair and eyebrows were falling out again. On the road to good nutrition, my mind began to work better and my thoughts became clearer.

I wonder where Dan is these days. I allowed my mind to wander to the secret pleasurable thoughts I'd treasured throughout my marriage. I pushed them away. *I need to concentrate on getting my little trio healthy.*

The thought that God had spared me dashed through my mind. *Too little too late. Besides, why would God help me? I'm not good enough.* I banished the notion, put a guard at the door of my thoughts, and forbade it to return. *I can do this myself.* I put my hope in myself instead, which scared me because my husband had groomed me to think like him. *Gotta carry on,* once again became my mantra.

Chapter Twenty: Carry On

The first things on the agenda were to find a car and a job. Through a co-worker, Dad found a car that belonged to a young girl who'd died. It had been sitting in the woods since she first became ill, and it had squirrels, mice, and ants living in it—but what a deal. So, I had a white 1975 Plymouth Duster and was ready to roll.

I rummaged through the glove compartment when my kids napped and my parents were at work. The dead girl's parents obviously never looked in there. There were 8-track tapes of 1970s hard-rock bands, a couple of gas receipts, an old pack of cigarettes, a few tiny marijuana roaches, and a roach clip for holding the little joint remnants too small to grasp.

I thought about death. When confronted with death—even that of a total stranger—one is forced to think about heaven, hell, God, and the people left behind. I allowed myself to entertain the thoughts. I wondered if the girl's family knew she partied, or if she ever thought about God before she died.

Even in my lost, lonely, and miserable state, I recalled the prayer in the park when I was thirteen, and recognized the tragedy it would be if she had died in her sins. She seemed like a girl I could relate to. I muttered a quick prayer for her soul, gathered the roaches, and smoked them in her honor. They were stale. Inhaling the smoke, I remembered her. My nostrils burned. I prayed for peace for her family.

Not long after we returned to Ohio, Samuel turned one. My parents invited a few relatives over to celebrate his birthday, and their love and concern surrounded me.

No one asked questions about our circumstances—they just welcomed us with kindness and fun.

∞∞∞∞∞∞∞∞∞∞∞∞

That spring they found Elaine Zeigler's body. Almost six years following her disappearance, authorities excavated her remains from the backyard of Billy Mansfield's family home in Weeki Wachee Acres in Spring Hill, Florida. Elaine was one of the victims in his and his family's gruesome string of murders. They sent her to her family in Parkman. She was finally home.

Her memorial service was surreal. It was nice to see school friends again. We were adults attending the funeral of a teenager. The church filled to capacity, and we sat in chairs in the foyer. It was closure for all.

∞∞∞∞∞∞∞∞∞∞∞∞

One evening a few weeks later the phone rang and I answered it. It was Dace. His words were slurred and he sounded drugged. "I'm just going to die."

"What do you mean? Did you take something?"

"It doesn't matter. My wife left me."

"Where are you?"

"I had to break into the apartment to get my guitar."

"Why did you have to break in?"

"The mother-effers changed the locks on me." His speech slowed.

"Where are you? What did you take?"

By now, my mother could tell what was happening. She hated the fact he still manipulated everyone from two thousand miles away.

"Do you want me to go up to Aunt Connie's to call his mother?" she whispered.

187

I nodded and motioned for her to grab my purse. I pulled out a small address book and opened it to Janice's phone number and his brother's number.

"No, my wife left me," he continued with garbled speech. "She prefers women anyway. Shannon told me."

"What are you talking about? I hate her. I wanted to punch her out. I do not prefer women. That's just stupid."

"No, she told me. She wanted you, not me."

I surmised that after I'd left, he'd tried to put the moves on Shannon and she said that to get rid of him. Was he suicidal or simply trying to get my attention? I couldn't take a chance. I kept him on the phone.

"What did you take?"

"Pills. Just some pills." He exhaled heavily. "Lots of pills."

"Where are you?"

"Doesn't matter."

My mom returned. "His brother says he knows where he is. He's going there now. Keep him talking."

"Listen, your brother's coming over. He'll be there any minute. What did you take?"

A brief, indistinct outburst of expletives, and he hung up. My gut twisted. Did my agreeing to bring our neighbor into our bedroom cause him to kill himself? If he was self-destructive because I left him, that didn't bother me. I had to leave. But if he played this out because of her, I thought I'd never forgive myself.

After I'd gone to bed, Janice called and talked with my dad. She reported they found Dace. He'd swallowed some pills, was taken to the hospital, and he'd be all right.

I didn't want to hear from him again, but was glad they found him in time.

The next day she called again to speak with me.

"Dace told me what happened."

"Did he?" I doubted he shared the events of that last night.

"Yeah. He said, 'Mom, I chipped her tooth,' and I said, 'Oh no, not her beautiful teeth.' Oh gosh, Kelly. I'm just so sorry. Hopefully he'll get himself straightened out now that we have him in the hospital. I just wanted to tell you he's all right and to tell you how sorry I am about what happened."

"Well thank you, and thanks for letting me know. Good-bye."

I found that hard to believe since they knew about the abuse even before the babies and I moved out West. "I'm sorry" didn't retract the indifference.

Chapter Twenty-One: They Gave Me Apple Butter

I soon found an apartment. It was upstairs in a house on the same busy road my grandparents had lived on. The owners of the house weren't unfamiliar to me.

While in high school, a few kids stood out as Jesus freaks, Sophie being one of them. I'd taken every opportunity to laugh at them. Other students might have been Christians, but we labeled the outspoken, evangelical ones, "Jesus freaks." There were a few girls and two boys. This was the home of one of the boys and his parents.

Despite my history of mocking their son in high school, they were loving and eager to help us. The long wooden staircase to the apartment was awkward for the children to climb. Still the price couldn't be beat. The woman had two cages of doves below the stairs, and Star and Sam often paused to look at them and enjoy their cooing.

Finally on our own, we needed temporary assistance. Independence was great, but frightening. The cupboards were bare.

I met with a welfare caseworker. I applied for AFDC (Aid to Families with Dependent Children), food stamps, Medicaid, and learned about the food program WIC (Women, Infants, and Children).

"Your WIC will kick in soon and your food stamps will start next month. Do you have food now?" she said.

That was one of those defining moments when you pause as your life flashes through your mind. *How did I ever get here?* I asked myself. Overwhelmed, I wanted to decline help, but my kids had no food.

"Not really. I could ask my parents, I guess."

She handed me a piece of paper. "No. You go to this church and they'll give you diapers and milk for the baby. I'm going to call them and tell them you're coming. They have a food pantry—they'll help you. It's getting late, so go there right now."

I slowly took the paper, quietly thanked her, and walked—trance-like—to my car. I buckled the kids into their seats and drove to the church.

The women in the office were kind and quickly led me to a spacious closet.

"This is our food pantry," one said, opening a paper grocery bag and sitting it on a large table. "You put some food in here. Now get enough to last you until your food stamps come."

It was strange. My head spun and I couldn't think straight. I saw myself reach up to a shelf and put a box of cereal into the sack. I took two cans of soup and a can of green beans. I struggled, trying to hold my daughter's hand and balance my son on my hip.

The woman returned and peered into my bag. "No, honey, that's not enough! You need more. Here, let me help you."

She snapped open another paper bag and grabbed items off the shelves so rapidly I couldn't see what she packed. Then I saw it on the shelf—a jar of red-brown apple butter. The label looked homemade. I heard my voice. "Oh, you have apple butter."

"Yes! A farm just up the road always gives us lots of apple butter. You're lucky there's any left—it always goes so fast. It's really cinnamony and good. I'd give you two jars, but there's just one jar left. Do you like apple butter?"

My eyes filled with tears. "Yes," I whispered. "I do."

The sun was setting as I drove back to our apartment. The red sky reflected pink on my precious babies' faces. Love engulfed me and I knew God and Gramma were watching over us.

After I got my children into bed, I gazed at the food in my cupboards. It was enough to last two weeks. Front and center sat a jar of apple butter. I dropped my head and cried. "Now I'm sure we're going to be okay."

I went to bed smiling that night. With tears streaming down the sides of my face, I looked heavenward. "Gramma," I whispered, "they gave me apple butter. Thank you, God."

My parents gave me curtains, a couch, a bed, a couple of tables and lamps, and a small black-and-white TV. They supplied all of our kitchen necessities. They also gave their grandchildren the twin beds that were Dad's when he was a child. They were the same beautiful dark wood beds with the carved pinecone finials that Sophie and I slept in during visits with our grandparents throughout our childhood.

The apartment had a stove, but no refrigerator. Dad had a co-worker with an old, pale pink refrigerator in his garage. He gave it to me. Staring at the rosy dinosaur, I began to feel my creative juices reawaken.

Scouring through Mom's magazines, I dreamed about my "someday" house and saw photos of a brightly colored kitchen I loved. Wanting to emulate it, I bought lime green spray-paint and rolls of duct tape in bright red, sunny yellow, and sapphire blue. One night when the kids were asleep, I spray-painted the refrigerator.

The windows were open for fresh air. I loved the cool evening breeze. I noticed a light coating of paint on the floor all the way down the hallway. I didn't even mind staying up most of the night scrubbing the floor. I was doing it on my own and felt so free.

The next night I measured, marked, and banded three strips of colorful duct tape horizontally on the back wall, down the side of the refrigerator, along the front, up the opposite side, and on the wall leading to the living room doorway. It appeared cheerful and I loved it.

I had a card table and folding chairs, but no booster seats for Star and Sam. They ate at a little metal Samsonite table set that was Sophie's and mine when we were children. I spray-painted the chairs and table shiny apple red and fitted the top of the table with a colorful vinyl tablecloth.

My kitchen shone bright, and the entire project made me feel alive and in control again. I did something I wanted to do—I felt creative.

Chapter Twenty-Two: Freedom Is a Slippery Slope

While receiving government assistance was humbling, I'd paid into the system since my first job at sixteen; it was reciprocation time. It wouldn't be forever, and my trio needed help right now. Still, my pride drove me to a grocery store twenty miles away to use my food stamps and WIC coupons.

I qualified to receive the cheese and white flour afforded the poor during the Reagan administration. I had to put my pride on the shelf as I stood in line with many others and showed my welfare card to receive a huge block of yellow cheese. Although bland fare, we loved it in grilled cheese sandwiches, and macaroni and cheese. Too much of the stuff and we dealt with constipation.

Waiting in line, I talked with the other people. We were all the same. Some were there because they'd lost their jobs. Some were single parents like me with little or no income. We were just people looking for help. The lessons I learned standing in the "gubment cheese" lines were priceless. The most important lesson is that richness can be found in poverty when you have a positive attitude.

My welfare caseworker helped me secure a job through a federal Summer Youth Program. At twenty-one years old, I was the oldest youth in the program and worked in the office at a small airport in Middlefield. The office was in a trailer on the dusty grounds of the single runway airfield.

One morning that summer, I saw a familiar face at the airport and was exhilarated. Dan was handsome and had kind, soft-blue eyes. He wanted to rent a plane. He'd taken flying lessons and was out for a flight.

We chatted for a short time outside the office trailer. I asked him about his family. His girls were doing well and he was engaged. My spirit sank.

He's got a life and you're still married. Besides, what would a guy like that want with someone like you? The flicker of desire sparked and burned out immediately. It was a sad end to a long-enjoyed fantasy.

It soon became quite clear minimum wage would never be enough for me to be on my own. My typing was second rate at best. I had no social skills, since the last time I'd been with people other than family was when Star was a baby. Most of the men in my life took advantage of me or hurt me. My oft-spoken phrase—"I'm sorry"—displayed my critically low self-esteem.

My caseworker suggested I go to the Ohio Job Service Department for a test to see if I qualified for free education. I met the criteria financially and they offered the opportunity to go to a school for fifteen months to learn medical transcription. I tested and learned I scored among the top ten of the class. I could choose to go to a business school to learn word processing instead—something new at that time.

I couldn't fathom I had the intelligence to score among the top ten. Having been hit in the head for so long and told I was stupid and irrelevant, I didn't think I was capable of
achieving . . . anything. This lit a tiny light in me—a light of hope.

Word processing was a six-month program. I saw it as a means of supporting my family and getting off welfare quicker. *I don't want to just design the album cover. I want to play in the band.*

The school was on Public Square in Cleveland, Ohio. There I studied word processing, transcription using a Dictaphone machine, and English. We learned on Tandy Radio Shack's answer to the word processor—the TRS 80.

My welfare caseworker said I could either receive a nominal stipend and relinquish my welfare benefits or stay on welfare and not receive pay. I chose the latter and my childcare was covered.

The leader of my childhood Girl Scout troop, my friend Gina's mother, was the at-home childcare provider for my children. I trusted her completely. I even carpooled with Gina because she also worked in Cleveland, several blocks from Public Square. I couldn't have been happier.

Being with the other people in my class was an education in itself. They were real people with real opinions. We were different races and from various backgrounds. This was something I wasn't used to, having grown up in a rural town. Aside from Leon's family, the only minority in our community was Amish. Becoming acclimated to people of diverse ethnic groups, cultures, and belief systems was interesting.

Judy repeatedly blew her nose during the class lunch period and Charlene told her to "take it outside" because it made her sick. Owen said I'd been pregnant since high school and could not relate to real life. Although correct, it hurt, nonetheless.

Josephine was older than me and had a nine-year-old son. She took any education offered to her—this being her third program. She'd rather learn than earn.

She advised me to tell the welfare people nothing. "The less you tell them, the better," she warned. "Don't tell them you have a phone. Don't tell them you have a car. Don't tell them when you get bread for anything. Just don't tell them nothin'." The posters in the welfare offices warning of penalties for welfare fraud compelled me to ignore her counsel. Real people with real opinions.

I learned new skills in school and my grades were good. At last, my future looked bright.

After my business school classes each day, I walked several blocks to the bank Gina worked in. I waited in a small foyer in the rear of the building until time to go home.

An elderly cleaning woman waited for her son to get her. She had scrubbed floors to help put him through college, and now he was a professional. I enjoyed her company.

"My son wants me to quit here," she confided. "But like I told him, what would I do? I can't just sit and watch the television. I like to work. It's hard, but it makes me feel good. You know . . . productive."

She asked me about my life, and I shared some with her.

"You get out now, you hear? Don't you stay up in that apartment and let yourself dry up. You get out and date."

I blushed and nodded. I didn't intend to grow close to another man for a long time. I was still legally married. Besides, I enjoyed my freedom far too much to end it with another man.

But freedom and happiness are both precarious. My power was too new and I wasn't aware I had to guard it—that it could slip through my fingers in an instant if I wasn't careful. And I wasn't careful.

When the children and I came home from school one day, I saw someone sitting at the top of the stairs. It looked like Dace. I felt joy, but cringed simultaneously. I had to admit, I missed him, but I still feared him.

He sat beside his guitar and a duffle bag.

"Hey."

He seemed somewhat uncertain of my response.

The children, carefully ascending the stairs, watching each step, didn't see their dad until they reached the top. Coming to a stop, they looked up. "Daddy! Oh look, Mommy, it's Daddy."

"Star, Samuel, did you miss me?" That fake smile again.

"Yeah, we missed you."

Just like him to manipulate their feelings.

"Daddy missed you both." They hugged him and tried to crawl on him.

The little landing made me nervous. "Be careful, kids. Let's get in the house." I reached past them to unlock the door.

"I missed Mommy too," he crooned as I guided them inside.

"Put your things in your room, kids. Then you can come out and play with your daddy."

Turning my attention to him, I said, "What are you doing here? How did you get here?"

"I flew and hitched from the Cleveland airport."

"Really? Must've taken you hours."

"All day. But I'm here now. Can I stay?"

"I guess you can stay. Why didn't you tell me you were coming?"

"I didn't know what you'd say."

"Where's the Rambler?"

"I left it at the airport. It didn't work right anymore anyway."

"You just abandoned it?"

198

"Yeah. Kelly, I want you to know that I've changed."

"We'll talk later, once the children are in bed."

I prepared dinner while they showed him their beds, toys, and books. He feigned interest, and I could see he loathed our moving on without him.

That night after putting them to bed, I sat on the end of the sofa.

"You gonna sit all the way down there?"

"Yeah. Let's talk. What are you doing here?"

"Well, like I told you, I've changed. I saw a counselor when I tried to kill myself. I got straightened out. The pain meds for my foot made me do stupid crap. I won't do anything like that again. I've changed. I mean it."

"You know, I want to believe you, but you've said that before." I controlled my voice, showing no emotion.

He squirmed, trying to hide his impatience. "Well, that's all I can say. You either believe me, or you don't. I said I've changed. What more can I say? I'm sorry? Okay. I'm sorry. What more do you want out of me?"

I was tired. It had been a long day and I just wanted to sleep. Although seeing this man was like seeing an old friend again, I remembered my last night with him and was afraid. I also remembered the vulnerability I'd heard in his voice on the phone that night at my parents' house.

Could he have really changed? He had come all the way there. He was unemployed. Did he come because he'd lost his job, or did he quit his job to come? My head spun. I so wanted to trust him. I still desired the happily-ever-after fairy-tale ending I'd always read about.

With trepidation, I leaned forward and gave him a hug. He scooted closer and held me. Part of me wanted to push him away so he couldn't control me, and part wanted to melt into his body and give myself to him.

He lifted my chin toward him and kissed me deeply.

"Let's go to bed," he whispered.

That's how he kissed Shannon. I tried to shut my mind off. *But he's kissing you now. Just shut up.*

I took him by the hand and led him into my bedroom, convincing myself I had control of the situation. Our reunion felt right. He was my husband and the father of my children. No guilt, just natural.

Several days later, I asked my landlady if she would let my husband move in, although he already had.

"Well, honey, families were meant to be together."

One morning, just before my business school courses ended, I woke with terrible pain in my hip. I couldn't put any weight on my right leg; my hip felt out of joint. Dace didn't have a car, and I called my mom, who took me to the doctor's office. My doctor was out of town, and his stand-in admitted me into the hospital.

Day after day, they ran tests. They kept me on Demerol, and I couldn't control my emotions.

My husband stayed home with the kids and called me at the hospital. Amid obscenities, he complained, "How can I look for a job when I have to stay here and watch these effin' kids?"

My heart broke. I was distressed he said that about his own children. He sure didn't sound like he had changed. I worried about their safety.

When Dad came to the hospital to visit that afternoon, I was crying. I reiterated to him what his son-in-law said. I couldn't believe I repeated the "f" word to my father, but I was unglued. He didn't react and assured me they would get the kids and take them home. They would bring them to their regular babysitter during the day when they worked and back to their house at night. I was so grateful.

My doctor returned, diagnosed me with tendinitis in my hip, prescribed medicine, and released me from the hospital. When I got home, Dace was still in my apartment. He said he'd leave when he found a job. I presumed my father told him to get out.

He bought an old Camaro painted in primer red and flat black. The ball on the stick shift was missing and the metal shifter rod dug into his palm. Thick smoke enveloped the cars behind him when he accelerated. I hated the car and didn't want the children to ride in it for fear of the exhaust fumes making them sick.

Next he found a job in Cleveland and moved out.

I finished school and registered with a temporary agency. My first job was at General Electric at Nela Park in East Cleveland. Word processing centers were fashionable, and they had converted part of a parking garage into a large open area where many word processing operators sat, typing for the executives upstairs. They sent their work downstairs and retrieved it later.

After I had typed all day, the center manager came over with the executive requesting the document.

"Are you finished, Kelly?"

"Yes, I'm done." I handed her the thick original document and the one I'd printed out.

"Where is it? What did you call it?"

I blinked and cocked my head sideways. "What do you mean?"

"When you saved the document, what did you call it?"

"What do you mean, 'saved' it?"

The manager's mouth dropped open and the executive rolled his eyes. "Where do you find these people?" He stormed out.

The humiliation and frustration beamed from my face and the manager took pity on me. "Didn't they teach you to save your document, Kelly?"

"No," I whispered.

"Well, don't worry about it, honey. It'll be typed again tomorrow and he'll get it when it's done. He'll just have to wait. They're all on edge up there anyway. The company's trying to do away with their secretaries and replace them with this word processing center. The guys hate it because they have to do so much themselves. It's killing them." She laughed and patted me on the back.

"Go home now, honey. I'll see you in the morning. Don't worry about it."

The man's hurtful comment bothered me, and I couldn't forget about it. I cried all the way home. I learned about saving documents that day, never to repeat the mistake.

When that job ended, I worked more temporary positions. With each one, I learned more about office procedures, professionalism, and human nature.

I got a job with a company that soon moved its corporate headquarters to Playhouse Square in Cleveland. I moved with them, and my temporary position became permanent. The pay was decent and I had insurance benefits.

Just before exiting onto the road one morning, the axel broke on my Duster. It wouldn't move and sat at the end of the driveway. My landlords wanted it gone. I didn't know what to do, so I called the father of my high school boyfriend. He was a mechanic and owned his own business a few miles away.

"Well, I'll tell ya. The junkyard will give you $35 for it and towing would cost $50. I'll come get it free of charge."

I worried he was taking advantage of me, but had no choice. Another car gone to appease an angry landlord.

My father found a 1976 Ford Pinto for me. It was ugly baby-poop green, but it ran well, and I was grateful to have it.

Chapter Twenty-Three: Trying It on My Own

My husband agreed to a Marriage Dissolution, a non-adversarial action that didn't require an attorney. The fee was $350 and we agreed to split it.

When the arbitrator asked the crucial question, "Do you want to end this marriage?" all we had to do was say yes. Dace said no. The mediator allowed two weeks for us to work out the answer, and then he'd close the case.

I was furious. With a bit of freedom in clear view I blasted him once we were out of the courthouse.

"Why did you lie?"

"I didn't lie."

"You did. You told me you'd go through with this and you said, 'no.'"

"I know. I'll say 'yes' next time. I will."

I stormed away. Two weeks later, we met in the courthouse. When the arbitrator asked the key question, "Do you want to end this marriage?" Again, he answered, "No." I couldn't believe my ears.

Led to the cashier, we had to pay the fee. He had no money. The burden of payment was mine because he didn't want the Dissolution. I felt hopeless and helpless. Even without my consensus, he controlled me.

∞∞∞∞∞∞∞∞∞∞∞∞

Trying to move on, I got an apartment in Mayfield Heights, a suburb of Cleveland, closer to work. I asked to see the place we'd be living in, and the manager took me to one of the many units.

He pointed to a few dark spots on the carpet in a thirty-six-inch radius. "You see there are some small spots on the carpet here." He sounded apologetic. "They're from an old mold problem that has been taken care of. You don't have to worry about it."

"Oh, that's all right. I can put a rug on top of it." I loved the apartment. The stairway was open and modern, but I worried about the kids falling through.

"I wonder if these are safe for my kids."

"Oh sure. Everyone loves these stairs. It opens the living room up. You can see the powder room underneath. Kids love 'em."

"I guess so."

"The owner of the complex is going to call you about the unit."

I thought it strange the owner cared about my opinion.

"Why?"

"Oh, she just wants to see if you are okay with the spots on the carpet. You make sure to tell her you saw them and it's all right with you."

"No problem."

In my gullibility, I waited in the office for the call and followed the agreed-upon script.

"You've seen the carpet?" the owner said. "You have no problem with it the way it is?"

"No, really. It's fine." I couldn't understand why she made such a fuss about a few little dark spots.

The next weekend, when my dad arrived with my furniture and boxes in his pickup truck, the manager told me I had to take a different apartment or none at all.

"That's not the one you showed me."

"Well, this is the one we have for you. Take it or leave it." He wasn't apologetic now. Gruff and exploitive, he put me on the spot.

The place he offered had suffered such water damage that mushrooms were growing in the carpet beneath the open stairway. Now I understood the owner's reference.

"I want to talk to the owner again."

"I don't have time to get her phone number. Besides, you already told her you'd take the one with the water damage. Move in or get that pickup the heck out of here."

I didn't feel I could inconvenience my father any more. He'd been patient, waiting in the truck for me to finish talking with the manager. Taking all of my stuff back to his house in the country and starting over again was unfathomable.

"I'll take it," I huffed.

Gray shadows swirled on the carpet in the dining area by the kitchen. Upon closer inspection—ants.

The sliding glass doors faced a grassy courtyard, but wouldn't open. Bullet holes peppered the window in the dining area.

I was stuck. We moved our things in.

I couldn't afford to have the gas turned on, so I cooked on a hot plate and in an electric skillet.

Out of my upstairs bedroom window, I could see a large Baptist church next door. Every Sunday morning I watched the people come and go in their fine Sunday outfits. I wondered if any of them were single mothers. I wondered if they would ever accept someone like me. A couple of times I had the notion to join them for service, but chickened out. *I'm sure they'd not want me there. I'm not like them. And my kids are so naughty.*

Discipline wasn't my strong suit. My children spent the day in day care, and by the time I brought them home, I was bushed. Getting them fed and bathed and playing with them for a while depleted my energy.

The laundry room was on the second floor of the building. I delighted to learn other tenants threw away their dryer sheets after just one use. Their trash was my treasure, and I used them regularly.

I met the young family that lived in the front by the parking lot. They had an adorable baby boy. I envied the mother's ability to stay home and have a loving husband support her.

∞∞∞∞∞∞∞∞∞∞∞∞

I never drank to be social. I drank to get drunk, and I got drunk on weekends. One Sunday morning I had a hangover and took the kids to McDonald's for breakfast. They wiggled and jumped in and out of their seats and were loud.

While hunched over my large coffee, I noticed an older man staring at me. His hair was gray and he had gold chains around his neck. I thought he looked handsome and fit. He struck up a conversation.

"Good morning. You look like you had a hard night."

I tried to smile. "Yeah. This coffee helps."

"Do you live around here?"

"Yes, we live at the Peppergate Apartments."

"That's not far from me. I'd love to see you sometime."

"Well, who are you?"

"Oh, I'm sorry. Of course. I'm Bob Venice. And your name is?"

"I'm Kelly Easton, and this is Star and Samuel. Say 'hi,' kids."

The children giggled and sang, "Hello," together in silly unison.

"Hello, kids. Nice to meet you."

I smiled at Bob and turned my attention to my chatty children. "C'mon, kids. It's time to go."

He followed us to the car.

"So do you want to go out with me, Kelly?"

My hangover subsided somewhat. If this dude could ask me out when I looked terrible, he was worth one date.

"Sure. How about Friday?"

"Oh. That's a week away. How about Tuesday night?"

"No, I'd better not. Getting a sitter on a school night is tricky. Friday's good."

"Okay then, if I can't convince you otherwise. I'll pick you up Friday at six and we'll go out to eat. How about that?"

"See you then." I gave him my work number. When he called me later that week, I gave him my address.

At the restaurant he told me about being part of an infamous Cleveland, Ohio, mafia family. I was twenty-two and didn't read the newspaper, so it meant nothing to me. He told me he was forty-four years old. He seemed ready to move into the position of Sugar Daddy. Although I'd have loved to be taken care of, I kept my guard up. I was still married and didn't even know where this guy lived.

He asked me if I'd go to a popular health club with him. It was located across the four-lane highway opposite my building. I agreed. While there, he offered to buy me a membership. *Great*, I thought, and he paid my initial sign-up fee with the agreement he'd pay the membership dues scheduled to start in sixty days. I signed the papers and made plans to attend often.

Mafia Guy brought me presents, but they were Avon jewelry. I asked him if he was married because men don't usually give Avon. He told me he wasn't. He wouldn't tell me his address, but told me he could see my building and car from where he lived.

A couple of times, he took me to the racetrack and out to eat.

When I told Dad about my new boyfriend, he blew his top. "That's a huge mob family in Cleveland. What are you doing, Kelly?" I laughed.

Sex with Mafia Guy was disturbing. He screamed obscenities and misogynistic contentions at me upon completion. It freaked me out, and he always apologized afterward. His screams frightened my children one night and I had to do some quick talking to comfort them. I began to search for a safe way to ease out of our relationship.

One day he scheduled an appointment for a permanent body wave in my long hair. He told the beautician he'd take care of the bill. They seemed to be close friends. After she rinsed the chemicals out of my hair, she set it in a variety of Velcro curlers and lowered a hairdryer over my head. She and Bob set off to the bar next door.

I sat under the hairdryer for over an hour. When the esthetician wanted to leave, she asked me where the stylist was.

"She's next door at the bar with my boyfriend!"

Irritated, she said, "I can't leave you here with the door open. I'll just lock you in. You can get out, but you can't get back in, so don't leave until you're really ready to go."

I jumped up and headed toward the door with a head full of colorful curlers. "Tell her that her *boyfriend* will pay for the curlers." I left in a fury.

When I burst through my door, I found Dace lying on the couch with Missy, my babysitter. I couldn't deal with it. Without pausing, I stormed into the powder room and began removing the curlers and ranting about what just happened, acting as if I didn't see them together. They jumped up.

"Ah, hi, Kelly. I dropped by to see the kids, but they were asleep. I'm just leaving. Um, Missy, want me to take you home?" She agreed and they left.

"At least I don't have to drag the kids out," I mumbled, still irate about sitting for so long while Bob stayed at the bar with the hair stylist.

The next day Bob stopped by and told me I'd acted immaturely. Unapologetic, he told me to meet him on Sunday at McDonald's.

I found the mystery surrounding Mafia Guy disconcerting. While helping my kids into my car on Sunday, he snapped at my son, "Get in there or I'll beat you within an inch of your life." The child looked frightened and hurried into the back seat.

"Do not talk to my kids like that."

"Oh, Kelly. I was just kidding. Grow up."

With that being the final straw, I knew I needed to break up with him immediately.

He wasn't happy, but said it was no big deal. The next morning I was late for work because someone released the air out of two of my tires. I was grateful they hadn't been slashed. *I will never date another Italian as long as I live.*

Dad did some investigation of his own. "Kelly, there is no way this guy is forty-four years old. I've checked him out and he must be in his mid to late fifties."

"Don't worry, Dad. I've kicked him to the curb. He wasn't nice to Sam. No more Italians for me."

He was ecstatic. "Good. Now don't do anything like that again, Kelly. I mean it."

Freedom from the old guy meant payments to the health club. I'd signed a binding contract and had no choice, but my budget had no room for this burden.

I began to date a man from work. Shawn and I agreed to keep it just physical. I learned that one time after a date, when he took Missy home, they stopped and made out. While my kids loved her and I thought she was a decent young woman, I'd lost enough dates to her and didn't hire her again.

Why couldn't I have been this bold two years ago?

With the forbidden fruit syndrome kicking in, Dace came back and wanted to date me. Since we were still married and the kids liked having him around, I agreed to see him casually. It seemed logical, and I could still be in charge.

Again, freedom and happiness are both shaky, and I wasn't careful. In short time he was in my life again.

He worked for an alarm company and had a tool the industry called a butt set. It resembled a telephone with wires hanging from it with alligator clips on the ends. He showed me how to hook it to the phone lines in the laundry room and use anyone's phone line. I couldn't afford phone service of my own and was grateful. I could listen in on conversations, too, but didn't have time for that. He left the tool with me, and I used it to make phone calls.

∞∞∞∞∞∞∞∞∞∞∞∞

I made several requests to the management company to have the ants exterminated in the dining area, the sliding door fixed, the mushroom fungus killed, and the windows with bullet holes replaced. They said the repairs were unnecessary and would not make them. I told them that until they fixed the problems in my apartment, I wouldn't pay rent.

When they took me to court, I asked my friends in the front of the complex if they'd testify for me about the condition of my unit. They said no, for fear they'd jeopardize their own place.

In court, I told about how the manager tricked me and how I'd offered to pay the rent after he dealt with the problems. The judge didn't believe anyone could be stupid enough to move into an apartment that bad, deemed me a liar, and ruled in favor of the management.

"So?" I snapped at the manager as we parted ways at the courthouse. "I'll just go bankrupt on you. I don't care."

I gave them a fifty-dollar check at the courthouse and pondered calling a bankruptcy attorney.

Chapter Twenty-Four: Choices

I prepared to move again. Dace wanted to come back, and exasperated with trying to live on my own, I agreed. I found a townhouse in another neighborhood in Mayfield Heights. Again, management tricked me into a terrible one.

"How could I have fallen for this *again*?" I moaned. "That's it. From now on, forget the model apartment. I won't sign a lease until I see the actual unit I'm given."

My husband smirked. "But isn't that what you did before?"

"Yeah, you're right. I guess that's how they get you. They switch it once you have the truckload of furniture there. I hate these people. You should've come with me."

"Nope. This place is in your name, not mine."

How handy.

Cockroaches ran throughout the residence we were given. They traveled from townhouse to townhouse the length of the multi-family structure. The 220-volt outlet for the stove was in the pantry in the kitchen, so I had to cook in that closet. The kitchen sink had no cabinet under it, exposing the pipes and holes in the wall. The stairway had no railing, and I had to monitor the children as they clung to the wall on the steps.

When I complained about the bugs, the management sent someone in when we were at work. They put blue powder along every wall throughout the entire place. When we got home I found a note saying not to allow pets or children around the toxic powder. I called the office right away and told them I had toddlers and keeping them away from the walls was impossible. After several calls, they agreed to let me out of the lease.

During our short stay there, Dace and I had a terrible fight. He became enraged and chased me down the stairs. Memories of previous confrontations flooded my mind as I ran into the pantry behind the stove. I crouched against the wall, covered my head with my arms, and cried, "Not again, not again, not again."

This must have caught him off guard because he backed off. I realized that night I needed to move out when he wasn't around.

I called my parents and told them he'd gotten mean again and I wanted to leave. They supported my decision and offered to help me move.

We lived in the townhouse for about three months. For two of those months I didn't have a menstrual period. I thought I was pregnant, and the idea of being a single mother of a newborn and two bigger babies was daunting. A maternity leave would mean no income.

I worked with an older woman named Sarah. I told her I feared being pregnant, but planned to leave my husband.

"Well, honey, can't you just go have a D&C?" I knew what she meant.

My mind returned to 1973, the year abortion became legal. I was thirteen and didn't watch the news. While at the county fair, Suzie and I perused the various mobile displays in vans and truck trailers. Most offered freebies, and we didn't miss one.

Stepping into the Pro-Life van brought us into a world that would solidify what every child instinctively knows—right from wrong.

Glancing at the photos and brochures, one in particular caught my eye—a picture of a garbage can full of babies.

214

"So a trash can full of dolls. So what?" I looked closer, and I nearly screamed. "Those are babies. That's against the law."

"No, I'm afraid it isn't," the soft-spoken response came from the corner. "They have recently made it legal to have an abortion anytime a woman wants one."

"What's an abortion?" In my adolescent innocence, I listened to the short version of the answer. *She's lying.* I studied the photos more carefully. "That's so wrong," I whispered. We left with handfuls of literature.

That impression cemented in my mind. Now there I was, preparing to make a hushed and hasty exit from my abusive husband and become a single mother of two tots. Two more weeks and still no period.

All the facts from those brochures shot through my mind.

"A baby's heartbeat begins at eighteen days post conception."

"A baby has nerve endings and can feel pain during an abortion."

I was torn. The thought of supporting my two children on a secretary's salary was menacing. Imagining having another baby, missing work, paying for day care, and trying to catch up financially, overwhelmed me. I chose to dismiss my conscience and follow Sarah's advice.

I called a woman's services clinic found in the phone book, was told they did abortions, and planned to schedule one following my initial visit.

I couldn't imagine calling Suzie about this. Melanie joined me instead. I cried all the way there.

"I know this baby's old enough to feel pain. I just hope it's quick and he doesn't have to feel pain long. I'm so, so sorry. This is wrong, but I feel helpless." Mel made no judgments, but listened.

We arrived a half hour earlier than my scheduled appointment. They gave me a pregnancy test, which read positive. When I asked to schedule an abortion, they said to take a seat in the waiting room.

Pregnant girls and their boyfriends filed in. One hour passed, then two. I asked when I'd see someone. They said to sit and wait. Three hours later, when the last pregnant girl left, they gave me another pregnancy test, which read negative.

Although my tests were inconclusive, they told me they didn't do abortions, nor did they refer them. I was livid and crying. I screamed at everyone about being liars and my having to pay a babysitter, and them disrespecting my time, peppered with expletives. I crashed open their screen door and slammed it behind me. Melanie whispered an apology to the gaping-mouthed staff and followed me.

Two weeks later, my period started. Although I didn't have an abortion, the guilt of deciding to abort haunted me for years. Dace never knew.

He sensed something was up and asked me not to leave him. He pointed out that he didn't hit me in the pantry and it should prove he'd changed. Still concerned about finances, I agreed to stay.

Together we rented a ground-floor apartment elsewhere in Mayfield Heights. My parents were disappointed, but tried to be supportive.

216

Chapter Twenty-Five: Manifestation

Dace got a job at another burglar alarm company. The violence continued, but I didn't dare tell my parents. Although we suffered, I still thought a happy life was attainable.

Craving family intimacy, I talked him into taking us to the circus when it came to town—I'd pay for the tickets. He hated to do family things, and his attitude was foul from the beginning of the day.

It was evening and the children chattered on the way to the arena. Walking toward the building their father told us to be quiet. Cars waited to take their places in the parking lot.

His demeanor made me nervous.

"I hope our seats are good," I thought aloud. Apparently, he didn't like my tone or words, and slapped me, sending my ornamental hair comb flying into the road. I ran back to get it, making the cars wait. My humiliation showed brighter than the headlights that seemed to spotlight my anguish. Everyone saw, but no one did anything.

Amid the circus gaiety, I swallowed cries and blinked away tears. Did any of these people recognize me from the parking lot? I pushed my embarrassment and sorrow down my throat and prayed the little ones would enjoy the show and my tormentor would be calm by the time we got home. This time, God seemed to hear my prayers.

∞∞∞∞∞∞∞∞∞∞∞∞

One day the following week during a fight, he seemed determined I wouldn't escape. I hurried the kids out the door. He followed us into parking lot as I rushed them into the car. I had always heard a key could be a weapon. He refused to allow me to shut my car door, and I lashed out with my car key, striking his cheek. Instant blood—it worked. His expression dropped and he stepped back. We sped off for hours.

Afraid to go home, I waited until dark, and he'd gone. He had met up with the two sons of his co-worker. He called the three of them the Serpent Brothers.

The Serpent Brothers spent much time together. When I'd come home from work, I'd often find them hanging out, getting high. Sometimes they played guitars. The few pieces of good jewelry I had disappeared. They were always stoned, and my Serpent just got meaner.

I'll never have a relationship with a musician again for as long as I live, I vowed.

The abuse escalated and he no longer attempted to hide his exploits. His voice, my screams, and the sound of flesh hitting flesh became inconvenient for the neighbors. The upstairs family routinely stomped on the floor and yelled for us to shut up, as we no doubt were interrupting their television programs. Yes, they knew, but no one did anything.

∞∞∞∞∞∞∞∞∞∞∞∞

Although we both worked, we still didn't have enough money to live on. His was unaccounted for, and I knew I needed to have a larger income in the near future.

Believing the lie that I wasn't smart, I decided to cash in on the one thing I supposed I had going for me— my appearance. I signed up for modeling classes at Dorian-Leigh Modeling Agency near where I worked on Playhouse Square. I made small payments, lifted from my grocery budget. My classes were on Saturdays, and he stayed home with the children.

At the school, I learned to apply makeup for daytime, nighttime, and the disco dance club, as well as

218

for color and black-and-white photography. Additionally, I learned how to walk down a runway in high heels and how to pose for the camera.

One of the modeling teachers was Amy Stoch, a beautiful blonde woman with joyful eyes and a broad smile. She eventually moved to Hollywood, changed her name to Amy Stock, and appeared in *Days of Our Lives* and movies. It was fun to see her on television and the big screen, thinking *I know her*. It gave me hope someone from small-town Ohio could become a success.

One day as I was leaving to go to class, my son said, "Where are you going, Mommy?"

"She's going to learn to be plastic," his father retorted.

"Mommy's going to learn how to make fifty dollars an hour, sweetie. I'll be home by lunchtime."

∞∞∞∞∞∞∞∞∞∞∞∞∞

The tension grew in our apartment. One night while the children watched television in the living room, my husband and I had a terrible fight in the bedroom.

Between shouts of obscenities, he grabbed my great-grandmother's mirror and threw it across the room. It crashed into the wall and shattered, drawing the kids' attention.

I ran out into the hallway, slipped, and fell. My tormentor stood over me kicking me in the side. Samuel, now two and a half, ran down the hall screaming, "You kicka my mama. You kicka my mama."

No one had ever confronted the monster about his abuse. Apparently he couldn't handle our toddler's remark and ran out of the apartment.

I held my trembling children close to me, reassuring them we were alright.

I had stayed with Dace at that point in my life because I thought, *he's the father of my babies, and for them I have to stay with him.* However, when I saw my baby fall apart, I realized that, for those kids, I had to leave.

By now, my modeling classes were drawing to a close and it was time to put a portfolio together. I needed money for that—money I didn't have. I found an inexpensive photographer in Cleveland.

Mr. Dill's studio was close to where I worked. I scheduled a Saturday photo shoot, borrowed some clothes from Melanie, and put my hair in hot rollers that morning. My long hair hung in soft, bouncy curls, and I had confidence I looked great.

Dill had asked me what sort of photos I wanted. I told him professional photos for modeling. He suggested something sexy for a well-rounded portfolio.

"I think every woman should have nude photos taken at the ripe old age of eighteen."

I disagreed.

He smirked. "At least bring a teddy for some intimate shots."

In his studio, I felt uneasy. Although not very tall, he was heavy, and I didn't think I could take him if he made an advance toward me. His studio had a dilapidated hallway leading to a tiny bathroom where I changed outfits. The "walls" were bare 2 x 4s with only outer drywall. I wondered if cameras hid amidst the lumber and electrical wires in the tiny, dusty dressing area.

Outside he took photos of me in Mel's gray suit and silky red blouse. I walked up the sidewalk with purpose. I posed by office building doors and leaned against a lamppost. Then we went inside.

"Take your jacket off," he suggested. I agreed and he continued to snap shots. Soon I was lying on my side with my head resting on my hand.

"Unbutton the top button."

I did.

"Just one more button."

"Umm, okay."

"Okay now, just one more button."

"Ahh, I don't think so."

"Ah, come on. Just one more. That's all."

I obeyed.

I changed into a black satin teddy and he took more photos. Being exposed, I felt vulnerable and unsafe. Within minutes, he finished and put his camera away. I dressed again and left.

For weeks, he wouldn't answer my phone calls. Finally, he phoned to tell me I could pick up the thumbnail sheets. He said to tell him which photos to reproduce and he would comply.

I took the manila envelope and opened it later. He hadn't given me the pictures of me wearing the teddy. I tried to contact him for two weeks. I wanted the negligee photos and negatives. I stopped by his studio during my lunch break and learned he'd left town. Maybe my husband was right—I couldn't make smart decisions.

In my paranoia, I thought every male professional in the city looked at me strangely, as if he'd seen my negligee shots or secret photos of me changing.

∞∞∞∞∞∞∞∞∞∞∞∞

I had heard it said the true meaning of insanity is continuing to do the same thing and expecting a different outcome. At last, I was getting it through my head Dace would never change. I gave up hope of the fairy-tale happy ending little girls dreams of.

Each time I left, I'd remember the few tender moments we had shared and would weaken again. Following his promises to change, I'd decide to try once more.

After vacillating in my commitment, my deceased Gramma helped me make the ultimate break from my abuser.

One night in a dream, I faced a wall made of stone. Light rays shone through a narrow aperture—a rectangular passage two feet wide and four feet tall. In my dream, I crawled up into the opening and, on my hands and knees, made my way through the thick stone wall. It was like a tunnel, and the stones were smooth but hurt my knees.

The crawl was short and the approaching sunlight was warm and welcoming. On the other side, the trees and grass were emerald green. There my grandmother stood, with her bright smile, welcoming me with her arms held wide. She gave me a much-needed hug.

"Oh, Gramma, is it really you?"

"Well, yes, my little chick-a-dee. It *is* me."

She continued to hug me. The warmth was real and the reassurance absolute. I allowed myself to melt into her arms.

"I miss you, Gramma. I love you so much."

I felt overwhelming love for her. I also felt shame. I was ashamed of my weakness. I had always been a firecracker with whom adults struggled. Now I was a wimp.

My grandmother held onto my upper arms firmly. Looking into my eyes she said with conviction, "Kelly, I am so proud of you. I love you. I always have."

Without further conversation, I knew I had to go. I had so many questions and wanted to stay, but it was time to leave. I entered the short, narrow tunnel. As I began to crawl, I paused to look over my shoulder. I heard a voice: "You can't come back here." A twinge gripped my heart. I paused and then moved on.

While sad, I smiled at having been with my beloved grandmother. I awoke with a renewed resolve to meet the future with determination. I thanked God for allowing me a few precious minutes with Gramma. I ached with a fresh feeling of loss.

Through my dream, my grandmother had given the encouragement I needed. Mustering the courage I had inside of me and the strength that comes from being her granddaughter, I gathered my babies and left—this time for good.

I called my parents and told them I was leaving Dace forever. I don't why they believed me, but they did.

They offered to buy a new mobile home in the country for the kids and me. It was furnished and, because it had been a model home, featured extras that made it warm and homey. I planned to pack our belongings, including the few family heirlooms I had left, and my parents would help us move.

Moving day came, and apparently the monster decided I wasn't going.

"You think you're moving today?" He hadn't dressed yet and wore his white briefs.

"Yes, Dace. We are leaving today—permanently. Mom and Dad will be here in a couple of hours."

I continued to bring my packed boxes into the living room.

"That's what *you* think." He grabbed me and threw me sideways to the floor. My feet flew into the air as I slid over the carpet. I rolled to get up, but before my feet could hit the floor again, he was above me, flipped me onto my back, and clutched his hands around my throat. His evil stare burned with hatred.

"You *think* you're leaving. How dare you try to leave me! How *dare* you! You and your effin' 'Dadly Do-Right.' You're not going *anywhere*."

My head began to feel numb and stars flashed amidst darkness as I choked and sputtered, trying to push him away. I was losing consciousness. He'd never choked me with that much fervor before. *He's going to kill me*, flashed through my mind. *The kids!*

A supernatural strength overtook me. I put my hands on his chest and pushed him, just short of me blacking out. He flew backward, stumbled, and banged against the wall. He lurched forward and tried to pin me again. Instinctively, I retaliated. It was surreal, like I was watching myself.

Still sitting, I again shoved him. He faltered but didn't lose his footing. I was on my knees now and he stood over me. A deep gravelly voice came out of my mouth, "It's the balls now." In one sweeping motion, I reached up and grabbed his underwear, tearing them from his body.

He jumped back with his ripped briefs hanging by the waistband. His eyes bulged in disbelief. What was he dealing with here? *Who* was he dealing with? It wasn't Kelly Easton anymore. He ran into the bathroom, slamming and locking the door behind him.

I sat alone on the living room floor and tried to gather presence of mind. Blinking and looking around, I breathed heavily, confused about what had just happened. *Where did that come from?* And such a vulgar phrase. I had never seen or heard anything like it. If it hadn't been in my favor, I would have been terrified.

I was flooded with understanding of how some women kill their husbands. I'd just fought back for the second time in our marriage. Was it battered woman syndrome? Temporary insanity or post-traumatic stress disorder? Was it the shear will to live? Was it heaven, or was it hell? Whatever it was, something had come over me. I couldn't wait to get out of there.

The kids ran into the living room. "What's wrong, Mommy? Why did Daddy slam the door?"

"Oh nothing. He just had to go potty. Do you have all your toys out of your rooms? Gramma and Grampa will be here soon. Go check your closets now."

By the time my parents got there, my abuser was dressed and smoking a cigarette in the rear bedroom, avoiding the living room where I continued to stack boxes.

My father entered first and saw the marks on my neck. His jaw clenched. "We're getting you out of here."

"It's okay, Dad."

Mom came in and saw me. She shouted to Dad, "Ray, did you see her neck?"

"Yes, calm down. We're taking her out of here now."

Their son-in-law sauntered past us and, without a word, left.

Dad grunted. "He'd better leave, if he knows what's good for him."

"Hey, Dad." I giggled. "He called you 'Dadly Do-Right.' You know—like the old Canadian Mountie cartoon?" I laughed and couldn't stop. "That's funny, Dad."

He and Mom studied me, motionless. He snickered. "Dadly Do-Right. What a jackhole. Let's go."

We rushed to leave before Dace returned. Out of spite, I took all of the light bulbs and toilet paper.

That night, we stayed with my parents in the country. My cousin Lisa came over and the two of us drove to the apartment to peek in.

There was a party going on. A sheet hung across the large sliding-glass door. We peered under and saw the ceiling fixtures had black light bulbs in the sockets. People lined the walls everywhere. There was no furniture. Lisa and I entered the apartment, recognizing no one. Once down the stoner and whore-lined hallway, we found the Serpent Brothers leaning against a bedroom wall. All three were stoned silent. We left, our curiosity satisfied.

"He's so wasted, he won't even remember seeing us," I snickered. She agreed. We went to a bar for a drink. I had only one.

A few days later, Dace flew back to Phoenix. Having him two thousand miles away made me feel a little safer. I vowed not to bad-mouth him to the children. "He's still their father," I told my parents. "They should respect him."

∞∞∞∞∞∞∞∞∞∞∞∞

A month away from our escape, I took time to review the event. *Where did all that strength come from anyway?* Having been so timid I couldn't defend myself, I marveled that I confronted my abuser and left.

Now I led my children through each day. Some days I didn't feel like getting out of bed, but for them I did.

I think my bravery came from Gramma. I saw her as a conduit for God's unconditional love, and strength was a byproduct of that love.

My advocate since infancy, my grandmother had always been my best friend. She listened to me gripe, and then sometimes tried to mediate between my parents and me.

We lived beside my grandparents in Middlefield for the first three years of my life. My relationship with Gramma is my first recollection of unconditional love.

Smiling, I remembered when I was three years old, telling her every swear word I had ever heard. I cussed that poor woman up one side and down the other. I pictured her reaction in my mind. She had feigned disappointment and shook her head slowly. "Oh, Kelly, my little chick-a-dee. Good little girls don't talk like that." I'd giggled and skipped home, secure in her love.

With patience, she welcomed my hyperactive visits throughout my childhood. She didn't squelch my energy or determination.

While my parents found it unacceptable for me to ask, "What did you buy me?" when my grandparents came home from trips, my grandmother never scolded me. I would whisper the question and she'd wink and tell me what she'd purchased—she always had something.

My grandparents had cashed in a certificate of deposit to purchase the Mustang for me to drive during my senior year of high school.

They allowed me to live with them when I ran away from home and Dad brought me back from Dace's apartment. She'd encouraged me to make up with my folks and move home, but assured me I was welcome there.

When I became pregnant the summer after graduation, Gramma quickly put together the sweet outdoor wedding for us. She and Grampa allowed us to live in the two-room apartment.

Always present, she had been my rock, my closest friend, my reason to carry on. For the first time in a long time, I honestly believed I could carry on.

Chapter Twenty-Six: Final Attempt

I answered ads in the Cleveland Plain Dealer for cattle calls—modeling calls for auditions. At one such interview, I sat in a woman's office while she perused my meager thumbnail photos. "You need a portfolio. These are too small. Who did these anyway?"

"A photographer on Playhouse Square—Mr. Dill."

"Ahhh, 'One-More-Button Dill,' ey? I see."

I was aghast. His filthy reputation preceded him. I had been just another one of his stooges. Where had he gone? What had he done with my negatives and the shots of me in the teddy?

Responding to another casting call, I went to where John Casablanca Modeling Agency was holding local auditions. After waiting for over an hour, they called my name. The receptionist took one look at me and presented a superior attitude. "Johnnnn Casablanca has NO models under five foot-seven, thannnk you." Her tone was patronizing. She leaned sideways and called around me. "Next!"

I already had a wounded self-image. With that added embarrassment, it was easy to let the modeling dream die.

∞∞∞∞∞∞∞∞∞∞∞∞∞

I needed a lawyer—a good one because I worried Dace would have unsupervised visitation with the kids. I had no money, but believed I could make payments.

Dan had custody of his two daughters. I thought that for a man to have guardianship, his attorney must have been excellent. Although I called to find out the name of his lawyer, I was secretly excited to have a reason to communicate with him again. *Maybe he's not married after all.*

He sounded somewhat annoyed. "Actually, her attorney was better than mine."

"But you have your daughters. Yours must've been better."

With a groan, he told me a few of the painful details of his divorce to prove I should contact his former wife's attorney.

"Mine was too nice—not very effective. Hers was more aggressive. You should contact him." Although kind, Dan obviously didn't care to discuss it.

I met with the lawyer he had suggested, who agreed to represent me in the divorce. He agreed it would be harmful for my husband to have unsupervised visitation, and called a psychological evaluation to be done on Dace in Phoenix.

In typical Dace fashion, he chose a female psychologist to administer the test. The report showed he had her eating out of his hand. She even used the term "charming" in her report.

For months, he fought my divorce attempts long-distance. In the end, he had to concede and fly back to Ohio for the proceedings. Wanting to get on with my life, I determined to make sure he would go through with it this time. The children and I picked him up at the airport. Star was four years old and Sam three.

At the airport, Dace sat on the arm of a chair in which Sammy rested. My sweet son, who was always smiling and quite jovial, solemnly looked at him and said, "Are you my daddy?"

Dace knelt in front of him, puffed out his chest, proudly raised his chin, and delivered his classic plastic smile. "Why yes, son, I am."

Samuel stared with his little deadpan face. He calmly said, "You broke the glass and kicked my mommy." He leaned closer to the man and slowly repeated, "You broke the glass and kicked my mommy."

Dace's face drained of all color. He slowly stood and walked away. Sammy's and my eyes locked. He was the only one who had ever confronted him for his actions. I never dreamed my knight in shining armor would come in such a small package.

My attorney had asked me if I had any witnesses to confirm my husband's abuse. I believed people knew, but throughout our relationship, society had observed the abuse and looked the other way.

I asked Lisa and my other cousins, Linda, Lori, and Lenny Jr., if they could help me. Lisa was going to go to Buffalo, New York, with her parents the day before the court date, but her siblings agreed to stop by the courthouse on their way to Buffalo. Their father, my Uncle Lenard, received treatments in a cancer center there, and they were going to support him. It touched me to think they would delay such an important trip just for me.

Of course Dace obtained a female attorney to represent him. With him came the other two Serpent Brothers. Even though cleaned up, they looked like scum.

I was the first on the witness stand. My representative was composed. "Has Dace ever hit you?"

"Yes."

"How many times?"

I exhaled with a little puff of air. "I really don't know. Many times."

"Would you say every day?"

"Just about. He'd go for a couple weeks and I'd think everything was going fine. Then he would have an outburst and scream about how terrible things were as he was slapping or choking me."

His attorney appeared confident. I wanted to shake her and say, "Sister, you're defending a man who abuses women in horrific ways. What are you doing?" I met her glare.

"Did you ever hit him?" she said with a smirk.

"Twice. Once when he knelt beside the bathtub backhanding our two-year-old and once when I was about to move out and he choked me."

Clearly not the answer she was looking for. "Tell me"—she obviously had a new strategy—"did you ever hit a police officer?"

I couldn't believe she had brought this up. Dace was scraping the bottom of the barrel with this one. I was irritated because it showed me he hadn't believed me at the time of the incident.

∞∞∞∞∞∞∞∞∞∞∞

Shortly before I had left my abuser, one evening after work, I had gotten a warning for having an expired license plate sticker on my car. I'd been annoyed because I thought Dace should be in charge of such things. I was preoccupied with trying to stay alive and keeping my children safe.

I'd planned to take the kids to the day care the next morning, buy and attach the sticker, and proceed to work. Getting out of the house had been hard. Dace had had a fit about something and had slapped me. Running late, I grabbed the kids and sprinted out the door before he could do it again.

On the way to the day care center, a police officer in Mayfield Heights stopped me.

"Step out of the car." His arrogance was palpable. "You have an expired sticker."

I got out and stood beside my car. "I know. I got a warning last night. I'm on my way to take care of it right now."

"Too bad," he sneered. With an obnoxious smirk, he handed me a ticket.

I snapped. I snatched the ticket away and muttered, "Effin' jerk."

Suddenly, I was against my car with my face pushed into the car roof. He cuffed my hands behind my back. My gray maxi raincoat got dirty rubbing on the side of the automobile. The brutal police officer read me the Miranda rights while my kids screamed in the back seat of my car. Without regard for my children, the cop tried to pull me away and put me into his cruiser. I lost it.

"You can't take me away from my babies! You can't take me away from my babies!" I was hysterical. The look on his face was shock and fear.

Officer D'Ford put my children in the police cruiser with me. They cried uncontrollably. Unable to hold them, I tried to calm them.

"Don't cry, kids. They just want money. That's all. As soon as Mommy gives them money, they'll leave us alone."

At the station, I sat across from the police chief's desk, and my children sat in chairs beside me. I repeated my ridiculous rant to my kids, totally destroying the coveted "The Policeman Is Our Friend" axiom for my children.

The chief freed my hands. He seemed like a nice, reasonable, "dad" sort of man.

"We normally would fingerprint you, but since your children are here, we're not going to do that."

I thanked him.

"Do you know why you're here?"

"Yes. I have an expired license sticker and I was on my way to buy a new one, and *this* guy arrested me."

The arresting officer stood beside his partner, who had remained silent throughout the entire incident.

"Officer D'Ford said you punched him in the face."

I couldn't believe my ears. I had sworn at the man. While he could've arrested me for disorderly conduct by course utterance, he obviously didn't know the law and thought he had to fabricate something, arresting me for disorderly conduct by hitting a police officer.

"What?" I glared at D'Ford standing there. He looked worried. "I swore at him. I didn't hit him. If I'd hit him wouldn't he at least have a red mark on his face? You can tell he hasn't been hit. He's lying."

The police chief didn't seem to doubt me. It made me wonder about D'Ford's record.

They released me, and I took the kids to the day care center and then drove home to cry. My tormentor was home. I plopped on a stool by the door and wept, ignoring his demands to explain why I'd come home. After I could talk calmly, I told him what had happened.

"You hit him, didn't you?" Any hope of receiving comfort vanished.

I was surprised he didn't believe me. Considering all the abuse I'd taken from him without fighting back, I was appalled he'd think I'd hit a police officer.

I called work to say I'd be late, and drove to the DMV. After putting the updated sticker on my plate, I went to work.

At lunch, I heard the company nurse say that while riding the city bus to work that morning, she'd seen "some poor lady" in a gray raincoat against her car with her hands cuffed behind her. I thanked God my face had been pushed onto the car roof and not facing the road.

Now Dace's lawyer had asked me if I'd hit a cop. I was irritated.

"No, I did not hit him. I cussed at him, I jerked the ticket out of his hand, but I did not hit him." Dace's jaw dropped. He was either shocked he was wrong or shocked at what he perceived as me lying under oath.

"Why did you swear at him?" she said.

"Well, I'd had a really rough morning and the cop stopped me for something I'd gotten a warning for the night before. I was on the way to get the new license sticker, and he gave me a ticket. I snatched the ticket away and swore at him. Then he lied and said I hit him."

It was my lawyer's turn. "What do you mean you had a rough morning?"

He obviously worked on instinct because we hadn't discussed the incident that had happened over a year earlier.

"Well, I'd been slapped before I left the house and was running late . . ."

"Slapped?" he interrupted. "By who?"

"Dace. He was mad about something and slapped me."

My matter-of-fact manner spoke volumes about my daily life with him. His representative seemed sorry she'd asked the question.

They called my opponent to the stand. His calm demeanor and politeness was infuriating. I had never seen him so sedate and cooperative. His fake grin made me sick. His attorney asked him how many times he'd hit me in the five years we'd been married.

"Eight or nine."

"How many times did Kelly hit you during that time?"

"More times than that."

Now my jaw dropped. Add perjury to his list of sins.

They called my youngest cousin, Lori, into the courtroom to testify. My other cousins waited in the hall, ready to help if asked.

"Did you ever see Dace hit Kelly?" my attorney said.

"I never saw him hit her."

"Do you have reason to believe he ever hit her?"

"Yes. One Thanksgiving Kelly, Dace, and baby Star came to the family dinner at our aunt and uncle's house. Kelly had a black eye that she tried to hide with her hair. She said she fell in the bathroom, but I don't think anyone really believed her."

Dace looked surprised.

My heart leapt and broke at the same time. Love, shame, and anger flooded over me all at once. So they had noticed. Why, oh why didn't anyone say nor do anything? Maybe they were all afraid of him. Maybe they thought it would make life harder for Star and me if they did. Instantly, love won out and I was indebted to Lori.

She was excused. As she left, my lawyer whispered, "Who are these two guys Dace brought for his witnesses?"

"Oh, they call themselves the Serpent Brothers. They're his party friends." His attorney heard me and saw my disgust.

"Do you have any witnesses?" the judge asked her.

"We have no witnesses, Your Honor." Her client's jaw dropped again.

This is just a jaw-dropping morning for him.

The judge granted the divorce, set child support, and visitation proclaimed. My husband agreed to everything far too quickly. I was in disbelief when I saw his large flamboyant signature on the papers. I didn't trust him. Everyone left.

My attorney told me his lawyer mocked him afterward. "He hit her *only* eight or nine times?" she had scoffed. "*One* is too many." His lies hadn't helped him.

My cousins waited on a bench in the hall outside the courtroom. When I walked out, they stood up.

"Is it finally over?" Linda wasn't talking about the hearing.

"It is." I smiled weakly.

She gave me a big hug, as did Lori and Lenny.

"We love you, sweetie," Lenny said.

That morning, my cousins had brought me spiritual life and continued on their journey to encourage physical life to their father during his cancer treatments. I was grateful for their support.

The next day Dace took a taxi to the airport and flew home to Phoenix.

My hopes for a normal life didn't transpire for awhile as the kids and I lived through the consequences of the previous five years with the monster.

Chapter Twenty-Seven: Serenity

Like seeing your life flash before you in an accident, the drive from the health spa to the day care after the divorce proceedings provided just enough time for my mind to encapsulate my life. *Snap out of it; you're here.*

I experienced a renewed joy as I entered the day care center. I had chosen alternative childcare options in the past, but the Kiddie Company in Lyndhurst was a perfect fit. The director was a registered nurse who also held a degree in elementary education. She'd been both nurse and teacher in her life and combined her knowledge and life experience to create a fantastic day care center in a church. A peaceful atmosphere rounded out the program. Maybe it was because it was in a church. Maybe it was the God about Whom the children sang.

When I had first brought the kids to the day care, Samuel didn't talk much. He was two years old and Star spoke for him. The director saw the predicament and separated them. It was difficult on these best friends, but it helped each of them to grow. Three-year-old Star could concentrate on being a child and not looking after her little brother, and he had to speak up to get what he wanted. His vocabulary grew quickly.

I stopped to collect my daughter at her room. Always a chaotic time, I tried to move the routine along swiftly. Hugs, "oohs" and "aahs" over creative four-year-old artwork, and then on to retrieve Sam. A smooth repeat and we were safely in the car traveling home.

After dinner and baths, it was time for bedtime rituals. "Can we sleep vis you tonight, Mama?" Samuel always sounded like a little German boy with his *w*'s being *v*'s.

"Oh, I guess so," I laughed. "You can sleep VIS me." They grabbed their favorite stuffed animals and tore down the hallway, through the living room and kitchen, and into my bedroom at the front end of the trailer. Snuggles, whispers, giggles, and the song followed. I sang without interruption, "You are my sunshine, my only sunshine. You make me happy when skies are gray. You'll never know dear, how much I love you. Never take my sunshine away."

"Don't take *my* sunshine away," they teased. I tickled first Sammy's tummy then Star's, back and forth. "No, *you* are both *my* sunshines. No one is taking these little sunshines away from *me*." I kissed their cheeks, told them goodnight, and shut the light off.

"I love you, Mama."

"I love you, too, Mama."

"I love you two sunshines. Now go to sleep. I'll be in later. Good night."

At long last, the day was over. Now came my time. The children were in bed and I shuffled to the kitchen and stared at the wall. More than just contemplate this day, I needed to summarize my marriage and pinpoint what went wrong. I certainly didn't want to relive that.

I made a cup of tea and settled onto the sofa to ponder the day. I heard Dace's harsh words again, "Only one person can sail this ship. Now sail your ship, Captain."

Would I be able to sail my children to safety? The divorce was over, but we still bore physical scars and experienced nightmares, untold humiliation, and a loss of self-esteem. My inner strength had gotten me this far. Would it sustain me through the tumultuous torrents of tomorrow?

I sensed a peace surround me. "Gramma?" I whispered. Maybe not. Maybe it was this God I'd prayed to on and off for years. I slowly exhaled. Whatever or whoever it was could be decoded tomorrow. *Gotta carry on.* I closed my eyes, relaxed, and sipped my tea.

With much healing yet to take place, I would draw from that strength many more times. And carry on I did.

1978 graduation party

Pregnant Teen Bride

Mr. Spots & baby Star Aries

Star & Baby Samuel Stone

My Little Trio

Mr. Spots

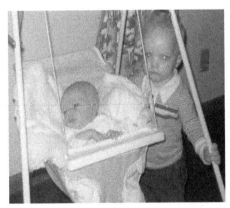

Two babies in sixteen months

Going away party

Flying to Phoenix, AZ

Phoenix Zoo

Back home safely in Ohio

Under 100 pounds

On our own in Ohio

Modeling thumbnail pics

Single parenting & working
two jobs

July 4 th camping

Sad Christmas - NO Jesus.

Happy Christmas -
KNOW Jesus!

First Christmas dating Jerry

Star's kindergarten graduation
(my famous candy cane dress)

We *all* got married that day!   We were a Package Deal.

Cutting the cake

We moved into Jerry's farmhouse
apartment, a happy blended family!

Part Two—Pathway to the Altar

Chapter Twenty-Eight: Sailing Solo May Be Simple, but Never Easy

1983—Chardon, Ohio

Afraid and feeling unsure of myself, I asked my cousin Lisa to move in with us. She had been laid off from her job, and agreed. I had the kids share the back bedroom in our trailer so she could have her own room.

She babysat while I worked, was my evening friend, and listened to me drone on about my problems and concerns. She even potty trained Samuel. She was a godsend for the months she lived with us.

Rushing to and from work every day became a mindless routine. Often, Steve Perry of Journey sang in the background of my thoughts. "Don't Stop Believin'" became my morning theme song.

I wanted a healthy family. I didn't want to be a bitter woman who badmouthed her children's father to them. *He's still their father, and they should respect him for that position, if nothing else. Maybe I can make my own happy ending.*

I encouraged Dace to communicate with Star and Samuel. The occasional letter was written for me to share with them, as they weren't old enough to read. "Tell your mother," was the prelude to snide remarks.

He always included a letter to me, excusing his lack of financial assistance. "So the kids need shoes. What's new?" "If I had a million dollars, believe me, I'd share with you. But since I have nothing, I can't give you anything." "When I find out where the money tree grows, I'll share it with you. Until then, you're on your own."

In his letters to me, he often tried to belittle me by putting the pronunciation and meaning of words in parentheses, insinuating I couldn't understand his vocabulary—his final sorry attempt to verbally abuse me, via the U.S. Mail.

He showed his lack of toddler communication skills in his letters to the children, often going into detail about his workday, peppering his sentences with comments like, "Don't let the dregs of society drag you down." Such remarks flew over their young heads.

He could comment on their colored pictures for only so long and soon stopped writing. I presumed he lost interest.

Meanwhile, I confronted my own financial distress and learned to stop using my last few drops of gasoline to drive home during my lunch break to check the mailbox for child support checks. The unpaid support continued to mount.

Chapter Twenty-Nine: Sinking My Ship

"Eff you."

Each morning when I looked into the mirror, I saw the broken blood vessels around my neck and across my left jaw. The jaw marks, reminders of that night before Thanksgiving when I used the forbidden word "divorce." The neck marks, ugly souvenirs of the day I broke free—my Independence Day symbols.

As I applied my foundation each morning, I repeated my curse. While I thought I said it to Dace, maybe I said it to myself for allowing such horror into my life and the lives of my kids.

Twice daily when I brushed my teeth and saw the chipped bottom tooth, I was reminded of that fateful last night in Phoenix. "Someday I'm going to have it capped."

I hadn't learned money management skills. I'd gone from not owning even a fuzzy toilet seat cover to having credit cards in my name. When I got depressed, I self-medicated with shopping, buying whatever I thought we should have. I bought a new wardrobe for myself and things for my children and our house. Every bit of money I received, I used on us and not on my bills. I soon fell behind on payments.

The trailer park owners insisted residents own storage sheds, but mine was empty. One evening during a winter storm, it blew through the yard into the road behind us. My dad dragged the dented structure back into place. I used the insurance money to buy Christmas presents.

The first Christmas without my ex-husband, I determined to prove we didn't need him. I used my holiday bonus from work to buy gifts. I bought three guinea pigs, two finches, one big yellow Tonka dump truck, an Easy-Bake Oven, many outfits, and more toys than two preschoolers need. I would show him—I would show everyone.

∞∞∞∞∞∞∞∞∞∞∞∞

Lisa was called back to her job. I still worked in Cleveland and needed a babysitter. I found one located in the country, close to the freeway.

Unforgiveness, stress, and booze kept my gut aching continuously. I drank lots of antacid and kept a large bottle of it in my desk at work, and another at home.

My priorities fell askew. I had no self-confidence and doubted my ability to please a man. In seeking affirmation of my desirability, I sometimes put men before my children. Star and Samuel became impromptu overnight guests at the babysitters'. I'd pick them up in the morning exhausted and take them to McDonald's or Chuck E. Cheese's.

In my ongoing fatigue, I was impatient with the kids. I didn't talk to them, I screamed at them. When that no longer controlled them, I screamed cuss words at them. I had become a bad mom—I was an angry mom.

∞∞∞∞∞∞∞∞∞∞∞∞

The Cosmopolitan was a dance club in Willoughby, a suburb of Cleveland. The disco craze was in full swing, and I hated everything about it. The otherwise normal people who fancied themselves John Travolta and Olivia Newton-John on the dance floor, made me laugh. The dance moves made me cringe, I thought the clothes were hilarious, and the music didn't appeal to me.

Live rock-and-roll bands played at the Cosmo on Thursday nights, and Melanie and I went faithfully. It was a good time for me to work out my frustrations through dancing.

244

One Friday night I returned to enter a legs contest to earn quick money. I'd never been in one and didn't know what to wear. In my remaining Midwestern country-girl simplicity, I'd missed the obvious implications and didn't show off my legs. I wore a shimmery silver dress I'd gotten for an office Christmas party. It fell below my knees and was more classy than sexy.

I didn't win the contest.

While enjoying a few gin and tonics, I stayed for a while after Mel left.

That night, I met a man and went home with him. Handsome and somewhat quiet, he seemed sweet. Being drunk and going home with someone affords you little in the way of local awareness. He owned his own home in a suburb—somewhere.

He showed me around his house.

"My brother and I inherited this place from our grandparents. Come see the basement."

It was what Northerners call a "finished basement," with a complete recreation room containing a pool table, bar, stereo, and ample room for dancing. Always hoping for future fun, I said, "This would be a great place to have a party." He looked intently at me and resumed his story.

"My brother and I lived here together for a few years. We had some nice parties." While he spoke, he racked up the billiards for a game. "I'd gotten into some gambling trouble. He knew I needed money, and he asked me to stage his murder." Not looking up, he continued. "Yeah; had me tie him up so it would look like a robbery."

My chest pounded. I controlled my breathing to hide my fear. *Don't stare at him.*

"He was depressed and didn't want to live. So he had me tie him up here in the rec room. Right there by where you're standing, actually. Anyway, he said I should hit him in the head with a baseball bat and then leave. I took some stuff and threw things around to look like someone had ransacked the place."

My stomach flipped, and I glanced about for signs of blood. Was he serious? He seemed so nice. Holding the pool cue, my hands trembled.

"He wanted me to make it look like a homicide so I'd get his insurance money."

"Did the fuzz buy that?" I found words to speak and tried to sound nonchalant.

"Aww, they thought I'd killed him, but could never prove it. They said they'd keep an eye on me. They weren't very happy. I miss my brother, but I did get the money."

He landed a striped ball in a side pocket.

Although creeped out, something inside me said, *remain calm*. I listened and didn't say anything judgmental, nor did I look at him. I took my turn at the table. *No eye contact*. I had learned from my marriage to a monster that sometimes it's safer not to run.

After he won the game, we went upstairs. I knelt to check out his record albums in the living room while he disappeared into the kitchen for a drink.

"You have a cool collection of LPs here," I called to him.

Upon spying Neil Young's *Zuma* album, a song raged in my head. I could hear Dace singing Young's "Stupid Girl" loud and clear.

Suddenly, dread rose from the pit of my belly. I sensed danger and instinctively wanted to run out the door. For a second, I considered the distance between the front door and me, and me and him in the kitchen. Instantly, calm cascaded through me from the top of my head downward, as though a blanket of tranquility draped over me kneeling by the crate of albums.

He entered the living room with two glasses of cola on ice.

"You're really sweet," he said. "I'd never do anything to you."

Can he tell I'm freaked out? Breathe deep. Relax. You have to ride this one out.

I giggled nervously. "Of course you wouldn't. You're a nice guy."

In the back of my mind, I wondered if I'd ever see my children again. No one knew I was there. I didn't even know where I was. My car was still at the Cosmo.

It was late and we were both exhausted. I needed to buy time and keep my eye on him.

"I'm tired," I said. "Can we take a shower?"

He appeared unsure of himself, like he was unaccustomed to having women over—or anyone, for that matter.

"My shower is really dirty. No one ever comes here, so it doesn't get cleaned very often."

"Oh, I'm sure it's okay."

We went into the bathroom. What I saw when I pulled the shower curtain back shocked me.

"See? Pretty dirty."

"Oh, it's fine. Let's just shower and get to bed."

Dark filth coated the bathtub. Was it black from dirt or . . . no, it was most likely just months, perhaps years of built-up grime.

We got out of the shower and he rushed into the bedroom.

"I don't change my sheets much," he said. "I have some new ones here though. Let me put them on real quick."

After seeing his tub, I couldn't imagine what his sheets must look like.

"I'll help you," I called into the bedroom.

"No! Just wait there a minute. I want to take these sheets off. I don't want you to see them."

My mind raced as I shivered in the bathroom waiting for him to invite me in. *I'm naked. No blood will be on my clothes if he kills me. What's he doing in there? Is there blood on the sheets? What's he going to do?*

I pushed the thought of never getting out of there way down inside me so I would appear calm and genuine. I rubbed my arms for warmth. It helped me relax. But then something changed. It wasn't a pretense, but natural. There was no struggle to hide my fear because there was none on the surface. I felt safe somehow.

"Can I help you put the sheets on?"

"Sure. You can come in now." He took sheets out of a package.

"You had brand-new ones? That's cool."

"Yeah, I bought some a while ago, just to have."

Strange. I helped him put the sheets on his bed, and we crawled in.

"I can't believe you're here," he said. "I can't believe someone as sweet as you is here with me."

Within an hour, we were fast asleep.

Early the next morning he woke me. "We should get you back to your car."

I jumped, scoping out the room to get my bearings.

"Oh my gosh, I have to go get my kids."

In silence, we each grabbed our clothes and threw them on. I was queasy from the alcohol, hunger, and disbelief I'd actually spent the night with this dude. My self-loathing rivaled astonishment that I was alive.

Would he have to get rid of me now? He'd shared so much. I grabbed my purse and headed toward the front door. Without deliberation, I sent a prayer heavenward in my mind. *Oh God, please get me to my children.*

He threw the front door open, and the morning sun welcomed us out. I squinted and inhaled the fresh air, savoring a moment of joy for being alive.

As we moved down the curved sidewalk to his car, he looked around.

"I hope my neighbors don't see you. They keep a close watch on me since my brother died. Maybe I *want* them to see you," he chuckled nervously. "Having a pretty lady like you leaving my house will show them I'm normal."

When we reached my car, I got out and thanked him, and he drove off. Opening my car door, I began to shake. I couldn't leave fast enough, eager to get my kids from the babysitter's house.

Their sweet happy faces jolted my spirit. They were the most important people in my life. Was it because of them he hadn't hurt me?

That afternoon as we played, watched television, and colored in coloring books, I pondered the feelings I'd experienced at that man's house.

I'd recognized an evil presence in the basement where he said he'd killed his brother. I'd experienced panic and the impulse to run, but calmness squelched it. There was an awareness of protection and control guiding me throughout the evening and morning, directing my every word and action.

Now, safe at home, playing with Star and Sam, I hugged them, and they squealed with delight. I sighed heavily, looked heavenward, and whispered a quick, "Thanks!"

I'd put myself into yet another dangerous situation. How did I ever get out of there alive? I vowed never to go home with a stranger again.

∞∞∞∞∞∞∞∞∞∞∞∞

Soon I was again desperate for money. I scoured the newspapers for a second job and saw ads for dancers at a gentlemen's club. I tried to call the number a couple times, but the manager never had time to speak with me.

One day while visiting my parents, I helped Mom hang clothes on the clothesline in the backyard. I soaked in the sunshine and longed to stay in the country. I ached for yesteryear.

Dancing at a club went against everything moral my parents had taught me. While I knew I couldn't ask my mother how she would feel about me if I took such a job, I couched my question in the classic "I have a friend" scenario, hoping she'd buy it.

"Mom, there's a girl at work who is thinking about dancing at a bar at night. What do you think of that?"

Sometimes my mother surprised me, like when she didn't condemn me for kissing Leslie goodnight that time in high school. Without stopping our chore, she said, "Well, Kelly, people have to think about these things. I do understand about needing money, but it's not a respectable thing to do. It probably doesn't have insurance. It doesn't sound safe to me either, and it'll be something that's with her always, for the rest of her life."

"Yeah, that's what I thought. I told her I'd ask you your opinion. I'll tell her Monday. Thanks."

Tucking her words into my heart, I searched for other jobs in the classified section of the *Cleveland Plain Dealer*.

It was about that time something in my head clicked.

I'm an adult. I need to stop arguing with Mom. I don't like how we treat each other. I'm just tired of it. I'm going to keep my sarcastic words to myself. I'm going to stop freaking out about her harsh words. She's important to me—I love her, and I don't want the kids to see us like that. I wouldn't want them to be that way with me.

Moving forward, I made the conscious decision to watch my words. The next time she made a move that would normally prompt my angry reaction, I swallowed and conceded. It caught her off guard. She was speechless for a moment, not knowing how to react; thrown off by a different step in the middle of the dance that had defined our relationship. It interrupted our normal routine. Even so, she regained her footing. We never yelled at one another again.

The following week I entered the legs contest at the Cosmo again. This time I was savvier about what they required. I wore short shorts that were cut high on the sides, giving my legs the appearance of being longer. I wore a snug knit top that hugged my ribs. To my surprise, I won.

Between songs, I tried to call the club about the dancer job again. The payphone was in an alcove between the restrooms—the quietest place at the Cosmo. This time I got the manager on the phone. Once more, he tried to put me off.

251

"I'm sorry, but you seem to blow me off every time I call. Is there really a job or isn't there?" My persistence piqued his attention. He said they had auditions for dancers on Saturday nights. Entrants got $20, and the audience chose the winner, who'd receive $50. I needed the money.

"So, what's my next step?" Again, my perseverance impressed him.

"Where are you at right now, Kelly? Sounds like you're at a club."

"I'm at the Cosmopolitan. I entered a legs contest tonight."

"Yeah? How'd you do?"

I chuckled. "I won, actually." That sealed the deal.

"I'll put you on the list for the tryouts next weekend. Why don't you stop by before Saturday night and get a feel for the place? Bring a friend."

I agreed, thanked him, hung up the phone, and squealed with excitement.

Monday at work, I approached a sweet co-worker who was recently divorced. Vivian wanted a family, but her husband wasn't interested. She'd worried what her Catholic priest would say, but he said she had grounds for divorce and didn't condemn her. She was saving money to pay for an annulment. It had to happen before she could ever consider remarriage in her church.

"Viv, I have a favor to ask of you."

"Sure, Kelly. What is it?"

"Well, I answered an ad for a job at night, dancing at a nightclub. I spoke with the manager, and he entered me into a contest for Saturday night to see if I could hack it. The winner gets fifty bucks!"

"Wow, that's good. Maybe I should enter too. Where is it?"

I told her, and she said she couldn't do it.

"He suggested I come by to scope it out first. Will you go with me Thursday night? I'll get a babysitter if you can come."

She agreed. We stayed after work and had dinner out. At seven, we drove to the club. Although in a questionable part of the city, the parking lot was lit up and the outside of the building looked well maintained. The man at the door wore a tuxedo and smiled as we approached.

"What can I do for you ladies tonight?"

"We're just here to check out the place. I'm scheduled for the tryouts Saturday night."

He welcomed us in. Once inside, a tall young woman wearing a black lacy corset with fishnet nylons led us to the upper level and gave us a table by the railing, overlooking the two main dance floors. A brass pole stood from ceiling to floor in the center of each of the lighted bases.

"What can I bring you to drink?" She had to yell above the house stereo where "Billie Jean" played from Michael Jackson's *Thriller* album.

"I'll have a Tanqueray and tonic with a twist of lemon, not lime, please."

Vivian smiled. "I'll have a red wine."

Within ten minutes, we were enjoying our drinks and studying the place. We were the only female customers there. A man's voice boomed over the speakers, "Helllooo, ladies and gentlemen! Welcome to the club where every night is ladies' night!"

Applause and cheers roared bringing our attention to the tables behind us—all filled with men dressed in business suits and ties.

"Let's start off tonight with Lila on the front stage and Bunny on the back! Have a great time guys, and remember if you like our girls show them with your cash in their garters!"

Two women took the stages to Irene Cara's "What a Feeling." As the tempo increased, so did their dancing, bringing men to their feet, howling and clapping.

As the second song ended, Vivian and I looked at each other. I was shaking and nauseated. "I feel like I'm in Satan's den."

"I do too." She leaned closer to my ear. "Kelly, do you really think you could do that?"

I shrugged and focused on the stage.

The dancers were waitresses who served while waiting their turn on the dance floor. Each dancer's set consisted of three songs. *How could I walk around like that in front of complete strangers?* But I had to admit, I loved how they cheered and showed their approval to the women—not just the dancers, but the servers too. Even the female bartenders, who didn't perform and were fully clothed, garnered smiles and kindness from the men.

Just as we were about to leave, the voice on the loudspeaker shouted, "Grand finale! Gentlemen, get your wallets out!"

All the dancers and servers rushed onto the front stage to the sound of Kool and The Gang's "Celebration."

After the big finish, we left. Outside the air was chilly, but fresh. I shuddered.

"I don't know, Kelly. It's exciting in there, but I couldn't do it. Are you going to go back Saturday?"

"Oh, Viv. I don't feel I have much choice. I need the money so bad. I'll think about it. See you tomorrow." We hopped into our cars and left.

My mind raced. How could I work there? What if my parents found out? *They wouldn't find out; they're forty miles away.* I tried to reason my mind into submission. *Besides, all that cash just for dancing and serving drinks!*

Chapter Thirty: How Low Can I Go?

Saturday night came, and I wasn't sure I could go through with the contest. When I entered the building, the man at the door asked if I was the one who had won the legs contest at the Cosmo. I blushed and nodded. He gave me a toothy grin and directed me to the dressing room.

My gut twisted until I thought I'd throw up. In the ladies' room, there were five other women preparing for the event. Some of them looked scared, but a couple of them were there to get their old jobs back.

"Freddy said I had to try out again if I want to come back. They know I can dance. They just want more people for their stupid contest."

Her friend checked her watch before tossing it into her duffle bag. "I know, Laura. But let's just get through this so we can get on next week's schedule."

A tall, husky man in his thirties came in.

The girls shouted, "Freddy, can't you knock? We're dressing in here."

"Like I haven't seen it all already." I recognized his voice from the loudspeaker on Thursday night. "Just wanted to make sure everyone has the right outfits. And remember, no contact! Don't let anyone touch you, or you're outta here, pronto!" He left to the murmurings of abuse from Laura and Angela, the two girls who wanted to be rehired.

A small group of us waited in the rear by the restroom until it was our turn. Shaking and nearly falling off my stilettos, I took the stage with another girl. We danced to a song I couldn't recognize and ducked into a tiny dressing area between the stages, at the back.

A tall girl waited for us there. I recognized her as Bunny from when Vivian and I came. Others crammed into the tiny closet.

"You all go out now for the Grand Finale," Bunny instructed. "Be careful you don't fall. Everybody on the pole. Watch you don't stab anyone with your shoes and don't fall. Let's go!"

Pep talks from our high school majorette instructor flashed through my mind. *Never had to worry about stabbing anyone with my marching boots, that's for sure.* High school football game halftime shows and marching in parades seemed so far away now.

Michael Jackson's, "Don't Stop 'Til You Get Enough" saw us to the end of the contest. We stood in a line onstage, and Freddy called out our names individually. The volume of cheers and applause determined who won. Laura had a following and easily won the fifty dollars. The manager took me and another girl aside and offered us jobs.

"You're pretty green Kelly, but Bunny can teach you some moves. You can start Tuesday night. It's slower then, so you can have some time before the weekend."

I accepted the offer and left.

Driving home, I rehearsed the evening in my mind. I couldn't believe I'd done it. A part of my spiritual heart turned black, shriveled, and died. I sensed Satan smile.

A few days later as I began my second job, the boss gave me some advice. "These girls make a lot of money, but they spend a lot too. After their shift, they often go out to eat. Easy come, easy go. Remember that. Now, what do you want your stage name to be?"

I hadn't thought about it.

"Kelly, I guess."

There was another Kelly, so she changed her name to Kit. I realized I shouldn't use my real name because I worked at a corporate headquarters on Playhouse Square, just ten minutes away. I changed my name to Sinda. *Seems appropriate.* Again, I knew Satan smiled.

Working two jobs, I rarely saw my kids. The babysitter had them for long days and sometimes overnight.

When I was at home, I was tired, inconsistent in my discipline, and felt guilty for not spending more time with them. Therefore, I spent too much money on toys and entertainment in an effort to show my love. I didn't consider they'd rather have an attentive mommy at home than a tired one who spent a lot on them.

In short time I was at ease with my night job. The difficult part was waitressing. Often my server number flashed on the lighted number strip by the kitchen and I didn't notice it. People got cold steaks and warm salads. Soon they took me off food and told me to take only drink orders.

Draft beers were seventy-five cents, and I could always count on a quarter tip with every beer. At the end of the shift, we each had to give the bartenders a percentage of our take.

A uniformed guard in his thirties stood at the door of the club. He was a police officer by day. A family man, he was earning extra money at night, just like the rest of us. He was kind and not forward like the other guys there. He reminded me of the Pillsbury Dough Boy because he was a bit plump. One evening he said, "Sinda, I'm worried about you."

"Me? Why?"

"You're getting too comfortable here."

I chuckled. "What do you mean?"

"Well, at first you were somewhat shy and unsure of yourself. Now, you seem very at home here. That's not good. I just hope you don't get jaded like so many of these girls."

I thanked him for his concern and tucked his words away. I became more aware of my demeanor each night. Perhaps he was right. I was at ease there.

I was presented with opportunities to make more money at private parties off-site, but I declined, always using my children as an excuse.

I didn't want to work there forever. Some of the women had been there for three or more years. One was working her way through law school. Two more worked during the day at a health club. Another girl wasn't twenty-one yet, so she just danced and sold items from a cigarette and cigar tray that hung around her neck. One woman was a frustrated dancer, having studied the art in college. She did high kicks and impressive spins, and brought an element of class to her sets. There were a few single mothers like me, simply trying to pay bills.

One man summed up my time there when he said, "You can't dance worth crap, but you're cute as heck!" I didn't make as much money as others. Even the bartender recognized the problem and sometimes took less from me than expected.

Men came in for bachelor parties, business dinners, and other celebrations. One man folded a five-dollar bill into a tiny square and dropped it into his beer. He enjoyed watching me fish it out. Each night I collected a stack of business cards. I never called anyone from the cards, but having them made me feel liked. Deep inside, I knew I was fooling myself—none of those men would be there for me if I needed help.

Once the cook saw me eating a customer's leftover french fries from a plate I returned for the dishwasher. "You hungry, honey?"

"Yes! Gin and Snickers bars don't stick with me all night!" I joked.

"Well, here you go, baby." From then on, she kept a platter of freshly made fries on the pickup window for all of us to pick at throughout the night. Her kindness touched me.

One night, the drivers' education instructor I had as a teenager showed up for a bachelor party. I saw a dude from my high school another night. One day, while walking along the street with co-workers from my office job, I heard a man behind us yell, "Sinda! Hey, Sinda!"

"What is that guy saying?" My friends turned around and looked.

I panicked. "I don't know. He's crazy, obviously. Just ignore him."

My second job was getting complicated. I needed the money, but was it worth the risk? The Rush song "Freewill" raged in my head. Clearly I needed to make a choice.

I began to worry about being recognized and losing my respectable daytime job. Once, as I rode on the elevator after lunch, three men stood behind me. When I stepped off at my floor, one whispered, "Your secret is safe with us, Sinda."

I rushed to the ladies' room and slammed the stall door behind me. I grabbed my chest and tried to slow my breathing. It was catching up with me. I couldn't lose my secretarial job—I just couldn't.

The manager of Human Relations called me into his office one day.

"Shawn in accounting told me you're working at the gentlemen's club, Kelly."

I gulped. My heartbeat drummed in my ears. My vision closed in until he was a tiny speck in front of me. Like looking into the wrong end of binoculars, he seemed far away as he sat behind his desk. I remained silent.

"I'm not going to tell anyone, so don't worry. I know you can boogie though, and I thought maybe you could come over to my apartment to teach me some moves."

"I'm not very good. I don't make much money, that's for sure."

"Aww, I'm sure you're very good. I think this Friday night around seven—you could come over and give me some lessons."

I was stunned. Did this man expect me to sleep with him? I'd long since learned that a business suit on a man didn't mean he was honorable. Could I trust him? Would he kill me once I got there? What if I told him I wouldn't come? Would he tell everyone about my dancing gig? Would he fire me from my office job?

"Um, okay. I have to get a babysitter, so I can't stay long. I can come dance a couple songs with you, but then I'll have to go."

"Great. Here's my address. I'm in an apartment, and it's easy to get to. I'll see you Friday night at seven. And don't worry, Kelly, I'm not going to tell anyone."

I was shaking when I left his office. *Oh dear God, what have I done?*

That Friday night, I went to his apartment in total fear. He gave me a glass of wine and put some music on his stereo. Was there something in the wine to make me pass out? I took only one sip.

I stood facing him as he feigned poor dancing—nobody could be that bad. I danced in front of him. He put his hands on my hips. "Show me how it's done."

A bundle of nerves, I stiffened and chuckled. "Well, like I told you, I'm not very good. This is all I can do."

He quickly got the message and stepped back. "Okay then. You can go. First I have to make a phone call."

He grabbed his phone and punched some numbers. The next few minutes seemed contrived to evoke a response from me. Into the receiver, he cooed, "Hi there. Yeah, it's me. Wanna get together tonight? Yeah, how about now? Uh-ha, that's right. Okay, I'll be right over."

He snapped to attention and ushered me out. Walking the hall to the exit, I said, "Thanks. I'll see you at work Monday." He didn't speak.

I tore out of the driveway. All my worrying was for naught, as he never brought it up again. I presume he didn't want anyone to know I'd rebuffed him. I was just glad I didn't have to discuss it with anyone and didn't get canned.

One night, at my second job, the boss met with us before the doors opened. "Girls, I want more fantasy costumes around here. The men who come in here should see things they won't normally see. No more teddies or negligees—they can get that at home. Dress as their fantasies."

No one was pleased about that mandate. Costumes were expensive. Still, we chatted about what we'd "come as" the next night. One performer worked with the local theater and had access to several costumes. Her big, wild hair was a wig. Now she complimented it with medieval garb she discarded during the first song in each set.

"I think I'll dress up like a little girl," I thought aloud. "I'll have a big lollypop and put my hair in ponytails."

"Aw, I was going to do that! Okay. You got that one," said a co-worker.

I thought about it that evening. Disgust and guilt overwhelmed me. As if someone whispered in my ear, my soul resounded with, *if you dress like a little girl, a child who might otherwise have a restful night sleep will be awakened when her father returns home. It will be your fault that "a child" aroused him.* I couldn't do it. I just couldn't. I realized I consistently put marriages in jeopardy with this live porn, but I couldn't blatantly hurt a kid.

I worked again that weekend. It was like Halloween with everyone checking out the costumes.

"I thought you were going to be a little girl, Sinda! I woulda worn that if I'd known you weren't going to."

I shrugged. "Changed my mind."

Lila, who had worked the night before, said, "Oh, I did that last night! I put a bow in my hair and had a huge lollypop. The guys went nuts over it. They cheered and I got so much cash. They loved it."

My gut jerked. My level of contempt for men went even higher, surpassed only by my self-loathing. Dace's porn had hurt me and now I was involved in hurting others. The irony didn't escape me.

I spent too much money on costumes from Frederick's of Hollywood. My life went from fun and exciting to distasteful. I had never learned to say no, and I hated the person I'd become. I was so sick and tired of my life and thought the kids would be better off without me. Again, I deliberated suicide.

One night around 2 a.m., I was coming home after partying with a friend out in the country. Before I'd left, she had requested I join her and her husband in their bed. I'd told her all the reasons why that wouldn't work. She'd assured me I wouldn't be the first guest they'd had in their bed. Still I declined, but she thought I was being judgmental. I assured her I was not—I had been down that road before and it wasn't a good path to take. When I left them, she appeared angry with me.

The first time I actually say no, and I get someone mad at me.

Dejected, I sighed heavily. *If I just die—if I just fall asleep right now while driving, I won't hurt anyone, and the kids would be better off without me. I'm just so very tired.*

I had decent life insurance through my secretarial job, but I knew it wouldn't pay on a suicide. Therefore, I made the decision to fall asleep. I drove underneath a train track into a tunnel and closed my eyes. An unexplainable peace came over me as I drifted off. My memory ends there.

The next morning I awoke in my bed. I had no idea how I'd gotten there. I was scared. I ran out to inspect my car, expecting to find dents or blood on it. It was fine, parked in the driveway perfectly. Somehow, I'd gotten the key in the house door and put myself to bed.

I pondered that extensively, surmising that God protected me and brought me home. He seemed to be with me, whether I realized it or not. Even when I was smack dab in the middle of ugly locations and immoral situations, God was there with me. I wondered why.

Chapter Thirty-One: My Fantasy Comes True

It was summer, and I joined some friends from high school for a girls' night out. My parents watched Star and Samuel, and I met my friends at Ruth's house. I agreed to drive. Dan, Ruth's older brother, wanted to come.

We went to the Riverside Bar. It was fun, but as usual, I drank too much too quickly. Before long, I was in the bathroom throwing up. Dan drove us home, and I slept at Ruth's house.

When I awoke the next morning, I was embarrassed and ashamed. I didn't drink for enjoyment. I didn't know moderation or social drinking—I drank with the sole intention of getting drunk. I was relieved to learn her family wasn't home.

I took a few days off from my jobs, and my kids and I went to a local campground for a Fourth of July vacation. I chose to stay in the primitive area. It was heavily wooded, and tents were pitched wherever there was flat ground. There wasn't a restroom close by, but it was cheaper. I borrowed Dad's tent and set out to camp with my preschoolers.

We enjoyed swimming and fishing and toasting marshmallows over the fire. We loved spending time alone with each other.

While sitting on the sandy beach at the lake, I met Dan's mother. She had his girls there for a swim. It was good to chat with her. She had been one of my Camp Fire Girls of America leaders in late elementary school. I hadn't talked with her since high school.

Each day we chatted while the kids swam. As we talked, I mentally counted blond heads in the brown water.

She filled me in on her son's ex-fiancée and how their breakup affected him physically. Dan was a truck driver and he and his girls still lived with his parents. I shared about my abusive husband and that I was now single.

I stopped midsentence. That blond head was not my child!

Leaning forward, I scanned the water left, right, and back. To the far left, amidst the cattails and reeds I saw a little blond head come up and go down again into the murky pond.

I jumped up and ran across the water like Jesus, to the side of the lake. Reaching into the grassy darkness, I grabbed something and pulled it up. It was Sam's arm. I yanked him up and out of the water. He choked and sputtered and bawled all at the same time. I held him tight as we cried together, mixing snot, mud, reeds, and dark pond water. I thanked a God I was yet to meet for allowing me to see that head as it bobbed up, maybe for the last time.

My son sat beside me on the sand for a while and then joyfully joined his sister in the shallow water.

The next day Dan brought his girls to swim. He smiled as I approached.

"Mind if I put my towel down here?" I asked.

"Sure." He had a lilt in his voice. He wore sunglasses, but I could tell he was checking me out. Then it was clear to me: his mother had been interviewing me. I guess I wasn't too bizarre for a recommendation.

We had a wonderful time at the beach. Afternoon waned, and it was time to go.

"Kelly, would you like to go to a party with me tonight? It's a '50s party at the Shangri-La Dam."

"That sounds fun. What do I have to wear?"

"Everyone is supposed to dress in 1950's styles like the people on *Happy Days*. Don't worry about it if you can't. Just come with me, okay?"

My insides jumped with excitement. "I'd love to come with you. I'll see if my parents will watch the kids."

We dressed and went to their house. They agreed to look after my children, and I said I'd pick them up in the morning since I'd be out late.

I borrowed a white button-down shirt from Dad and white ankle socks and sneakers from Mom. I rolled my blue jeans up and put my long hair into a ponytail. "Good enough."

That night we had fun at the party. It was on a lake by the dam. I vaguely recognized his friends from high school.

The two of us had a wonderful time talking all night. I determined not to drink too much. Still, I had enough to get drunk. I would have agreed to go home with him even if I was sober, but the alcohol made it easier.

In no time we were going together. We laughed and talked for hours at a time. I loved being with him. Now and then, throughout the years I'd thought of him and his little girls. I had fantasized about being his girlfriend. Now my dreams were my reality. He was everything I hoped he would be, and we were both very happy.

∞∞∞∞∞∞∞∞∞∞∞∞

Dace had it added to the divorce settlement that I would see a psychologist because he thought I needed counseling for my poor decision-making skills. Maybe he thought it was a bad choice to leave him. Actually, the counselor commended me for that final decision.

Talking with the analyst one time would have fulfilled my commitment. However, I'd thought, *what if there is some merit to what he says? Maybe I should continue for a while just to be sure I'm all right. Besides, my insurance pays for it.*

I saw the counselor a few times. I called Wednesdays my health days because I'd go for my mental health and then to the health spa a couple miles away for my physical health, visiting Melanie for a half hour or so in between. She noticed I was more down on myself after I saw the counselor and suggested I stop going. I did and began to feel better about life right away.

∞∞∞∞∞∞∞∞∞∞∞

Dan had seen a psychiatrist after his fiancée dumped him. We joked about what our therapists would have to say about most situations, giving our responses in terrible Austrian accents—our versions of Sigmund Freud. We opened ourselves to each other, and those dynamic sex hormones bonded us immediately.

I also got to know his two daughters. They were sweet and adored their grandparents, who were like parents to them. I fell in love with those delightful girls, and they treated my children like jewels.

I once mentioned to him that flowers melt a woman's heart, and his oldest daughter, who was seven, overheard me. The next time I visited, she gave me a small box with wildflowers in it. Maybe his girls needed a full-time mommy as much as my kids needed a daddy.

We often talked about getting married. The talk changed to plans. We planned where we'd live, what I'd do after we were married, what school our kids would attend, and if we'd have more children together. It was fun to plan a future that looked healthy.

My drinking didn't stop, however. I still drank to get drunk. I liked drinking and the escape it provided. I looked forward to it. However, many mornings, I thought, *I paid money to feel this way?* Still, it didn't dissuade me from grabbing every opportunity to get smashed. I started missing Mondays at my secretarial job.

In October, Dan and I planned to wear costumes to the clubs for Halloween. I wore an elaborate turquoise silk-and-chiffon harem girl costume from Frederick's of Hollywood. My gold-colored accessories included a thin chain around my waist, slave bracelet on my upper arm, dangling earrings, and a thin rope with gold leaves across my forehead. Lastly, I super-glued a rhinestone button into my navel.

My parents agreed to babysit. My father saw the rhinestone.

"How'd you get that in there?" His forehead vein began to protrude.

"Umm, I super-glued it in," I laughed trying to ease the tension.

"I hope you like that in there." His eyes bugged out. "I hope you like it darn well because you're not getting it out!"

"Oh, Dad. It'll be alright. Thanks for watching the kids!"

That night as we danced, Dan got irritated with me. I had become a sensual dancer and was enjoying myself. I'd had too much to drink and ignored his comments.

"Can't you dance without having your arms above your head?"

Inebriated, I teased him by dancing with my hands just below my ears, palms down. He was not amused. We left that club and went to a bar without a dance floor. *He showed me!*

At the end of the evening, we returned to his room in the basement. As I rolled over to fall asleep, the rhinestone button dropped out of my navel. I grinned and drifted off.

∞∞∞∞∞∞∞∞∞∞∞∞∞∞

Club regulations at my second job stipulated that boyfriends weren't welcome. Time had proven that strange men staring at girlfriends in seductive outfits didn't sit well with them. It was a logical rule. When my boyfriend came to the club, he was enraged. Quiet quips, dirty looks, and he left before the bouncer noticed him. When I refused to quit, he wouldn't talk to me for days.

Our fun relationship became tense. His friends teased him, saying that their experiences with women proved the attractive ones don't stay.

"They only stay if you hit 'em. They don't stay with nice guys like us. They stay with guys who beat 'em."

Insulted, I determined to prove them wrong. I complimented Dan often and tried to make him feel appreciated and loved.

He tried to change me. "Why do you wear makeup when you aren't at work? I prefer you to be a jeans and T-shirt kind of girl."

"I'm happy with my look."

"I hate coordinated casual wear. You don't need to dress up."

"I'm relaxed on the weekends and comfortable with what I wear."

I actually didn't "dress up," but wore cute tops and colored shorts or jeans.

"Why don't you wear jean cut-offs and my shirts more often?"

I liked my own clothes, but he never seemed satisfied. His discontentment grew.

On New Year's Eve 1983, we went to a dance at the Middlefield Town Hall. I wore a black leather-look jumpsuit and curled my hair. He met me at my parents' house because they had agreed to babysit.

An old friend from Dan's class in high school was home visiting for the holidays. She lived in Las Vegas, and rumor was she was a schoolteacher by day and a showgirl by night. He seemed captivated by her. When the clock struck midnight, I looked around for him. I found him on the dance floor kissing her.

"What the heck are you doing?" Everyone stared at me. I repeated, "Dan, what are you doing?"

"Grow up," he snapped, and turned back to her.

I got my coat and left. As I headed down the road, teetering in my high heels over small piles of snow, a police cruiser pulled beside me. A female officer said to get into the car. I crawled into the rear seat.

"What's your name?"

"Kelly."

"Kelly, it's cold out here tonight. What are you doing?"

"I'm going home." I tried hard to sound sober.

"You had a fight with your boyfriend and now you're walking home, right?" She was not being condescending; she was kind.

"Yeah."

"It's freezing out here, but you can't tell because you have a few drinks in you and you're feeling warm, right?"

"Yeah."

"Well, we can't let you walk tonight. Where can we take you?"

I asked her if she could take me to my house in Chardon. She said it wasn't in their jurisdiction. I asked if they'd take me to my parents' house in Parkman, and she said they couldn't for the same reason. She said they'd take me to the station so I could call my father.

"Hi, Dad. You were sleeping, weren't you?"

"That's okay, K.J. What's wrong?"

"I'm sorry, Dad. I know it's one in the morning, but Dan and I had a fight and I was walking home. The police said it's too cold and won't let me. They won't take me home. Can you please come get me at the police station? I'm not in trouble; I just need a ride."

"Sure. I'll be right there."

He was sweet. So was Mom. The next morning she didn't yell or ask a million questions. I was sad and told them what had happened.

Days turned to weeks and Dan didn't come to see me. *For all he knows I was killed that night. He doesn't care.*

"Dan and Mommy aren't friends anymore," I told Star and Sam. Just another man to come and go, leaving them confused and sad.

Chapter Thirty-Two: Messy Places

I loved the first line in the Beatles song "Norwegian Wood" I'd been exploited enough. The thought of me being in charge was appealing.

In my mind, men existed for my use, and I had no respect for any of them. As I continued to live a promiscuous lifestyle, a deep hatred for them grew. To me they were good for just two things: honey and money. The line between being picked up and picking men up blurred. I believed they didn't have me—I had them. It didn't matter—I did what I wanted.

I seldom brought men home. However, on one occasion I did bring one to my house. He took note of the tiger décor in my bedroom.

"You dig tigers, huh?"

"Yeah. I think women are like tigers."

He chuckled. "You do? How so?"

"Well, we're soft and beautiful on the outside, but deadly on the inside."

"You are, huh?"

His patronizing smirk annoyed me. Expressionless, I stared at him, mentally bidding him gone. I'd used him for what I wanted and no longer needed him. His value had expired. After years of exploitation by men, it felt good to reverse the roles.

"Yes, we are. You think we are cuddly, but we can kill you in an instant, if need be."

He made small talk for another five minutes, excused himself, and left. Maybe he felt he was in a potentially messy place. Perhaps he was.

While partying at a club one weekend, I heard a voice in my head say, "You are Satan's little princess."

Satan's Little Princess. Somehow, that idea made me feel special—powerful.

One night at work, I met an unusual man. Bruce didn't seem like the depraved voyeurs who frequented the club. He had gentle blue eyes and soft, curly blond hair. He asked about where I lived, my family, my life— like he was interested in me.

"You have a long way to drive home. You're free to stay with me at my house tonight since it's Friday and you don't have to get to your other job in the morning."

"Oh, I don't know. Sounds tempting, I'm so tired."

"I'll put my mattress on the floor. I won't try anything, I promise. I'm worried about you driving so far when you're tired."

Although the boss forbade us to date customers, I agreed to follow him. I ignored my promise to not go home with a stranger.

He and his ex-wife shared custody of their two children. Every other year he had guardianship for twelve months. That meant each year their sons lived in a different state, attended a different school, and lived with the other parent. That also meant every other year, each parent paid child support. It was his year to have them. It worked for them, and there seemed to be no animosity. Their kids appeared stable too. I guess time would tell how well they fared.

He made a late dinner for us. His brother lived with them, and Bruce slept in the attic when his kids were there. He slid the mattress off his bed and put it on the floor beside him, as promised. He was a gentleman—a *real* gentleman—not like those wolves in business suits at the club.

This happened four times. Then on the fifth evening he asked if he could join me on the mattress on the floor. His control, kindness, and courteous behavior impressed me. I was falling in love with him. He cared about my wellbeing—a real turn-on. With an agreed-upon "no commitment" relationship, this continued for weeks. My children became frequent weekend guests at the babysitter's house.

On the nights I didn't stay with Bruce, I struggled to stay awake on the ride home. There was an all-night Kentucky Fried Chicken about halfway there. I'd hit the drive-thru and order an entire meal. Eating helped keep me awake.

Once I entertained myself by encircling a semitruck. We were the only drivers on the highway. I drove on his left, dropped back, pulled forward, and drove on his right. Next I sped up, pulled in front of him, and drove on his left again. I rotated this cycle a couple times.

To me it was just a way to stay awake. I guess he took it as a summons to get in my pants. He drove closer and closer to my car. It woke me up. I sped faster and faster, but he stayed right on my tail. At nearly one hundred miles per hour, I lost him and spun away at my exit. *That could've been messy.* I didn't do it again.

A couple weeks later, while I danced at work, I had a visit from God. The second song ended and I swung around the pole and leaned into it. I'd had lots to drink and used the pole to hold me up. At once, a brilliant illumination shone on me. Not the regular spotlight, but a distinctive light—one that came from further away than our building. I knew in my spirit it was God.

How can you look at me, God? I learned in Sunday school that you turned your back on Your own Son, Jesus, when He hung on the cross, because He had taken on the sins of the world and You can't look at sin. How can You look at me right

275

now? You know I'm Satan's Little Princess because I lure men away from their wives . . . and from You.

I sensed God call out to me within my soul. I was ashamed. I felt I'd gone too far for Him to love me still.

I've gone too far, God. With that thought, I turned my back on the light. I knew immediately that physically showing my back to God was symbolic of me ignoring Him and turning my heart away from Him. It was a conscious decision. I believed He could never forgive me again.

Soon after that, on a Saturday night after my second job, I went out with a co-worker and two guys she'd just met. We both wore skimpy outfits, mine from Frederick's. I hardly knew my co-worker and didn't know her friends at all. We drank, smoked weed, and snorted cocaine. The clubs were closed and we drove to a house in a rough-looking neighborhood.

I was intrigued with what I learned was an after-hours joint, something new to me—a private residence with a bar in the living room. Couches seating four or five people lined every wall. Chairs, bar stools, and kitchen chairs filled each smoky room. *So this is where people go after the bars close.*

We walked throughout the house as the two men greeted people they knew. We were the only Caucasians there, and I the blonde. Reality slipped further away the more stoned I got. I heard bits and pieces of conversations. It seemed they were discussing my coworker and me. Soon they led us out a side door and into her friend's car.

They'd shared their drugs and bought us drinks at the house; surely they'd want something in return, I thought. I would have to go along with it. After all, it was expected, wasn't it?

I was surprised and somewhat scared when they dropped me off at my car without incident. Too wasted to drive home, I somehow made it to Bruce's house. Although late, he seemed to be expecting me. Perhaps he heard me pull into his driveway. He met me at the front porch.

Motioning for me to be quiet, he led me through the darkened kitchen to his room in the attic. I sat on the mattress on the floor beside his bed and told him about the party house I'd been to.

"That's an after-hours joint, Kelly. You shouldn't have been in that neighborhood."

I told him about the snippets of conversation I'd heard. His eyes widened and his jaw dropped.

"Kelly! They said, 'trade the blonde' and 'all the coke you want'?"

I nodded.

"Kelly, they were talking about trading you for cocaine." He pulled me close and held me for what felt an eternity.

"That was so dangerous. You're lucky to be here," he said, drawing back.

I was exhausted and stoned. Following a quick session of what felt more like making love than just having sex, I fell into a sound sleep.

As I drove home early the next morning, I pondered the previous night's events. I had been the only blonde there. They had indeed said, ". . . trade the blonde" and ". . . all the coke you want." Why hadn't that dude traded me for cocaine? He didn't know me. No one knew I was there. I would've just disappeared and it wouldn't have been connected to him. On the surface, I was perplexed, but deep inside I heard a voice say, "It's for your children."

I couldn't wait to see Star and Samuel. It was Sunday. I picked them up at the sitters' house and we drove to Chuck E. Cheese's. I kept them supplied with tokens bought with cash from the previous night's tips, while I sat in a stupor and waited for my hangover to subside.

The normal Chuck E. Cheese noise was amplified in my throbbing head. To me the pizza was tasteless and the soda pop flat, but it filled the gap in my stomach. I tried to make sense of the previous night. Was it God? How could He . . . why should He . . . help me?

Soon the day ended and I put my kids to bed.

Tomorrow is another workday. I feel lousy, but don't dare miss work.

I had been warned that if I came in late or missed another day at the office before the end of the quarter, I would be fired.

That night, my hangover morphed into flu-like symptoms. My abdominal cramps got worse, and I finished the bottle of Pepto-Bismol. I put pillows all around me, but wasn't comfortable. I thought it just a combination of the booze, cocaine, weed, and maybe the nasty pizza and pop. By the morning, I couldn't stand up straight.

I had no patience and snarled at my kids.

"Hop in the car. Just get in there."

I didn't realize poor little Sammy had only one shoe on. I drove them to the babysitter's and, unable to straighten, hobbled to the door with them.

"Here are the kids. I'm sick."

"You okay?"

"I'm going to the hospital. I'll call you later."

At the hospital emergency room I signed myself in. While waiting, I asked Mae Lunk, one of the aids, to call my employer to tell him where I was. I told her if she didn't do it, I'd get fired.

Mae had stolen my boyfriend in high school. I had lured him back, and she and I always had animosity between us. She didn't make the phone call.

They catheterized me, checked my blood, pumped my stomach, and waited for the ER doctor to tell them what to do next. Two hours later, one nurse advised another of my white blood cell count.

"That's high!" She clenched her jaw and mumbled something about an appendectomy.

"I told Pacer!"

Dr. Pacer apparently didn't view my case as an emergency.

They summoned another doctor, and within the hour, I was in the operating room to have my appendix removed. Just before going under, I saw the surgeon waiting by the wall.

"Come here," I whispered and motioned with my index finger.

He approached and leaned toward me.

"I model part time," I lied. "Please, small scar?"

He agreed.

While in recovery, a nurse asked who I wanted her to notify. I gave her my parents' number and asked if Mae had informed my boss. She didn't know, but said she'd tell my office again, just in case. I later learned I had lost my job, until my office got the late-afternoon call from the nurse. With hopes the appendectomy would remedy my frequent absenteeism, I was reinstated.

When I was in a room, my dad phoned.

"Oh, Dad, can you go get Star and Sam from the sitters?" I gave him directions.

"We sure will, babe. We'll take them and pick them up until you can come home. Don't worry—we'll take good care of them." I knew they would.

Mom and Aunt Connie went to our mobile home to gather clothes for the kids. I'm sure what they saw shocked them. Cheese puffs covered the kitchen counter. Clothes, toy ponies, wooden building logs, books, dolls, and train pieces lined the hallway.

Together they cleaned my house. Mom collected the mail from my box.

My parents paid my delinquent trailer lot fees and mortgage, bringing my bills current. Although I appreciated all my family's help, I kicked myself for not keeping the place neat and staying on top of my bills.

The doctor came in to talk with me two days after surgery. He checked my incision and pointed. "See? Here you are tan and here you are white. I cut you in here. No one will see." He was pleased.

I thanked him and breathed a heavy sigh.

My parents brought us home, and for the next two weeks, I stayed on the couch, as per doctor's orders. I watched my children play—so happy to be home with their own toys and their mommy. Even though I didn't move much, they loved having me home. Maybe their contentment came because I was stationary.

While I lay there studying them, I was offered a lifeline.

I heard a voice speak into my soul just as clearly as the one I had heard in my head that called me Satan's Little Princess. This voice was different though. It was firm and loving. With authority, it said, "Now observe. Appreciate the gifts I have given you."

Without doubt, I knew in my spirit it was the voice of God. I wept. How had I missed that? Having these little people in my life was a tremendous blessing. I'd pushed them off on other people while I partied, pleasing my own desires, and chased the ever-elusive dollar.

From working two jobs to lying flat on my back, I was a captive audience, and God spoke. He had me right where He wanted. He reached into my self-induced messy place, pulled me out, and sat me on the sidelines.

I listened to, played with, and nurtured my children. I ate right and allowed time to cleanse the drugs and alcohol out of my body.

During those weeks, I regained a closeness I'd lost with my daughter. I hadn't been there for her, and she learned to trust me again. Also, I got to know my son better. I really didn't know him that well. A humorous kid, he enjoyed making people laugh. I liked him! I also realized he and his sister had become best friends, with him keeping her laughing during the tough times. They had been there for each other when I wasn't there for either of them.

Acknowledging the role reversal—Dace had been cruel to me and, once he was out of the picture, I'd become neglectful to Star and Samuel—was sobering. He had been the jerk, and now I was the jerk. I didn't want to perpetuate the cycle. Again, I cried, promising myself things would change henceforth. However, in no time, the cares of the world pressed in on me once more. My bills still weren't paid, and I was still lonesome for adult companionship.

The doctor signed off on a five-week sick leave. When I could drive again, I went to the Cosmo to enter another legs contest, hoping to make quick money. I didn't win, but I met a handsome man named Russ.

Russ was about my height and had dark wavy hair. His brown eyes twinkled and his smile was bright. We shouted to converse above the loud music.

"Where do you live, Kelly?"

"I live in a small trailer park out in the country."

"Where?"

"In Geauga County. I'm sure you've never heard of it."

"Maybe I have. What is it?" He made me nervous. Why did he want to know exactly where I lived?

"I live in a town called Chardon."

"Which trailer park?"

Is this dude for real?

"Why do you want to know?"

"My sister just got married and moved into a trailer park in Chardon, and I wondered if it's the same one."

I was sure he was telling me what he thought I wanted to hear. Without a doubt he was lying, and it irritated me.

"It's Leader's Trailer Park."

Now *he* looked startled. "My sister lives there. She is in the eighth trailer on the left when you take the road to the right at the entrance."

I got goose bumps. I was the ninth on the left and knew the man beside me recently had a woman move in with him. Maybe she was Russ's sister.

"I'm ninth on the left. She lives beside me." I smirked and downed the rest of my gin and tonic.

His face lit up. "My sister is Dawn, and she married David."

"You should come visit me sometime," I yelled over the music. We danced, talked some more, and parted ways.

Desperate for money, I showed up at the gentlemen's club on a Saturday night to enter their contest and get my job back. I hadn't told them about my hospitalization; I'd just stopped coming to work.

A large bandage still covered my incision. During the pre-contest preparation in the locker room, Freddy came in.

"Sinda, you're back! Bunny said you were in the hospital."

"Yeah, Freddy, I had my appendix out. I'm sorry I didn't call."

"Show me your scar."

I pulled back the leg hole of my cave girl costume to show him the gauze dressing.

"Is it gonna show?"

"Nope. The doctor put it inside my tan line."

"Okay. You can't be in the contest tonight with that bandage. I'll put you on the schedule though. Can it be gone by next Tuesday?"

"Sure. I'll just wear a regular bandage."

"Well, if we make it a week from Tuesday can you lose that thing by then?"

"Yeah, for sure."

"I dig it. I'll put you on the schedule for a week from Tuesday. That better not show. Wear your costume and don't be late. This is your last chance, Sinda. Go home now."

Relieved and frustrated, I left. On the drive home, I berated myself for losing money on the night. I'd paid for a babysitter and wasted gas going into Cleveland. I didn't even receive the twenty-dollar contest entry pay.

As the day to return approached, I felt queasy.

God spoke to you. He's doing something in your life. He's helping with your kids. Are you going to throw this gift back into His face?

The Tuesday came for me to work at the club, and I just couldn't do it.

I don't know how I'm going to have enough money to live, but I just can't return to that job. God help me. Sounded sort of like a prayer. I tore up my stack of customers' business cards, vowing not to look back.

One day the next week, there was a knock on the door. A delivery person handed me a bouquet of red roses and two pink sweetheart roses. Dan had sent them. I was thrilled, and the children reflected my excitement.

"He still loves me," I shrieked. I gave them each their rose, and mimicking me, they jumped up and down yelling, "Dan still loves us! Dan still loves us!"

I didn't have a phone but, while at my parents' a few days later, called to thank him.

"How did you know I was in the hospital?"

"I didn't. I wondered why you didn't call sooner."

"I don't have a telephone, remember? I had to wait to use the phone at my folks' house. Yeah, I had an appendectomy."

"Oh. I was going to give you a few more days and then just write you off."

We made plans to get together that night, and my parents agreed to babysit.

"Why didn't you come after me on New Year's Eve?"

"I thought, you're a big girl—if you could walk out, you could find your own way home."

That bothered me, but it was great to see him, so I let it go. We started dating again. The sex had always been good with Dan, but now something was missing. I no longer loved or trusted him.

"I thought, you're a big girl—if you could just walk out, you could find your own way home," echoed in my mind. *"I was going to give you a few more days and then just write you off,"* chimed in. I built an emotional wall and couldn't completely give myself to him again.

By this time, the Mayfield Heights mushroom-and-ant apartment management company found me and demanded the balance of my lease. My Christmas of giving extravagant gifts to prove I didn't need a husband had caught up with me as well. I'd maxed out my credit cards, and my financial options were gone. It was time to declare bankruptcy.

I contacted the attorney who had processed my divorce.

"I'm going to let Gil handle this one," he said.

Their secretary scheduled an appointment with his colleague.

Gil was short and stocky. He was nice, but didn't have much of a sense of humor. His eyes flashed when we met. He wanted to discuss my finances over lunch and picked me up at work.

I had borrowed a white suit with a soft, rose-colored blouse from Melanie.

"Well you don't look poor," he laughed.

I grinned. "I borrow clothes from my rich computer programmer friend."

He read my financial report, and his forehead narrowed into a frown.

"Wow. You really *are* poor, aren't you?"

This appeared to trigger something nurturing in him, and he asked me out for what became the first of many dates. As long as it was lunch, during my work day, I agreed.

Getting to know one another, I learned that Gil was kind and liked kids. I also learned he was an atheist. While I wasn't a total Jesus freak, I believed in God and knew I could never allow the influence of a nonbeliever on my children.

After lunch one day, he dropped me off in the lobby of my office building. Just before I boarded the elevator, he kissed me. I guess he meant it to be a romantic kiss, but I was unimpressed. It was gross—like kissing your brother. I was alone and screamed on the elevator all the way up to an upper floor where I worked.

Later, he said he wanted to go to the health club with me. I agreed, and we met at the spa one night.

"Kelly, why don't you marry me," he shouted playfully from the pool.

"Yeah right!"

He became serious. "No, really."

He was sweet—I didn't want to hurt his feelings. Trying to keep it light, I laughed, "How can I marry you, Gil? You don't even believe in God."

The question came up again later, and I politely said I wouldn't marry him.

Eventually, the court granted my bankruptcy, and we soon parted ways. His proposals tempted me, certain my financial problems would be over. Still, I couldn't have an atheist help me raise my daughter and son. Besides, there was no chemistry at all.

With the bills off my shoulders, I searched for a job closer to home. Driving to Cleveland was a race against time. I couldn't risk being late again.

I read an ad in the paper for an assistant dispatcher at a local trucking terminal. It required office and computer skills, so I applied. I got the job and gave my two-week notice at the office in Cleveland.

I loved the short commute and extra time I had in the evenings working just one job.

One weekend, I felt energetic and cleaned my house. I didn't clean very often, and it took all day. My kids played in their rooms while I ran the vacuum, dusted, scrubbed floors, disinfected bathrooms, and sanitized the kitchen.

There was a knock at the door. I couldn't imagine who it could be and peeked through the window. There stood Russ. *Maybe he wasn't lying after all.*

With my sweaty clothes and greasy skin, and my hair pulled into a disheveled ponytail, I reluctantly opened the door.

He beamed. "Hi! You said I should stop by the next time I visited my sister and her husband. Here I am."

"Wow. Come on in. I've been cleaning."

"It looks good in here."

"It's rare so enjoy it. Have a seat." My mind reeled as my party world clashed with my mommy world. My preschoolers rushed into the living room to see who was there.

"Kids, this is Russ Wiseman."

"Wismon," he corrected. "Wis with an *s*, not a *z*."

"Oh yeah," I laughed. "The three wise men came to the baby Jesus." Those old Sunday school lessons came in handy on occasion.

He greeted them, and they said something irreverent and silly and ran off to play. I was embarrassed. Discipline hadn't been my strong suit. In my perpetual working-mother exhaustion, I was as inconsistent in my instruction as I was in my housekeeping.

He began to come over regularly. We dated, and he offered to pay for my babysitter, often employing his sister. Having Dawn next door was convenient, and my kids loved her.

Soon, Russ and I started a physical relationship. With him, it was perfunctory—simply do it and go back to watching TV. It didn't seem right, but I wanted to be near him. Something about him was sweet. Besides, saying "no" had never been my forte.

Chapter Thirty-Three: New People, Ageless God

One day, while washing clothes in the trailer park laundry building, I met another resident who lived there with her husband and their four children. She was kind, but a bit reserved. We chatted for a few minutes and she invited me to her church. I agreed to attend that weekend.

It was a Baptist church. We arrived after service had begun and sat toward the back. Since it was Sunday night, seating was not a problem. The evening started with a water baptism.

I sat behind our neighbor, and she turned and, in hushed tones, chatted with me. A teenage boy slid into the pew in front of her. Through tears, he talked about the person being baptized. When he left, I asked her why he was crying.

"Oh, he's just emotional. I mean, you know, God is touching his heart."

I knew what she was talking about. I remembered feeling God reach out to me while I was dancing. I also recalled hearing God speak into my spirit while I was lying on the couch following my appendectomy, as I watched my children play.

The pastor began to speak. Trying to keep my kids quiet had already worn me out. They were best friends out in a new setting and were being silly. My daughter took a Bible from the back of the pew in front of us and began to write in it with a pen she found.

I snatched the pen out of her hand and yelled in a whispered tone, "You can't write in Bibles."

Turning to my neighbor, I said, "We're going. They can't behave in church, so I'm taking them home."

"Please stay," she whispered. "It takes time to teach them. They'll learn."

I forced a smile and rushed them out.

For some ridiculous reason, I expected them to know what I knew. Did I think they'd just absorb my experience and knowledge? I had grown up going every Sunday. I knew how to behave there. I had never taught my kids the importance of church reverence or even what a Bible was.

On the way home, I cried aloud, "Oh God! I know I should have my kids in church. I am so sorry. I need to get them in church. Please forgive me."

Two weeks later, I ran into that neighbor again in the laundry room. She encouraged me to return to her house of worship with her family. She shared that her father had been a deacon when she and her five siblings were little. He had had an affair with another woman in the congregation and left her mother to raise the kids alone, without support.

I was touched. This woman didn't know me. She could see I dressed provocatively. Yet she was willing to obey God, take a chance with me around her husband, and bring me to church.

She must really want us to go with her. I would consider going again—sometime.

Not long afterward, after we returned from a date of dancing at the Cosmo, Russ said he wanted to take me to his church in a suburb of Cleveland by Mayfield Heights, where I used to live. He said his sister and brother-in-law, our next-door neighbors, wanted to take Star and Samuel to their church in the country. I agreed. The next morning I wanted to sleep in, but I liked Russ and elected to go.

I got my preschoolers dressed in their best clothes and walked them next door. Dawn and David buckled them into the back seat of their car, and off they went.

Russ arrived then. I longed to crawl back in bed, but feigned excitement and joined him. His was the First Assembly of God in Lyndhurst—much different from the Baptist one we had gone to with the laundry-room neighbor.

That morning the pastor told all the people to speak in tongues. Even children were speaking in some other language. I looked around. Panicked, I wanted to run out.

"What are they doing?" I whispered.

Russ leaned toward me. "Speaking in tongues. I'll explain later."

I was turned off and didn't want to return.

The next week, I agreed to go, thinking it would be the last time. The pastor stood at the pulpit and apologized for telling the people to speak in tongues the previous week. He said tongues are to strengthen the faith of a believer and there may have been unbelievers who were confused. He stood there and answered every question I had in my head, but hadn't voiced to anyone. It was as if I was having a private consultation with God.

Meanwhile, my kids loved Dawn and David's Assembly of God church in Burton. They came home with stories of the fun they had and the lessons learned. Soon I was taking them to Russ's big church in the city, on my own. Occasionally he brought us to Burton Assembly, where his parents also attended.

He introduced us to his whole family—three sisters and a brother. Mr. and Mrs. Wismon were kind and loving, often inviting us to their home. Star and Samuel had very few manners and were a handful. Still, his family loved us unconditionally.

That summer I ordered a black teeny-weeny French bikini from a catalog. It had long strings on the top that crossed in the back, looped through the sides of the bottom, and then tied in the front around my waist, drawing the bottom into a *V*.

When it arrived, the ruching on the front of the bottom was tearing out. Knowing Mrs. Wismon was a seamstress, I asked Russ if she would sew it for me. She sewed the ruching back in and returned it without criticizing me or my choice of swimwear. No one in his family judged me, my lax parenting skills, or my bratty little kids—they just loved us.

His sister Tammy was a year younger than me and had a daughter Star's age. I joined Dawn at Tammy's house several times while the children played. She'd married an older man and was living a comfortable life in a nice neighborhood.

Once, while visiting, I followed her upstairs when she put away the laundry. As we talked, she opened a hall storage closet. I was amazed to see that rows of Band-Aids, mouthwash, cotton swabs, and more filled the shelves—rows of soap beside rows of toothpaste. My mouth dropped open. I surmised she was rich to be able to afford all of those things before she needed them. To have such an inventory sitting there boggled my mind. I struggled to buy soap and toothpaste when we were out, and I couldn't imagine a life like that. I envied her.

Soon Dawn became my weekday babysitter. It supplemented her family income, and it was an enormous help to me. She was strict. My offspring were a challenge for her, I'm sure. Still, she was fun and they loved her, her guidelines, and her creativity. Her rules seemed to make them feel safe.

∞∞∞∞∞∞∞∞∞∞∞∞

Russ knocked on the door. I invited him in, and after a quick greeting, he drew a deep breath, puffing out his chest. Like vomiting words, he exclaimed, "I'm watching Star and Sam, and David is paying for you to go on a women's retreat with my mom and sisters."

"Ooookay. If it's that important to you, I'll see if I can take off work to go."

He relaxed. I felt shanghaied.

I asked my boss at the trucking terminal if I could have Friday off to go to a church conference.

"You gonna get saved, are ya?" he joked.

I grinned and shrugged.

He smirked. "Oh, sure. You can go."

The women met at Burton Assembly of God so we could travel in a caravan of cars. As I waited by the door, Jerry Stigliano, the principal of the Christian school there, came into the lobby. He smiled at everyone, his brown eyes twinkling. I could tell he enjoyed chatting with the ladies.

I rode three hours south with Mrs. Wismon, Dawn, and Tammy. Tammy, who was in her third trimester of pregnancy, drove.

When we got to the Hyatt Regency Hotel in downtown Columbus, we checked into our rooms and gathered together in one room to eat sandwiches, fruit, and snacks some of the women had brought.

I sat cross-legged on the floor in silence. Maryann, the pastor's wife, sat on the cooler. She gazed down at me and munched on her sandwich. Cocking her head sideways, she said, "So, Kelly, when did you get saved?"

I had gone to high school with her. She had been on the drill team when I was a majorette. I never liked her and her goody-two-shoes ways. She always fluffed her long auburn hair, trying to make the curls bounce. Now her question annoyed me. I seethed. *How dare she ask me that?*

"Oh, I got saved when I was thirteen."

I had said a salvation prayer with those boys at the park in Pennsylvania that year, so I believed it true.

She stopped eating and stared at me.

"Huh. Thirteen. Really?" She emanated judgment with each syllable.

"Yeah, thirteen." She ticked me off and I couldn't wait to get out of there.

That night the conference kicked off with a general session in the grand ballroom. There were a variety of classes offered amidst a few general sessions the next day.

While there, I watched the other women closely. They weren't at all like me. My clothes fit tighter, revealing my figure. Theirs were looser and modest, yet in fashion. I was quiet and guarded. They were relaxed, joking, and shared their feelings with each other. They didn't drink, smoke, take drugs, or even swear. Yet, they had fun—I couldn't figure it out. Still, I saw something in them that appealed to me—a freedom and sisterly love I didn't have. They didn't seem to have the bitterness I did. Deep inside, I wanted to be like them.

I felt compelled to leave one of the main meetings in the ballroom the next day. I went to my hotel room and into the bathroom. I knelt on the floor and bowed my head.

"God, I hate my life," I prayed aloud. "I know I'm not a good mother to Star and Sammy. I want so much more for them. Please help me. I can't do it alone anymore. Please come into my heart. Please make me complete—*save* me."

I waited in silence. I opened one eye and then the other. The room looked brighter than before. A smile took over my face. I felt lighter and sprang to my feet with a squeal of delight.

That lifeline fit perfectly. I ran out of the room and bounced to the elevator, eager to get back to the meeting to hear the speakers.

Since I had already declared salvation, I couldn't share the great news of my real born-again experience. Bursting with enthusiasm, throughout the day I jumped in the air with jubilation when no one was looking.

All too soon, it was time to leave. On the way home, our car ran out of fuel. Dawn and I trudged through a field beside the freeway to a farm and got a gallon of gas. Although enough to get the car started, we didn't go far before we ran out again.

I secretly believed we could pray the car to a gas station. I had faith to propel the car forward, but remained silent. I suppose it was my pride. I didn't want a fuss made over me or my decision. As Dawn and I began to walk up the road again, another group of ladies from church stopped and took us to a gas station.

At work on Monday my boss sneered, "Well, did ya get saved?"

I beamed. "Yep, I did."

"Well, ya don't look saved to me."

As if they were testing my resolve, my co-workers ramped up their vulgarity. I often knelt in the bathroom and silently prayed for God to give me strength and peace. I prayed He'd help me keep my mouth shut. Most days, my knees revealed small square tile indentations from the bathroom floor.

I began to spend my lunch hours at a nearby park reading a Bible Mrs. Wismon had given me. Everything looked different. The trees had individual, perfect leaves. The flowers were more brilliant. Even the bumblebees were flawless and wonderful. It was as though I'd put on glasses—spiritual glasses.

I loved that little Bible. A Counselor's Edition of the New Testament and Psalms, it had categories for specific issues such as suicide, financial problems, health problems, etc., each with pertinent scriptures.

Sitting in the park by the flowering bushes, bees often buzzed me. "Fear, fear, fear," I'd mutter, and fumble to the correct section. I would read the verses about fear, and the bees no longer worried me. Devouring every word I read, I grew spiritually.

Just like when Satan spoke to Jesus during Jesus' forty-day fast, the devil used scripture to try to persuade me. I read 1 Peter 3:1-2, "Wives, in the same way, submit yourselves to your own husbands so that, if any of them do not believe the word, they may be won over without words by the behavior of their wives, when they see the purity and reverence of your lives." (NIV)

My interpretation was that I should marry Dan. I fantasized that I'd talk him into taking more over-the-road trucking trips and I'd stay home with the kids and teach them about Jesus. He'd see by the changes in me and the children, that he should accept Christ as his Savior too.

Several months earlier, Sophia had sent me a large box of clothes. At the time, I'd modeled the long cotton skirts for my kids and we'd all laughed.

"Aunt Sophie wants Mommy to look like a schoolmarm." They had no idea what that meant, but if I thought it funny, so did they.

Now, as I read the Bible and began to view things differently, those skirts didn't seem dumb anymore. I started to respect myself and dress more modestly.

Russ brought over several of his Christian rock band record albums. I laughed. "Christian *rock*?" It sounded ludicrous.

"Don't laugh yet. Just listen to them and tell me what you think. You can keep them here."

The quality surprised me. "Sounds pretty good," I muttered as I stacked several for continuous play on my record player.

Leslie Phillips sang, "Dancing with Danger," and I danced around the house. Her lyrics hit the spot. I felt she knew my story.

David Meese hit something within my soul that craved classical piano music. The lyrics to "We Are the Reason" brought me to my knees.

The variety of music Russ gave me met my needs through every mood. If I wanted to dance, I could. If I needed to relax, I could. If I required encouragement, I got it. Music still led me, but now it led me on a healthy path.

David and the Giants, The Imperials, Amy Grant, Steve Camp, Mylon LeFevre and Broken Heart—the songs seeped into my spirit, vying for space in my mind. They competed for airtime in my brain with Styx, Rush, Foreigner, Bob Segar, Aerosmith, Ted Nugent, and more.

The songs we sang in church comforted me. They touched a place in my soul I didn't realize was there. They ushered my spirit into a holy place where God could speak to me and help me grow.

As the emotional, physical, and social cleanup began, "Amazing Grace" crept into my thoughts. The wretchedness of what I'd allowed my life to become came into clear view as when watching a Polaroid picture develop. I recognized the impoverished state of my spiritual life.

Songs of freedom resonated throughout my being. "Trust and Obey" was a necessary reminder when I felt discouraged. "Love Lifted Me" kept the realization of my rebirth fresh in my mind.

∞∞∞∞∞∞∞∞∞∞∞∞

The son of the trucking company owner took over the terminal I worked in and moved me to the night shift. That didn't work for me as a single mother, and I was laid off.

More lessons were learned. When one has very little, it's easy to identify every blessing, and each day held several. I often pitied the rich. *If you have plenty and your day-to-day needs are met, where can you see God work?*

I learned again there is much richness in poverty.

As I registered for unemployment, I also signed up for food stamps and Medicaid. I learned numerous money-saving ideas. I also learned to be creative with my money.

The food stamps came in booklets of ones, fives, and tens. When I had no gasoline, I used a one-dollar food stamp coupon to buy a pack of gum. I'd receive actual change in return. When I collected enough change, I'd put gas in my car. I was a new Christian, and still struggled to get it right.

We received so many food stamps, there were some left over from one month to the next. I tried to give some to my maternal grandmother.

"No, honey," she'd say. "These are for you and your children. You need them."

I assured her I had more than one woman and two preschoolers could ever use, but she insisted I keep them.

With the excess, I began to have what I later called a cookie ministry. My children and I were full of love, and we wanted to show that love to others. We delighted in making batches of cookies, and anonymously left dozens of our sweets on paper plates wrapped in tin foil, on the doorsteps of friends who'd been kind to us. In retrospect, I wonder how many neighborhood dogs enjoyed cookies during that time.

Chapter Thirty-Four: Subtle Seduction

Sammy was about to turn four years old. My former mother-in-law and her new husband were traveling in an RV and wanted to come celebrate his birthday. I agreed. They said Dace was joining them.

I told Russ they were coming, and while not thrilled, he agreed to stay away for the week they visited.

Seeing my children's father again wasn't as scary as I'd feared. The ex in-laws parked their RV in my driveway, and in just a couple days, Dace stayed in my trailer and we were in bed again. The last time we'd been together we were husband and wife.

Now our sex was familiar, but different. Through my promiscuity I had learned more about myself and about what men desire. I was more confident and less concerned about what he thought about me. This was attractive to him, and our passion ignited. Still, he would leave soon, and I kept a safe distance emotionally, something I'd learned through encounters with near strangers.

He started talking about reconciliation and the kids and me moving to Phoenix.

As we listened to Genesis, Phil Collins sang "Follow You Follow Me." The lyrics touched me, and hope tried to creep in. My ex-husband made it sound appealing, and for a minute I was excited about retrieving a long-forgotten "happily forever after" dream. Without firm commitment from me, I allowed him to talk about a future for our family in Arizona.

My precious children loved having their father and grandparents there. Hungry for a daddy, Samuel called him Daddy Dace and seemed to forget the past. I saw myself in my sweet son somewhat, but recognized the danger for him, Star, and myself. Our future was precarious at that moment.

I was a new Christian, still sorting out right from wrong, but I discerned the seduction of the old trap. I silently prayed for direction. I felt an answer and purposed in my heart to set Dace free. I was secure in knowing my children would not be hurt again.

I didn't tell him of my decision for fear of his response. He said he'd continue to write to me. Soon he left with his mother and her husband.

The lyrics of Journey's "Open Arms" reverberated throughout my home. I openly wept as I sang aloud.

My head argued with my heart. I knew he wasn't what was best for us. Still, I wanted a companion so badly.

Russ came the next week and I told him I'd slept with my ex. Surprisingly, he wasn't angry. He was hurt, sad, and disappointed, but didn't write me off.

I was seeing Russ and Dan often, but they didn't know about each other. Throwing Dace into the mix just made me more confused. I was learning about the Lord and what He expects from His children. I understood sleeping with someone who wasn't my husband displeased Him. Sleeping with three separate men was a definite no-no. I began to pray for guidance and strength to say no.

One weekend, after dinner with Dan, we ended up in his bed in the basement of his parents' house. No one else was home.

While fooling around, praise songs from church ran through my mind. They grew louder and louder. Soon the choruses blasted in my head and I sensed a spiritual battle in the air over the bed. It roared in my mind until I couldn't hear myself think. My ears actually hurt from a din audible to only me. The short distance to the basement ceiling seemed nonexistent. An unseen struggle took place in a vastness I couldn't yet comprehend.

Suddenly, amidst the thunderous cacophony, I heard a voice say, "Let there be a child conceived."

Where did THAT come from, I wondered. I tried to concentrate on the task at hand and ignore the skirmish raging above.

The following weekend, Dan came over after the kids were asleep. I didn't want to fool around, so I sat on my bed and put my sock drawer in front of me. While I sorted its contents, he reclined on the floor.

We talked about our families, his job, and our lives in general. The conversation transitioned to the future we once thought we would have. We had planned to wed, but those plans had changed. We discussed where we were at that moment.

"The weirdest thing happened," I said without looking up from my sock piles. "When we were in your bed last weekend, I kept hearing these songs roar in my head. And then I thought I heard a voice say, 'Let there be a child conceived.' Weird, huh?"

"Yeah, I wondered about that."

I stopped and looked at him. "You mean you heard it too?" Chills danced up and down my spine.

"Yeah, I didn't know what you meant, but then I thought, 'Whatever.' I didn't want to ruin the moment, if you get my drift."

"You mean *I* said that? Was it *my* voice?"

"Yeah, I guess. It wasn't me. I didn't know what you meant."

"Wow. That's weird. I heard it too, but didn't know who said it."

While he wrote it off, I realized at once it had everything to do with the intense spiritual battle I'd felt booming over the bed. Satan was trying to ruin God's plan for my life. I had been Satan's Little Princess for a long time, and he wasn't giving up without a fight.

The thought that God had a plan for *my* life made me feel special. I knew I was now a Daughter of the King—I wanted to please Him as my Heavenly Father.

∞∞∞∞∞∞∞∞∞∞

I continued to read the Bible to learn what God expected from me. I prayed for Him to show me the way to live my life as a Believer.

Russ wanted to take me out one weekend and offered to provide and pay for a babysitter. I was still unemployed and thanked him. When he brought his neighbor, Francie, to my house, I was thrilled. She was tiny and cute. She played with my children, and they thought she was fun.

The next weekend, he brought her on his motorcycle. She watched them while he and I spent the morning together. That afternoon, I peered out the window as he prepared to take her home. My insides twisted when he lovingly tucked her hair into her helmet. I realized then I'd lost another boyfriend to a babysitter.

The next time we went out, he brought her over, and while on our date, I confronted him about their relationship. He admitted he'd kissed her. There was no way I could compete with her, and frankly, why would I want to?

We had a huge fight and he refused to pay her for me, saying it was my responsibility.

Back home, I told her since he had agreed to pay her in the first place, I wouldn't. "As long as you're screwing my boyfriend, you can collect your money from him."

The next day was Saturday. My preschoolers and I prepared to go swimming, and I was in my bikini. At 8:30 a.m. I heard a knock on my door. When I opened it, a large woman stood there yelling at me.

"You have to pay my daughter because she babysat for you and you owe her the money." I realized she was Francie's mother.

"Go get your money from Russ," I barked.

As I tried to shut the door, she pushed her ample body halfway inside so I couldn't. I began to push the door into her squishy torso. I felt an instant reprimand in my spirit and jerked the door back.

She said she wouldn't leave until I gave her money. I assured her I had no money and she needed to leave or I'd call the police. She refused. Because I didn't have a telephone, I took a step out onto the porch and caught the attention of a teenage boy walking on the street.

"Call the police," I yelled to him. He stared at me. "I need help—I don't have a phone. Please, go call the cops!" He nodded and ran.

"Fine," I snapped into her bulging red face. "Stay here! The cops are coming now. They'll make you leave."

"Oh, I'll leave," she hissed back at me. She looked over my shoulder toward my car.

"I see you have a 'God loves you' bumper sticker on your car. Well it's a good thing He does because no one else on earth ever could!"

Satan knew just what buttons to push. The old insecurities flooded back.

"Get out," I whispered.

She smirked; satisfied with the blood she'd drawn.

"You'd better get that money to Francie."

I stepped past her and shut the door. My chest was still pounding when the police arrived. I told them a woman tried to push her way into my house and wouldn't leave at first, but finally did. They assured me it was a matter between us, but if she returned and I needed their help, not to hesitate to call them.

My spirit wounded, I learned the meaning of contrition that morning. The reality of my disdain of the words "I'm sorry" became clear to me. Always feeling like an inconvenience, I'd spent my life apologizing for anything and everything. But when truly at fault and needing to apologize, the words tasted like gall.

The Holy Spirit told me clearly in my spirit, I needed to apologize for pushing the door into that woman's body. Further, I needed to ask Russ for his forgiveness.

It was still early. I dressed and gathered all the money I had in the house. I owed $18 to the babysitter but only had $14. I told the kids we'd go to the beach later, but first Mommy needed to run an errand. We got into my car and headed toward the Wismon house.

First, I went to where Francie lived. Her mother answered my knock. I told her God told me to tell her I was sorry I pushed the door into her and that I had just $14. She said she'd ask her daughter if that was enough. I waited on her doorstep while she disappeared into the house. Within minutes she reappeared. "Francie said that will be fine."

"Thank you. Tell her 'thank you' for me. Again, I'm sorry I pushed the door on you." Without compassion or appreciation, she made a snide remark, pushing the invisible knife further into my heart and, with much joy, gave it a twist. She sneered and closed the door.

That was terrible, Lord. I HATE apologizing.

I drove down the long driveway next door. My children waited in the car while I walked through the house to Russ's bedroom where he was sleeping. No one else was home. I knelt beside the bed and whispered, "Are you awake?" He didn't answer. I repeated the question and he grunted. He was awake, but angry and wouldn't look at me.

I apologized for telling him to pay for my childcare. I told him if he wanted to date Francie it wasn't my business—I'd leave him alone. Then I told him I gave her mother all the money I had and she'd said it was enough. He didn't raise his head or look at me. I apologized again and left.

"Did I really have to do that, God?" I asked out loud in the car. I determined that morning I would try to control my temper and obey Him for the rest of my life. That's how much I hated to apologize. I never wanted to do it again.

With my spirit broken, I reverted to the mindset of a battered woman. I moved through the motions of life on autopilot.

About a week later, as I helped my kids out of the back seat of our car, Dawn opened the window of her trailer and called out, "Hi there, neighbor."

"Oh, hi, Dawn."

"Hey, neighbor. When was the last time you ate?"

I thought about it for a minute, turning my head slightly. "About nine days ago, I guess."

"You'd better eat something, neighbor—you're getting skinny."

I chuckled politely. "Thanks. I will."

Once inside, I sat on the edge of my bed. *Nine days.* I hadn't realized that much time had passed. *Nine days. What is wrong with me? I need to eat.*

As I sat in the kitchen eating a peanut butter and jelly sandwich with my kids, I thought about what was going on with me. After lunch I went into my bathroom and wept.

I had allowed a female Dace to abuse me back into a complacent, paralyzed state, almost not functioning. I wasn't being a good mother. I wasn't being a good daughter. I wasn't being a good Christian. I needed to snap out of it and move on.

Chapter Thirty-Five: A Quiet Whisper

In time, Russ re-entered my life. I was full of questions about God. One night we sat on the floor in my living room, cross-legged, knees to knees. One table lamp lit the room, casting a warm amber glow in my fourteen-foot wide trailer. I shot questions at him one after another about God, the Bible, heaven, hell, and everything else I had pondered since my salvation experience. Hours passed.

At one point I said, "How do you know these things? How can you be sure?"

He was calm, his expression soft and somewhat perplexed. He chose his words carefully.

"I don't necessarily know all these things, but I can tell when it's God speaking through me, and He is right now."

Hmmm. Maybe it is "Wise man" after all.

Again, a loving God who would use a fallible man to speak truth and love into my soul was a God I wanted to know more intimately.

Russ left. With a sense of awe and reverence, I drifted to sleep pondering God, His complexity, and His mercy.

The kids and I continued to go to First Assembly of God in Lyndhurst. It was an expansive round church, and the kids often ran the opposite way when I tried to get them out the door. One day I was furious by the time I got them into the car.

"When we get home, I'm going to beat your arses!"

They were crying in the back seat. Between sniffles, Star said, "Mama, Jesus doesn't want you to beat our arses."

My spirit winced. Hearing my precious daughter use my bad language back at me broke my heart. I resolved immediately to stop swearing at my children. My words would lift them up and not tear them down, just as I had read in the Bible in Ephesians 4:29.

∞∞∞∞∞∞∞∞∞∞∞∞∞

Always a list-writer, I created a new one. One night after the kids went to bed, I wrote "Pro" and "Con" across the top of a blank sheet of paper. Along the left side I wrote, "Dan," "Russ," and "Dace"—the three men in my life at that time. I needed simplicity and obedience. That meant not dating three men simultaneously.

For Dan, I had pros such as he was good in bed. He loved his daughters. He was a hard worker. His cons outweighed his positive traits. He had told me Jesus was for Sunday mornings only and to leave God at church.

Although I had imagined I would encourage him to take long-haul trips with his truck and leave me at home with our children where I'd teach them about Jesus and His love, it was just a fantasy. Further, he started to speak sharply with my kids, and I hated that. Sam called him Daddy Dan, and that worried me. I realized I loved his daughters more than I loved him. That would never work.

For Russ, I noted he was kind, giving, and spiritual. At the same time, he had a wandering eye and liked skinny girls. How long would I be skinny? Too risky. Besides, there wasn't the necessary chemistry for a forever relationship.

Dace was . . . well, he was Dace, and that was scary. I bore physical scars from him. The kids and I had emotional scars from him. He seemed to carry baggage from a traumatized childhood of various abuses. While sex was nice the last time we were together, he had little

309

going for him on the pro side other than the fact he was the father of my children.

There has to be someone right for me.

I flipped the paper over and wrote "Mr. Just-Right-For-Me" at the top. I thought and thought. *What would my ideal guy be like?*

I began to write. He had to be godly and want to be the spiritual head of the household. He had to be kind to my children and me. It would be awesome if he treated me like a lady. He had to be a hard worker and be devoted to God first and family second. He had to be good in the sack, but that would have to be left up to God. I pretty much understood by then sleeping with someone I wasn't married to, didn't please God.

Knowing no one is perfect, I wrote the drawbacks a man could have that I felt I could handle. He could flirt some. He didn't have to be rich. He could even be a musician—a feature I'd sworn to avoid, after my ex-husband.

Once satisfied with my list of Mr. Just-Right-For-Me, I laid the paper on the bed. Smoothing it out, I looked heavenward and prayed, "God if he's out there, please let me have him." I folded the paper and put it into my dresser drawer.

The next day I proceeded to tell all three guys to get lost. I refused to go out with Dan when he called me at my parents' house. I wrote to Dace that I wasn't interested in reconciling. I told Russ I wasn't dating for a while. Meanwhile, I concentrated 100 percent on serving God and living a life pleasing to him.

After having had a problem with alcohol, it was remarkably easy for me to stop drinking. Smoking marijuana and having sex were the last two things to go in my life once I asked Jesus to come into my heart. Abstinence would be difficult, but I desired to obey God.

I had very few friends and became lonesome and sad. First Assembly of God had a single parent home fellowship group that met during the week at night. I went twice, but they didn't have childcare, and it was very far from my house, so I stopped going.

There were churches closer to home, but the big one in the suburbs drew me back. Although Russ stopped attending, my kids and I continued to go each Sunday morning and many Wednesday evenings.

I still struggled with ulcers and colitis. I carried a large bottle of antacid in my purse. I was thin and grew more pale and fragile each week.

One especially despondent week as I agonized over my unpaid bills, romance woes, and ailing stomach, I prepared to take the kids to Wednesday night services. They enjoyed the children's programs, and I could sit in peace while the pastor preached.

Driving there, I listened to my children chatter. They were excited to go. Sadly, I didn't share their enthusiasm. I felt defeated.

Why am I going tonight? It's the middle of the week, and it'll be past the kids' bedtime when we get home. I have to go to the WIC office in the morning, and the car uses too much gas to come here.

We arrived, and they ran toward their classroom. I followed, and greeted their teachers. "Hi there. Thanks for serving tonight." I tried to sound cheery as I hung the kids' jackets. "You kids behave and have fun."

Trudging down the hall toward the sanctuary, I grew more pessimistic with each step. *Samuel will need a new coat this winter. Where will I find the money for that?*

The lights were low and not many people were there. The sermon didn't uplift my spirits as I'd hoped. I sat motionless when the pastor dismissed the meager congregation.

I'd better pick up the kids and head home. I dreaded the slow, dark drive into the country.

I stood and looked around. A few groups of people greeted one another here and there across the massive, darkened auditorium. I had no friends there.

Why am I even here? I've wasted enough time and money coming in the middle of the week. I'm such an idiot.

Chastising myself, I turned to leave. About six feet along the pew to my left stood a tall, heavy older woman. I hadn't noticed her during the sermon. She was alone. I sensed her staring at me. My head hung low, but I glanced up and smiled at her. She held my gaze and stared into my eyes.

"How ya doin'?"

I was surprised she spoke to me. She didn't know me. I took a couple steps toward her and sighed heavily, "Oh, I'm okay." I forced a grin. "Gotta go get my kids." My fake cheerfulness didn't fool her.

Facing me, she held out her arms. "Come here, baby."

Without even thinking about it, I entered her opened arms. "You look like you need a hug, sweetie." Her ample arms enveloped me, and I melted into her bosom.

Uncharacteristic of me, I stayed there for several seconds, my head resting peacefully on her chest. Beyond her physical warmth, she radiated the love of God. Confidence, strength, joy, and wellness that can only come from the Lord Himself flowed from this large, lovely woman into my boney, sickly frame.

312

As I stepped back, she held onto my upper arms. "You go get your babies now, and you have a good week, ya hear?" I nodded, still surprised at my own reactions and the release of love I'd felt from her.

As I walked to the kids' classroom, peace overwhelmed me. I was overcome with a profound love for them.

I helped them put on their jackets as they excitedly told me what they'd done in class that evening. I found it hard to listen and couldn't shake the feeling I'd been embraced by someone intensely close to Almighty God.

Suddenly I snapped to attention. "C'mon kids, there's someone I want you to meet." I hurried my children into the sanctuary. "Aww, she's gone."

I stopped two ladies who'd been behind me. "Excuse me. Do you know the lady who was in the pew right there?" I pointed to where she had been sitting.

"We didn't see anyone there. What did she look like?"

Smiling, I described the woman with the simple dress and cardigan sweater. "No, I didn't see her," they each responded.

"Well, we'll find her Sunday. Let's head home."

I left church that night feeling well physically, emotionally, mentally, and spiritually. The adoration that poured out of me onto my children was a renewed, unconditional love from God.

My circumstances would not make me that downhearted again; I was filled with hope.

For the next several weeks I searched for that sweet lady. I searched on Wednesday nights, Sunday mornings, and even Sunday evenings, but never saw her again. Clearly she was an angelic messenger sent just for me.

The love infused in me when encircled by her arms was affection straight from heaven.

It was life transforming and contagious. I was living with optimism, my cheerfulness was genuine, and I effortlessly lavished unconditional love on family and others.

Soon thereafter, I signed up for water baptism at my church. Melanie came and so did Mrs. Wismon.

After my baptism, Mrs. Wismon gave me a big hug and told me she was proud of me. Mel had to leave early but left a loving note on the windshield of my car. I was on a good road paved with love and hope.

Before long the weather got colder and my son needed a winter coat, but I had no money to buy one. Thankfully, his sister could still wear hers from the previous winter. The Goodwill store didn't have any boys' coats large enough, so I bought the smallest women's coat I could find. It was bright blue and puffy with individual sections filled with goose down. I brought the sleeves up two sections and hand-stitched them into place. Sweet Samuel looked like a blue Michelin Man.

Not wanting anyone to see his coat, I quickly removed it when we entered church and didn't put it back on him until just before we left. Still, one day after service, a woman commented on his jacket. Irritated, I explained what I had done; noting he was warm and that's what mattered.

"Have you asked God to provide a coat for your son?"

My blank stare answered her question.

"If you ask Him, He'll provide one. You should ask."

Frankly, that hadn't occurred to me. I thanked her and scurried away.

That night, with my childlike faith, I simply asked God if He would please supply a winter coat for Sam.

Later that week, a woman I didn't know approached me in the church parking lot. My little blue marshmallow was already in the car with his sister.

"Excuse me," she called to me as I opened my car door. I turned toward her and smiled. "Both sets of my son's grandparents bought him a winter coat this year. He doesn't need two. Would you like one for your little boy?"

I was embarrassed, humbled, and grateful at once.

"Yes, thank you so much."

Without a second to say anything else, she handed a stylish little brown coat to me, wished me a good day, and dashed off, disappearing into the parking lot.

I leaned into the rear of my car and passed it to my son. His eyes widened with excitement and wonder.

"Sammy, I asked God for a jacket for you and He gave you one." I could hardly believe my words.

"It has tags on it," they squealed, giddy with excitement.

The next week another woman buttonholed me in the church foyer and asked if I wanted her son's winter coat from the previous year—he had outgrown it.

"Oh, thank you, but Samuel already has one."

"No, I insist. You take it."

I thanked her and took it. Now he had two winter coats. I was amazed all I had to do was ask. God really did care about the little things in our lives.

I lengthened the sleeves of the thrift store down jacket and used it for myself when I played outside in the snow with my children. We were all warm—until the heater in our car broke.

With a forty-five-minute drive to and from our church in Lyndhurst, a working heater in the car was necessary. I kept a blanket in the back seat for the kids. Still the long ride was miserable. One Wednesday night we came out and it was below freezing. The thought of driving home without heat made me teary-eyed.

"Dear God," I prayed. "You gave Sam a winter coat when he needed one. I know You care about everything in our lives. Our heater is broken and this car is freezing. Would you please fix the heater for us?"

I exited the church parking lot and turned on the heater. Full of faith, I believed it would begin to purr out warmth. Nothing happened.

The car has to warm up first, I told myself. A few miles down the road, I tried the heater once more. Again, nothing.

My Dad planned to fix it that weekend, so I tried to forget about it and sing the songs we'd sung in service that night. About halfway home, I realized I wasn't cold. Was I just numb and freezing to death?

"Hey, kids," I called into the back, "are you guys cold?"

"No, Mommy," they chimed in unison. "We're warm. We don't need this blanket."

Huh, isn't that remarkable? All I have to do is ask.

I had learned in church God would meet all of our needs, and we were living it. I saw His provision on a weekly basis. If I had a want I perceived as a need, I would pray, "Lord, You said You'd give us the desires of our hearts. Please meet this desire or change my heart." He always did—not always in my way or in my timing, but always to His glory, showing His divine mercy.

Chapter Thirty-Six: Cleaning up My Act

Winter storms finally gave way to warmer weather. Like raking fallen leaves out of flowerbeds, God cleaned the garden of my soul. The kids and I continued to attend church and Sunday school regularly. They were like sponges, soaking up the Bible stories and the love of Jesus Christ.

God taught me to be a good mommy that summer. He made my negative words taste terrible in my mouth. He made my heart hurt every time I hurt Star and Samuel's little hearts. I learned compassion and the unconditional love I'd seen in my grandmother and the Wismons.

On many Sunday nights, my children crawled into my bed. We'd go over their Sunday school papers again, and they'd tell me what they had learned that morning. We took turns praying, asking God to take care of us and thanking Him for every single thing. They even thanked Him for their boogers, as kids will do!

God showed me how I often treated my kids' buddies better than I treated them. I began to show my own children respect—to say please and thank you and be patient with them. I learned to be kind in my words and actions.

Summer drew to a close, and the thought of enrolling Star in school became more and more terrifying to me. I'd gone to the local public school and remembered the harshness and apathy of some of my teachers.

The thought of Christian school kept popping into my mind. I wanted to enroll Star in Geauga Christian School, housed in Burton Assembly of God, where Dawn and her family attended.

You can't afford that, I reminded myself. *God, please meet this desire or change it. Star is Your child. Please tell me which kindergarten You want her in.*

I read the Bible and learned about tithing—giving the first 10 percent of my income to God via the church or other godly work. I collected unemployment, received some welfare benefits, and made the occasional fifteen dollars for ironing shirts. From that, I gave 10 percent to God, and He met all of our needs.

Walking in my new faith in God, and believing His Word and His promises, I enrolled my daughter in Geauga Christian School kindergarten.

The school principal was the same dude who chatted with the women in the lobby before we left the church to go to the women's retreat in Columbus.

Jerry Stigliano was a tall thin man with big, round brown eyes that twinkled behind his glasses when he smiled. An Italian, his thinning hair was dark and he had nice skin. He showed me throughout the school and made me feel welcome. I struggled with the correct pronunciation of his name, but after three tries, I said it right.

Occasionally Mrs. Wismon invited us to their church. The kids had attended several times with Dawn and David and were comfortable there.

One Sunday morning I sat diagonally behind Mr. Stigliano and stared at him. Something about him attracted me. I studied his profile.

He's too old for you, Kelly, I thought.

After service, I milled around where he stood talking. I wore a red and white striped dress, looking like a giant candy cane, yet he didn't notice me. I retrieved my children from their class and loitered in his area again. Even then, it seemed I was invisible.

318

To mark the end of summer, the congregation of Burton Assembly had a picnic at a park. Mrs. Wismon invited us to join her. She thought it would be an opportunity for my kids to meet some of the other children Star would go to school with. It rained that morning, but the forecast predicted afternoon sunshine. I made a huge taco salad, dressed the kids nicely, and off we went.

They joined the others on the playground equipment. I spotted Mr. Stigliano right away. He wore white jeans and played volleyball on wet grass, and yet avoided getting muddy. He greeted me when we arrived and smiled at me a couple of times throughout the day. My heart leapt, but I reminded myself I wasn't dating— especially an Italian.

Maybe this guy is different, I thought, but snapped to my senses. *Yeah, right. His gold chain is probably hidden under his shirt.*

The next week, school started and I found it more difficult than I'd anticipated. When we had our family photo taken in August, the basic package I'd purchased included a little round photo charm. I put it on an old chain and let Star wear it the first day of school. I told her Sammy and Mommy would be with her all day. If she ever felt alone, she should look at the picture and know we were there with her.

We took her into her classroom and got her settled. Sam and I returned to the car. I hated leaving my little girl there. He and I went home and, for a fun diversion, had a picnic for lunch.

When I picked his sister up from school, she was tired, but excited. Her teacher approached and handed me the picture charm. The chain had broken and someone

319

found it in the parking lot. I fixed it, and Star wore it for many weeks thereafter.

Tammy and I agreed to alternate driving our daughters to school. I was spoiled by not going to work and hated rising early. Still, I wanted to make sure they had a good day, so we prayed and sang songs on the way there.

Soon after school started, Tammy asked Dawn how I could afford Christian education.

"She prays," Dawn responded. "She prays, and every day she goes to the mailbox to check for 'her blessing' because she has faith she'll get a blessing in the mail. She looks for it daily."

Her sister filed that information away to ponder later.

∞∞∞∞∞∞∞∞∞∞∞∞

Russ's family was precious to me—I loved them and they loved us. The kids and I visited his mom at their house one day. We sat in the backyard while they played on the tire swing.

Mrs. Wismon said, "Kelly, you know what you need? You need an older, more mature man who can take care of you—and handle your children." Her eyelid twitched.

Confession time. "Well, you know I've kind of had my eye on Star's principal, Mr. Stigliano."

She was eager to share. "Oh, he's available! He's been single for six years."

"Yeah, but he doesn't even notice me. It won't work."

Although I didn't know it, Mrs. Wismon had her own "phone-a-friend system" and called her pastor's mother-in-law, who was the former secretary at the Christian school.

I didn't have a telephone, and a couple days later Dawn came over, smiling.

"Mr. Stigliano wants to see you in his office at ten o'clock in the morning."

I was scared; sure it was because my first tuition payment had been late and now my second tuition payment was late. All evening long, I practiced my spiel. I stood in front of the mirror and recited, "Mr. Stigliano, I realize my first tuition payment was late, and I apologize. I understand my second tuition payment is late. I get my unemployment check in two weeks. I promise I will pay you then."

To my wonder, it doesn't matter how old you are, it doesn't get any easier going to the principal's office. I sat in the "bad girl" chair across from his desk and steadied my shaking knees with my sweaty palms. Junior high school déjà vu!

He smiled and sat at his desk. He made polite chit-chat and then casually dropped the bomb.

"Someone has anonymously donated eight hundred dollars toward Star's tuition. Can you pay fifteen dollars a month?"

I about fell out of my bad-girl chair.

"Yes!" I nodded, thinking, *Even I can come up with fifteen dollars a month.*

Next, to my complete shock, he asked, "Are you seeing anyone?"

"Um. No."

"Would you like to go out with me sometime, then?"

"Sure," I said quietly, although a riot banged in my head.

He asked me out! Two prayers answered in five minutes. This God is good! This Christianity is working out for me!

"Great. My schedule is full of school stuff. This Friday is free though. Would you join me for dinner Friday night?"

"Sure. I'll have to find a babysitter. I don't go out much and don't have anyone I regularly use."

"Oh, I'll get one." He saved the day. "I'll ask one of Liz's daughters. The Guildons are my friends. They're wonderful people and their girls are responsible. I'll pick her up and I'll pay her too."

"Ahh, thanks so much!"

"Okay. I'll pick you up Friday. How about six thirty?"

We set the date, and I left in a fog. My mind whirled with excitement, anticipation, and trepidation as I remembered the numerous dates I'd lost to sitters in the past.

I borrowed a shirt from Melanie. She loaned me a loosely woven, course cotton shirt with a charcoal background and a thin plaid pattern. It had a large fold-over collar with buttons on the side, three-quarter sleeves, and a belt. It looked good on me.

Jerry told me months later he had asked his boss, school administrator Dr. Robert Black, where he suggested he take me for our first date. He'd recommended a fondue restaurant in Mentor.

"It'll give you something to do in case the conversation lags," he'd advised. Jerry had driven there the previous evening so he'd know where to go.

When he arrived at my house Friday evening, he brought Carrie Guildon to babysit. She was the oldest of three girls and was smart, responsible, talented, and cute.

Just knowing she had Jesus in her life made me relax. She was confident and firm with my kids. They responded with respect—impressive.

At the restaurant the waitress asked if we'd ever eaten there before. We hadn't, and she proceeded to explain the courses, fondue forks, methods of dipping and cooking, etc. However, she forgot to tell us to pierce the tiny potatoes prior to plunging them into the oil.

We talked while our speared potatoes cooked. Suddenly, POP! One of the potatoes exploded and hot oil splashed into my face and onto Mel's beautiful top.

"Are you alright?" Jerry asked with concern. I was embarrassed, but unharmed.

"Yeah. I think I'll go to the ladies' room to clean up."

In the restroom, I leaned into the mirror and looked for burns, blisters, or blotches. Nothing.

Thank God I'm wearing a heavy coat of makeup. I chucked and dabbed the shiny oil spots off my face and out of my hair.

I examined the shirt. "Oh no." While I couldn't see oil on it, I knew it was there. *I'll wash it out at home. She'll never let me borrow anything again if I've ruined this.*

When I emerged from the powder room, there was a new glass of soda pop on the table.

"The waitress came over to see if everything was alright," Jerry said. "I told her what happened. She said she was sorry for not telling us about the potatoes. She gave us some free drinks. Are you alright?"

"Yep, I'm fine." I just wanted to forget about it. We moved on to other subjects.

Sinking a cube of chicken into the oil, he asked, "So do you like this dinner?"

"Yes, I like playing with my food."

He laughed. He appeared to enjoy my company. My chest thumped with excitement throughout the evening. This guy seemed so nice and had an innocence about him unlike any other guy I'd spent time with.

On the way home, he asked me if I'd consider another date with him. I chose to be honest about what was on my mind.

"You know, I've been through a lot. My kids have been through a lot. If there's one thing we don't need, it's another man in our lives who is just going to come and go. Exactly what are your intentions here?"

Surprisingly, he didn't drive the car off the road. He grinned and swallowed.

"Well," he spoke slowly, choosing his words with care, "if you're asking me if I ever intend to get married again, I guess the answer is that I'm not opposed to getting married again. I'm certainly not ready to yet. But if the Lord brought the right woman along, I guess I wouldn't fight it."

"Alright," I responded matter-of-factly. "I just didn't want to go down that road again. I'm not ready to get married either. I just didn't want to waste my time, and frankly, my heart can't take much more."

When we arrived at home, he came in with me.

"How were they for you?" I asked. Carrie gave a polite response for what was probably a difficult evening with my challenging offspring. I thanked her and Jerry, and they left.

To my surprise, I did not scare him off. The next week when I was collecting my daughter from school, he came out to my car and asked if I'd like to have coffee with him Friday night after the school open house. I said yes and planned to have my parents babysit. The kids and I would stay at their house that night.

I couldn't believe the way I felt. I hardly knew this man, yet I was drawn to him.

It's just because you've been out of the game for so long, Kelly. You're just horny.

Yet, I wasn't thinking about a physical encounter. I realized an emptiness—a yearning in my spirit.

I'd never met anyone like Jerry. He was the same man at school in the capacity as principal, that he was at church as a song leader or parishioner; the same man when we were alone. Most important, he was kind to my children.

When the open house was over, I got a taste of life as a principal's wife. We had to hang around until the last person left and he locked the building. I rode with him to The Same Place, a local pizzeria. We ordered a medium pizza, and while we waited, he leaned into the table and fired rounds of questions at me, like in an interview.

What's your favorite color? What's your favorite food? What's your favorite movie? What do you like best about the school? What is the hardest thing about being a single parent?

He said he played the bass guitar.

Oh no—a musician. He's Italian and a musician. No way.

It was not a fun date. I disliked the questions and wanted him to stop. I finally spoke up.

"This sounds like a job interview."

He laughed and lightened up. The rest of the date was less intimidating. I relaxed and enjoyed Jerry's natural warmth.

I learned he had three sons from a previous marriage. They lived with their mother in a town thirty miles away. She'd divorced him when the youngest was a baby. He visited them at his mother's house for convenience, and desired to see them more often.

When he brought me back to my car, the school parking lot was somewhat dark, illuminated by just two lights. I wondered if he was going to kiss me goodnight. He didn't seem to be moving in that direction, and I thrust my arms forward to give him a hug. One of my arms accidently went inside his suit coat. My hug was awkward with one arm outside his jacket and the other inside. This embarrassed me, as I didn't want him to think I was being too forward.

Driving to my parents' house, I rehearsed the hug over and over. I got mortified with each review.

He has to learn about your past sooner or later. The negative self-talk started. Maybe it was Satan trying to ruin my mood and dash any hopes of a future with this man. By now, I was more aware of the ongoing spiritual battle for my soul.

Wait until he finds out about your old job and the guys you've slept with. He'll be all "ends and elbows." You know it.

"Shut up!" I shouted into the darkened car.

∞∞∞∞∞∞∞∞∞∞∞∞

School responsibilities claimed many weekends, and I often joined the principal. I met his mentor, Dr. Black, at an alumni banquet one weekend. I later learned Jerry had asked him what he thought about me.

"She's a classy lady, Jer. I like her."

Having his respected friend and mentor give me his seal of approval helped move his feelings for me forward.

During our interrogation date, Jerry learned about my ulcer. Later, he brought me a large bottle of Maalox. He also gave me a hardback Bible. I thought the gesture priceless—caring for me physically and spiritually.

I studied the Bible, drank the antacid when necessary, and slowly returned to good health.

Not too long after Jerry and I had our first date, Dan somehow learned about him. Late one night, while I was home watching television, Dan knocked on my door. It was 2 a.m. and he'd been drinking. I invited him just inside and stood while we chatted for a moment. Then I sat on the sofa, but didn't ask him to join me.

There he stood—my original fantasy. I had dreamed of him for so many years. I'd had him and loved it. Now he was here again. Could I resist him?

He leaned against the doorpost, tried to act casual, and questioned me about my date. I attempted to tell him about Jesus and the unconditional love available to him. He got agitated, as did I.

Tough love is what he needs, I thought in my new Christian exuberance.

"You know, I don't know why Jesus even bothered to die for people like you," I said. "You don't appreciate the fact He was beaten and hung on a cross for your sins."

"Leave it at church," he retorted. "That's not a fact; it's figurative. I'm not going to change my whole life for anyone."

My unloving, fixed response probably made Dan move even further from God.

"Yep. I don't know why He even wasted His time dying for people like you."

With an exaggerated, sarcastic wish for my happiness with my God, he left, slamming the door with all his strength, shaking the entire mobile home. My children were awakened and ran into the living room frightened.

"What's wrong, Mommy? Did you slam the door? What's wrong?"

I held them next to me. "Oh, don't worry. It was just Dan. He's angry. He doesn't want Jesus in his heart, and he got mad and slammed the door."

"Is he coming back?"

"No. No, I don't think we'll see him again. Don't worry; he's just mad. He'll get over it. He's not coming back. We're alright."

I kissed them and hugged them, thanking God for helping me realize their worth. I was warmed by my ability to chase away their fears and nurture them as a good mother should. I tucked them into bed and read my Bible for a while before going to bed myself.

Chapter Thirty-Seven: He Wouldn't Let Me Go

Satan wouldn't give up without a fight.

The Burning Bed, a television movie starring Farrah Fawcett, was on one weekend. It was based on a true story, adapted from a book by Faith McNulty, about Francine Hughes, an abused wife who killed her husband. I found it terrifying and somewhat relatable.

I'd asked Dace in a letter if he'd seen it. In his return correspondence, he mocked the movie and me. He ridiculed the notion that I might have felt a connection to the battered wife portrayed.

"I never punched you and never sent you to the hospital. You're delusional. (di loo' zhun al – a false belief or opinion that is contrary to fact or reality)"

There was a time when I believed him. As a brainwashed wife, I'd thought that if a fist wasn't involved, it wasn't really wife beating. Chipped tooth, bloody head, and bruises aside, I wasn't to feel like a victim.

Now there was enough space and time between us for my mind to clear and I realized that wasn't true. Mistreatment can come in a variety of methods. Open hand slaps, choking, kicking, or closed-fist punches—it was all abusive.

It was true that he had never struck me with his fist. It was also true that I'd never been hospitalized. However, Francine Hughes stayed with her husband for over ten years. I left my husband before our fifth wedding anniversary. Who knows what might have happened if I'd stayed? Bruises can lead to broken bones. Choking and kicking can lead to hospital visits—or worse. Furthermore, for years I'd prayed for God to kill him or give me courage to do it myself. I just wanted my misery to end and didn't think I could escape alive. I secretly envied Hughes' courage to murder her husband, as portrayed in the film.

Now I was sorry I'd asked him if he'd watched the picture. As I read his mocking response, old wounds opened again. The letter sat in my lap as flashbacks of his physical attacks on me pervaded my thoughts.

When I heard the commercials for a television rerun, something inside me snapped. In classic "first-degree murder" fashion, I planned a night of getting drunk while I watched The Burning Bed. It was a planned personal pity party.

As if in a fog, I drove to the liquor store. For the only time in my life, I left my children in the car while I went into a store. They sat alone in my Ford Escort, with the "God Loves You" bumper sticker on the rear bumper, in the parking lot of the booze store, as I bought a pint of Tanqueray gin and a bottle of tonic water. My old favorite of "Tanqueray and tonic with a twist of lemon not lime, please" was going to happen in my own home—in my renewed life.

I moved in robot-like fashion as if on auto-pilot as I put the kids to bed early, turned on the TV, and proceeded to drink myself into a stupor. I didn't see the entire movie.

I remember lying on the carpet in the living room, being sick, with the sounds of Farrah Faucet screaming in the background.

The thin shag carpeting in my living room didn't insulate the floor very well and the cold air that circulated under our mobile home chilled my body.

As I lay there in my mess, I felt the warmth of a hug. I clearly sensed someone cradling me. It was as if arms were through the floor, wrapped around my shoulders, holding me tight. In my spirit, I heard the Lord say, "It's alright. I understand and I'm here with you. It's alright—I love you."

I felt overwhelming love—unconditional love.

When I woke up it was early morning and I was still on the floor. I could hear the children playing in their bedrooms. They always came out in the morning. This morning, however, they did not. I breathed a quick prayer of thanksgiving.

I had to get moving so they wouldn't find me in that condition. I dragged myself up. My long hair stuck to my face and neck. I quietly staggered into my bathroom, washed my face off and pulled my hair back. I crept back into the living room to clean up the mess. There was a little gin left in the bottle and I poured it down the kitchen sink.

Without letting the kids know I was awake, I snuck into the bathroom down the hall to take a shower. My head was pounding and my body ached. As I stood under the hot water washing the filth of the previous night's sin off of me physically, I cried out to God spiritually. In silence, consumed with shame and guilt, I wept.

How did I let Satan win? Why did I knowingly drive to the store, leave my beloved kids in the car, exposing my bumper sticker—and God—to ridicule, outside the liquor store? Why did I premeditatedly get drunk? I am so, so sorry God. I am so ashamed.

I shook with sorrow as I sobbed and leaned against the wall of the shower. No punishment would be worse than how I felt at that moment.

And yet, He loved me still.

The condemnation I perceived was not from God. I'd lived for the evil one for years and he wasn't giving up without a fight. I allowed the enemy to taunt me and try to convince me I was a failure and shouldn't even try to live a Christian life.

Nonetheless, God held me, forgave me, and gave me strength to fight future temptations.

Jerry came to my house the following weekend. He said he had almost come over the previous weekend because he was available sooner than he'd expected. He said at the last minute he'd changed his mind. He didn't know why. He just did.

Months later when I told him about my planned pity party puke-a-thon, I said I'd lain on the living room floor all night. I was visible through the small rectangular window in the door. I asked him what he would've done if he'd seen me like that. He said he wouldn't have returned.

I also asked him, if I'd been pregnant from my time with Dan, when we heard a voice say, "Let there be a child conceived," if he would have dated me. He said he would not have dated a single woman who got pregnant while professing Christianity.

God had my back. I wouldn't put Him to the test again. My desire is to please Him. I have not had a drink since. Except one time . . .

Jerry wanted me to meet his family. Carrie babysat, and he took me to his parents' house in Niles, Ohio. His sister and brother-in-law from Beaver Falls, Pennsylvania, came over, as did his other sister and brother and their spouses, from Niles.

Ron, his brother-in-law from Pennsylvania, owned a grocery store. He fancied himself quite the weight-guessing expert and asked me how much I weighed.

I said, "I don't know. One twenty? One twenty-five?"

He lifted and sort of shook me, then plopped me back down. "One twenty-five, I'd say."

Embarrassed, I wanted to be anywhere but there.

We drove to Pittsburgh to a Samurai Japanese steakhouse. I loved the ambiance. The Asian décor and grill seating thrilled me. The chef sliced and tossed, grilled and steamed our food. With a quick flip of his cooking tools, our meals landed on our plates—a delightful show.

Then they brought out the sake, an alcoholic beverage made from rice.

I can't drink that! I fretted.

My heart raced when they passed the bottle around, filling each little sake glass. They all looked at me. I inhaled deeply to regulate my breathing. I smiled and took a quick sip.

"Oh, it cleared my sinuses!" They laughed, and I left the rest in the glass.

The next time we got together, we went to an Italian restaurant. That seemed more natural to me since they were Italian. The server poured red wine into each glass.

And these people call themselves Christians? I judged them from my dogmatic world of young Christianity.

In the course of the evening, I switched my full glass with the empty glass belonging to Craig, the brother-in-law beside me. He didn't notice.

I was amused to learn later that he joked with Jerry's mother. "Yeah, that Kelly's a nice girl. Too bad she has such a drinking problem."

If only he knew, I think he'd be surprised! Or would he? Maybe he saw me at the gentlemen's club. He is a salesman, and salesmen take clients there. Hmmm. I have to tell Jerry.

Chapter Thirty-Eight: Gifts

I was quickly falling in love with Jerry. *It's now or never*, I thought. *I'd better tell him about my past. Otherwise it will hurt too much when he leaves me.*

He came over for dinner, and I fought a nervous stomach throughout the evening. After I put the kids to bed, we sat on the couch.

"Um, I have something to tell you." I was uneasy, already ashamed and worried he would judge me harshly. Surely, he'd leave after I shared my history.

Would he depart angry, slamming the door like Dan did? Alternatively, would he go away dejected as Russ did after I told him I'd slept with my ex-husband?

I sat sideways on the couch beside my guest and steadied my breathing.

He looked concerned. "What is it?"

Speaking slowly and deliberately, I said, "There are things in my past I think you should know."

"Go ahead. I'm listening."

I proceeded to tell him about the many men in my life, my last time with Dace, and my job at the gentlemen's club. I didn't go into detail, but was straightforward with him, spilling out most of the skeletons in my closet.

"Come here." He pulled me close and held me. I heard him sniffling. He was crying. I held onto him, my eyes widened until I thought my eyeballs would fall out.

Who was this guy? I had laid out most of my darkest, ugliest secrets, and he hugged me and cried. Again, I forced myself to breathe.

A couple minutes later, he pulled back and looked at me.

"Why are you crying?" I inquired. He hugged me again.

"You poor thing," he whispered. "You've been through so much."

That sealed it. I wanted to marry this guy. Frankly, at that moment, I wanted to sleep with him.

We talked for a while and he assured me he didn't view me in a different way, except he admired my strength. What I perceived as weaknesses, he viewed as obstacles I had overcome. Amazing. Just amazing.

After a wonderful deep kiss, Jerry left with the promise to return the following week. He was one man whose word was true.

∞∞∞∞∞∞∞∞∞∞∞

The principal often joined us for dinner or dessert following school functions. We chaperoned student outings for many of our dates. We enjoyed roller skating, bowling, attending banquets, and other fun nights. I fell deeply in love with him.

I prayed, "God, please show Jerry that he should marry me." It was nice to pray about a man without asking God to kill him.

He'd been single for over six years, and the women at his church gave him baked goods throughout the year and knitted scarves for him at Christmas. He loved it and ate it up. Still, I knew I was the one for him.

In my mind, I saw a vision of me taking down a wall, one brick at a time. That thought made me smile since he worked as a brick and stone mason during the summers. God impressed on me that I had to be patient, but it was difficult.

Our relationship became more intimate, and I went on the birth control pill. One evening when the kids were snoozing, I cuddled up beside my man on the couch.

"I'm on the Pill now," I cooed.

He pulled away and said matter-of-factly, "You didn't need to do that because of me. I'm not going to have intercourse until I'm married."

Humiliated, I rattled off some spin about taking the Pill to help alleviate my menstrual cramps and regulate my period. Although not fooled, he didn't press it. My face burned red.

I went off the Pill. What was the point? As Cher said, wearing one-piece footie pajamas to close the 1975 debut of *Cher*, her post Sonny & Cher solo television show, "Why wear a parachute if you're not going to fly?"

After we'd been dating a few months, while cleaning, I found that "pro-con" list. I marveled at the goodness of the Lord as I read the qualifications of Mr. Just-Right-For-Me. Jerry had every single requirement. He even had every drawback written down. I struggled to be patient. *When will he see I'm the one for him?*

Christmas was coming and my finances got worse. I struggled to pay my bills and worried Star and Sam would be terribly disappointed on Christmas morning. The previous year there were tons of presents. This holiday, I was unemployed and bankrupt.

However, this year we had Jesus. I prayerfully sorted through the aspects of my life, deciding what must go and what could stay. I told my kids that Christmas is about the birth of Baby Jesus and not about Santa Claus.

They latched on to our new, positive way of life with total abandon. Still, being children, I wasn't sure how they'd take the information. To my surprise, there were no tears. We would still have a tree and presents. The real gift was the overwhelming love that filled our home and the Gift that would never leave—Jesus.

I instructed them not to share their new knowledge. "The other kids might believe in Santa, and we don't want to ruin it for them."

Telling my parents would be another story. Afraid they'd be angry that I told Star and Sam the truth, I coached them to keep the secret.

"Let's not tell Gramma that we know there is no Santa Clause, okay?"

When we visited my parents, Mom said, "What do you kids want Santa to bring you this year?"

Eager to share his news, my little chatterbox said, "Oh, there is no Santa."

Star quickly retorted, "Sammy, hush! Gramma doesn't know!"

While not pleased, my parents didn't say anything to me about it.

One snowy morning, my son and I had to check into the WIC office. It was in the upper level of an old building in Chardon. I held his hand as we slowly ascended the steep, icy stairs. Once in the office I realized I'd left the paperwork in my car.

The women working in the small area greeted us warmly when we entered.

"Could I please leave Samuel here while I run to my car to get my papers?"

"That would be fine."

They engaged him in conversation while I carefully descended the icy wooden steps. Upon my return, they stared at me in silence. My little boy stood where I'd left him.

"What's going on?" I inquired.

"Well," one woman spoke softly. "We asked Samuel what he wanted Santa to bring him for Christmas this year . . ." Her silence told the rest of the story.

"Oh, and he *told* you?"

She slowly nodded. "Yes, he told us."

Apparently, he evangelized the ladies in the WIC office. I quickly took care of business and we left. While they certainly didn't see me as Mother of the Year, I was proud he could verbalize the true meaning of Christmas. I felt I was making a positive difference.

Days passed and my tension grew as I prepared for the holiday. With very little money, I had to be imaginative when planning gifts. Again, I realized that poverty breeds creativity. Looking around my house, I found items that were new, nearly new, or could become something else with some effort.

Among my repurposed gifts, I took my great grandmother's antique framed black and white picture depicting a Bible story with Jesus in it. I repainted the frame glossy black and flicked gold paint on it with a brush. Believing someday he would marry me and I'd get it back, I gave it to Jerry for Christmas.

Gifts for my children came from thrift stores. I knew they'd be happy with anything they got, but they were sensitive and would notice if I didn't have a gift to unwrap. I found a little black purse at Goodwill and wrapped it for myself, and tagged it, "From Gramma and Grampa."

The special morning came, and they were thrilled with their presents, even though they knew Santa didn't bring them. I didn't feel poor at all. We were rich because unconditional love filled our hearts. Our living room was warm with heavenly love that chilly Christmas morning.

We later joined my parents for dinner. They more than made up for what I couldn't provide. Among other things, they gave their grandchildren a large plastic rocking horse on springs. They gave me a 19-inch color television set. Before I knew it, the day was over.

That night, after I put the kids to bed, I read Matthew 13 in my Bible. The parable about the sower and the seed touched my soul. I learned the wheat was the good seed sown by Jesus and the weeds are sons of the evil one, Satan. Pondering the meaning, I realized I'd served the evil one long enough. I desperately wanted to be the good seed. I desired all God had for me. I was a poor, single mother with a contrite heart. I prayed for Him to show me how I could become better—a better mom, daughter, sister, and Christian.

Taking out paper and pencil, I did what I'd been doing since a teenager—I poured my feelings out in verse. I applied the words in the parable to my life and spoke to God in the following poem.

Let the Wheat Grow

When all the gifts were in place
And I stood back to see,
What I saw was Your sweet grace
Taking care of me.

All my worrying did no good.
You provide all we need,
We have a home, clothes, and food
And all Your love, indeed!

This Christmas came upon us so fast—
Lack of money made me despair.
But all my worries are now past
Because, Dear Lord, You care.

And when the tree was shining so bright
I felt how much You love me.
I've learned that Your Word was surely right,
And now, Dear Lord, I see.

You take care of all our needs
And You always will, I know;
As long as I keep out the weeds
And let the pure wheat grow.

That turned out to be the best Christmas for my little trio.

Chapter Thirty-Nine: A New Reality

With an ever growing, tangible awareness that I could no longer afford to live in the trailer, my parents offered to make their barn into a tiny house for us.

That barn had been several things in my life. When we were kids, it housed my sister's wild pony and her midget foal.

It had been Mom's women's clothing store when we were teenagers. With no overhead, The Jean Barn offered low prices to anyone willing to venture out to our dirt road.

It had housed my father's antique cleaning and repair business.

I'd hosted slumber parties in the second floor of the barn throughout my teen years, and now it would be home to me and my children.

I was excited to think of shedding the mortgage and monthly trailer lot fee. It couldn't happen fast enough.

Dad put a wooden floor over the cement base in the barn. He partitioned it off to include a living room, kitchen, and bathroom. Upstairs he put rolls of insulation into the rafters of the roof and walls. He built a wall, making two bedrooms. He fashioned a clothing rack out of 2 x 4s and a metal pole. It was rustic, but he made progress. Finally, he and Mom said we could move in.

For months I advertised to sell the mobile home, continually dropping the price. The extras that made it a quality model home made no difference. It was still a two-year-old, single-wide mobile home in a trailer park. At last, a family from Burton Assembly bought it.

My father came home one day to find a pink slip on his back door. It was a Cease and Desist Order. The county building inspector refused to approve transforming the barn into an apartment, saying two families could not share one septic system.

My dad pointed out that several Amish families living along our dirt road had trailers and renovated barns with people living in them on properties zoned for one family each.

It didn't matter—we were pink-slipped.

He stopped work on the barn. He said it was a waste of time since he couldn't install a toilet, tub, or sinks. We stayed in the unfinished building and used my parents' bathroom. That soon grew old and tension rose.

Jerry lived in an apartment in the back of an old farmhouse outside of town. The owners lived in the house and ran the dairy farm. I mustered the courage to ask him if we could occasionally come to his apartment to bathe. He said we could.

Each Thursday evening he was out of town practicing with New Destiny, a Christian singing group with which he sang and played the bass guitar. He said he would leave the key for me in an envelope at school.

The next day I received the envelope when I collected Star from kindergarten. The note inside said, "Here is the key to my apartment. I wish I could give you the key to my heart as easily." He signed it, "You Know What, Jerry."

While it was cute he couldn't even say "Love, Jerry," it just exacerbated my impatience. I knew he was the man God had for me to marry. How long would it take him to acknowledge love for me? I obediently remained silent on the subject.

The kids and I bathed at his apartment about three times a week. It was inconvenient and uncomfortable to use his bathroom this way. Still, to keep the peace at home, we did.

He invited us to dinner one evening and made his specialty—spaghetti. It tasted delicious, and we ate our fill.

I still suffered from colitis, and it didn't take long before I had to get home. We carried my sleeping children out to the car. Our host said, "Have you ever asked God to heal your colitis?"

That hadn't occurred to me. "No, I never thought about it."

"Well, you should ask Him. It's a problem from your old life. You're a new creation in Christ now. You should ask Him to take it away. Just ask."

I looked at him, tilted my head sideways, and thought about what he'd said. "Hmm. Okay, I'll ask. Gotta go. Talk to you later."

Driving home, I remembered asking for Samuel's winter coat and for heat in a cold car.

"He's right," I prayed aloud. "My colitis is from my old life. I am a new creation. God, would You please take away my colitis?"

Instantly, I felt warmth deep within my lower back. By the time I arrived home my symptoms vanished. Indications of colitis were gone forever. All I had to do was ask.

∞∞∞∞∞∞∞∞∞∞∞∞

I had registered with a career placement agency, and they called me about a job in a computer sales office. The people at the agency coached me not to talk about my previous employment history or about money. I understood not mentioning wage because it was their responsibility to negotiate that, but couldn't understand

343

why I shouldn't discuss my skills or previous jobs. After hired, I learned why.

I got lost going to work on my first day. When I arrived, fifteen minutes late, everyone was in a staff meeting. They greeted me, and the boss introduced me.

"This is Kelly, who will replace Shirley."

Sighs, moans, and mournful smiles came my way. I later learned Shirley had committed suicide the previous month. She'd worked in operations at the sales office.

When they explained the details of my new position, I realized why I hadn't been permitted to discuss my job history. I had been a secretary and knew word processing. In operations, I was in way over my head and had no idea how to perform my duties.

About a month after I started the job, I saw everyone stop working and look toward the front door. There stood a short, balding man who appeared disheveled and weary.

I couldn't hear him as he spoke with Norma, the receptionist. His hands were out in front of him, palms up in wonderment, and he cocked his head sideways. Norma touched his arm and shook her head.

The room filled with whispers. "That's her father."

After he left, I learned he was Shirley's father and he wanted to know—again—if she'd ever given any of her co-workers any indication of why she killed herself.

"Did she say anything at all? Did you see any signs?" Those are the questions that are never answered when a loved one commits suicide.

It was sobering to witness the confusion and devastation her death left on those around her. Like giving me a tiny glimpse of life for others if I had killed myself, the Lord spoke loudly through that experience.

The owner of the company was Jewish but practiced EST (Erhard Seminars Training). **(Endnote 3)** An EST recruiter, he often made his employees attend seminars that utilized brainwashing techniques.

My co-workers relayed accounts of EST meetings wherein leaders' vehicles blocked their vehicles in so they couldn't leave. They said it was common practice for the organizers to pack attendees into a small room and turn the heat to unbearable temperatures, and then the air conditioning until they thought they'd freeze. They said the leaders yelled at them, called them names, and afforded minimal restroom breaks during sixteen-hour sessions. I dreaded the day I would be told I'd have to attend such a seminar.

Could the strange EST practices have influenced my predecessor and her decision to die?

∞∞∞∞∞∞∞∞∞∞∞∞

I didn't have a telephone in the barn, and one evening Jerry came over after the children were in bed. I was pleased to see him.

"What a nice surprise! Come sit beside me and watch television."

"Kelly, would you mind shutting the TV off?"

"Of course." I snapped it off. "What's up?"

He held my hands, cleared his throat, and slid on the couch toward me. R-I-I-I-P! The spring that poked just below the fabric of my low-quality mobile home sofa, caught his trousers. He refused to acknowledge the tear and proceeded to sing "Walk Hand in Hand."

Thoughts ricocheted through my mind. *I think he's proposing to me! He tore his pants. Ignore that!*

He sang the first verse with sincerity. He had such a nice singing voice. But the rip!

Think about death and famine. Death and famine.

Singing about our love being like a harmonious song, his eyes twinkled.

Don't laugh. Don't laugh.

As he sang out about being with me always, my heart leapt. But the rip!

Crescendo! Those poor starving people!

He sang the chorus beautifully, declaring his desire to walk hand in hand with me. When finished, he paused and smiled.

"That was beautiful. I'm sorry you ripped your pants."

"Don't worry about that. Kelly Jean Easton, will you be my wife?" He put a beautiful, modest diamond engagement ring on my finger.

"I'd love to!" I threw my arms around him and smiled until I thought my face would split. Not because he tore his pants, but because I knew God fulfilled His promise to me, and Jerry was listening to Him.

We snuggled on my sofa and talked softly.

"What would you think about a Christmas wedding?" he asked. The thought of having a wedding anniversary at Christmastime made me feel cheated. The thought of Thanksgiving without Jerry as my husband made me feel sad. The thought of living in that freezing barn until late December made me shiver.

"How about just before Thanksgiving? That way we could spend Christmas as a family." He liked that idea.

"That doesn't leave you much time to plan though." He was right.

The next day at work I couldn't stop looking at my ring, nor could I stop smiling. Everyone congratulated me.

∞∞∞∞∞∞∞∞∞∞∞

When I was first hired at the computer sales company, my boss said one evening every three months I'd have to stay until 9 p.m. to close out the quarter. However, one weekend each month I worked until midnight or later. That left me in a pickle with my babysitter.

The company added salt to my wound when they said I couldn't claim those hours for extra pay because I was exempt. My gut burned more than ever.

While visiting the doctor for my tummy complaints, he told me he wouldn't prescribe anymore Tagamet.

"Whatever it is in your life that is causing you to have stomach problems, get rid of it."

How could I? How could I not? My belly hurt more and more. I remembered the diagnosis of an ulcer when I was eighteen. God hadn't healed that and I didn't want to enter into a marriage with health issues.

Between the words of the doctor, my problem with late nights and babysitters, and the threat of having to attend an EST recruiting meeting, I decided it best to give my notice.

By the next month, I once again registered for welfare benefits. I worked temporary office jobs and got Medicaid only, but I was happy because I was getting married to the man of my dreams!

Jerry suggested we seek premarital counseling at a Christian therapy center in Akron called Emerge Ministries. I was nervous about it.

"What if they tell us we shouldn't get married?"

"Why would they?" He was certain about his decision to marry me and believed the counseling would help ensure a successful marriage.

Our counselor had us take the Minnesota Multiphasic Personality Inventory (MMPI). The questionnaire had hundreds of questions ranging from our dreams to physical issues.

We learned that Jerry had exhausted his patience in his first marriage and I had exhausted my submission. The doctor said because my fiancé was a leader all day at work, perhaps he wouldn't want to make decisions or lead at home. He offered suggestions, and we often referred to the sessions. Going there was a good idea.

Plans for a small wedding could continue with confidence the marriage to follow would succeed.

One Saturday we drove to the home of the printer to pick up the invitations we had ordered. We planned to run in, get them, and come right back out. Star and Samuel were in seatbelts in the rear seat of Jerry's new used Plymouth Reliant K car.

"You kids stay buckled in. We'll be right out."

The printer wanted us to sit and look the invitations over. Soon my daughter ran through the door, too hysterical to make sense. Between sobs we understood, "Sammy," "pulled the handle," "car rolled back," and "hit a tree."

We ran outside to see the blue Reliant on the edge of a ravine, resting on a small tree.

Samuel had unbuckled himself, hopped into the front seat, released the emergency brake, and put the car into neutral. The car rolled backward with both children inside. It headed toward the ravine, but curved and hit a tree measuring four inches in diameter. There it sat with the tree in the middle of the bumper. The bumper and trunk were dented. My son was hysterical, and I got him out of the car.

Star cried, "I saw the tree coming closer and closer and couldn't stop! We hit it and I got out to go tell you!"

Jerry and the print shop owner assessed the situation. My fiancé pulled the car onto the driveway. The children and I waited under a tree. We knelt, and I thanked the Lord for protecting them.

What would Jerry do now? This was a test, and I feared the outcome. The invitations were printed, but I would cancel the wedding if he handled this with anger and abuse.

We gathered our invitations, thanked the man, and got into the car.

I was worried. "What are you going to do?"

"I want to wait to see what my insurance guy says."

It pleased me that he didn't lash out in anger. Perhaps he put on a calm show for the printer. I was still apprehensive.

Once we reached Jerry's apartment, he called his insurance representative. After a short discussion and a polite chuckle, he hung up.

"Okay, Samuel. Come here."

This is it. If he lays one hand on him for this, I'm bookin'.

I knew Sammy's disobedience caused the accident. I also knew it was our fault for leaving them alone in the car. He was a curious little daredevil, and I didn't think he deserved a spanking for this.

"Samuel, my insurance man said it's covered. I'll have to pay some money to have it fixed. You know you did wrong, don't you?"

"Yes." My son was hesitant. I wondered if he remembered Dace's temper.

"You know you have to be punished, don't you?"

His chin began to quiver. "Yes."

"I'm going to discuss it with your mother, but you will be punished for this, Sam. I'm not going to spank you because I know we shouldn't have left you and Star in the car alone. We were in there longer than we planned to be anyway. You go play with your sister while I talk with your mom."

Sammy ended up with two weeks without television, something hard for a four-year-old who loved cartoons.

After dating men who treated my kids with disrespect, this guy had to pass this huge test. I praised God he passed.

The wedding plans continued. I contacted the sweet woman who owned the house with the hardwood floors that Dace and I had lived in. Mrs. Willis had always been kind to me, Mustang banishment notwithstanding. I remembered she made delicious stuffed cabbage rolls.

While visiting her one day, she made an enormous meatloaf—something I'd never seen. She added several cups of breadcrumbs to stretch it. A helpful lesson learned.

"Well, honey, I'll make the cabbage rolls for you, but you have to buy the ground beef. I'll supply the other ingredients." Sounded fair to me.

Next, I contacted Suzie's mother. She made delicious Hungarian pastries and cakes. When I asked if she could make my wedding cake, she not only agreed, but insisted it be our gift from her and her husband.

We wanted chicken and, of course, pasta. I ordered several cases of chickens. To keep the price down, Jerry and I cut them ourselves, although neither of us knew how. As a result, we offered strange new cuts we affectionately referred to as "breastwings."

350

His family made Italian cookies and pans of lasagna. He had friends at church who owned a catering business and volunteered to serve, as their gift to us. Other church members offered to help with the decorations, set up, and tear down.

We were excited as we began to formulate our plans. We had attended Jerry's church for awhile by then. They had just redecorated the sanctuary, and the colors would match our chosen wedding colors beautifully— mauve and gray.

Sophia was going to come from Wisconsin to be my maid of honor. Lisa, Dawn, and Mel agreed to be bridesmaids. Mrs. Wismon said if we would supply the fabric, she would make all of the dresses for the wedding as a gift to us. There was a lady at church with the singing voice of an angel, who agreed to sing at the wedding.

One of the men agreed to be our photographer. The groom's brother would be his best man. Two of his bandmates and his best friend, Roy, would be groomsmen. Of course Star and Samuel would be flower girl and ring bearer. I was overwhelmed by the outpouring of love.

"We have loved Jerry for six years," the soloist said. "We've seen him serve at the church and school all this time. We love him and have come to love you and your kids too."

Chapter Forty: Unexpected Foes

Jerry's pastor was a recent Bible college graduate and rigid in his beliefs. Pete had lived with him after completing his degree. Pete married Maryann and they both taught for Jerry at the school. His mother-in-law had been the secretary. His sister-in-law and her husband, Roy, Jerry's best friends, led the singles' group at church. They were the ones who told him of my interest in him. While those involved seemed to love us, pride got in the way.

Pete said since ours was a remarriage, he must contact Jerry's former wife. He said he called her and she said she'd always love her ex-husband. That was it—he wouldn't marry us, nor could we use "his" church. Jerry was furious. I was hurt.

The pastor had performed the marriage ceremony for his mother-in-law and her husband, both previously divorced. However, he said the principal couldn't remarry. Further, if he did, they wouldn't renew his contract at the school.

The young man quoted 1 Timothy 3:2 and Titus 1:6 from the Bible wherein the rules for deacons, or leaders, list "the husband of one wife."

My fiancé argued the scripture verses meant one wife at a time—a statement against bigamy. But no—Pete dug his heels in and made his opinion known to everyone. Soon people started dropping out of the wedding party.

"My voice is a gift," the soloist stated. "I have to be careful where I sing, or the Lord will remove His anointing."

Jerry contacted the former pastor/school administrator, Rev. Koveto. He said he would not marry us because doing so might step on Pete's toes. He said if we'd asked him first, he would have, but couldn't now.

The photographer backed out. Dawn backed out. My own sister backed out. Roy reluctantly backed out.

"I have to keep the peace at home, Jer,"

My fiancé said we would "storm heaven" and God would make Pete change his mind.

Apparently, God wanted us to walk through that trial because nothing changed. The pastor said we should wait until Jerry's former wife died. In an attempt at humor, he said Jerry could kill her.

"So if I killed my ex-wife and went to prison, when I got out you'd marry us then?"

With a condescending smirk, Pete said, "Yes."

I was steamed when Jerry relayed the conversation.

"And meanwhile what are we supposed to do?"

"Pete said we're supposed to just wait and date."

"What would that do to the kids?"

"Well, obviously we're not going to do that," he tried to calm me down. "That's just stupid."

We sent out wedding invitations. Many RSVP cards returned marked "no" without a name on them. One had "NO!" scrawled across the top in thick red marker, mailed from Cleveland for anonymity.

"Coward."

It was hard to go to church. I hated people there, especially Pete and Maryann. Their hypocrisy was insufferable. Jerry insisted we continue to attend each Sunday morning to show we had nothing to hide.

"We have heard God and are doing what we know is right."

Still, on Sundays before I entered the church, I begged Jesus to help me.

"Lord, please be my bandage."

He whispered into my spirit, "I won't be your bandage. I will be your Healing Balm." I held on to that statement, anticipating the day when the sting of rejection would subside.

I struggled to deal with the duplicitous people. Jerry had been my first encounter with a born-again Christian man. I thought they'd be like him—transparent and steadfast in their faith. Not so.

Christians disillusioned me. Yet, something in me wouldn't let me run away from God. I kept my eyes on Him and His goodness and tried to ignore the people.

My cousin Lisa became my maid of honor, Mrs. Wismon a bridesmaid, and another friend became a groomsman. The groom's sister played the piano, and another friend whom he'd known for years, sang beautifully.

Years earlier, Jerry had met a Baptist minister, whom he respected. He met with us, we explained our position, and he agreed with our interpretation of the scriptures. He consented to marry us—but where? Retired, he had no church.

Jerry had another friend whose father pastored a Mennonite congregation. He graciously opened his doors to us. So, we were two Pentecostals married by a Baptist minister in a Mennonite church.

We chose Hebrews 11 for the message. It speaks of faith and reflected us going against man and walking in trust. We had prayed—stormed heaven. Still, while we knew we were right in our decision to proceed with the wedding, we moved in direct opposition to man's ego and ruling.

My groom chose to sing in the wedding ceremony. We would speak from our hearts to one another. He'd sing to me, and the minister would preach on Hebrews 11. We'd say the traditional marriage vows, with "promise to love, honor, and respect" replacing "promise to love, honor, and obey."

We planned to sing "Household of Faith" together. I had never sung in front of people. My voice wasn't great, and Jerry practiced with me at church one evening.

The kids were rowdy that night, and Jerry's patience wore thin. Although we told them to sit in the pews and not run around, the darkness and emptiness of the sanctuary was too tempting. Star laughed and laughed at her silly brother scooting on the floor under the pews.

Jerry paused, put the microphone onto the stand, and came down just as Samuel scooted out into the aisle. The little boy started to get up, and the angry man yelled, "No, you just stay there." He grabbed Sam's coat from the pew and threw it on top of him. "Stay there!"

A mixture of fear and anger pounded at my chest. My son was visibly frightened, and the thought of someone scaring my kids boiled my blood. I tried to say something about it, and Jerry snapped, "Let's just practice this one more time and get out of here."

My mind raced, and I cried out to God. *What does this mean? Is Jerry going to be mean to my kids? He was nice when Sammy wrecked his car. Do I leave? Oh God, should I leave?*

Although just days from the wedding, I could still call it off. I sensed God calm my spirit. Although fighting doubt, I began to feel peace and relaxed. Unprompted, Jerry later apologized to my son for losing his temper.

I tucked a promise to myself into the back of my mind. I vowed to divorce him if he proved to be someone other than the man I believed him to be; if he got mean with my children, I'd kick him to the curb right away. I knew I could.

With the wedding approaching, I had to choose a birth control. Jerry convinced me five children were all we could handle financially. I'd looked up to him as a wise and educated man, so I complied. Just two weeks before the special day, I had a tubal ligation, and regretted it for years to come.

I'd always wanted at least three children. Years earlier I'd made a pact with Dace that if I wasn't remarried by age twenty-five, he'd father another baby with me. I wanted all the children to look alike and assured him he wouldn't have to support the third one any more than he supported his first two.

When I turned twenty-five, I worried about him popping up ready to lend a willing swimmer for the cause. Thankfully, he didn't come back.

∞∞∞∞∞∞∞∞∞∞∞∞

Jerry and I had our first date in November, and were married the following November. The ceremony was precious and evangelical. Our families were there with us. The people who attended from the school and church proved to be true friends.

The children and I moved into Jerry's little farmhouse apartment. It was cozy, and we enjoyed life as a family.

I got closer to God and prayed our marriage would work. I had been too submissive when with Dace — submissive into sin. Although in charge when alone, I hadn't been successful in that capacity either. Balance would be a challenge. I continued to read the Bible, pray, and listen for God's guidance to find success as a Christian wife.

I looked forward to having a voice in decisions but not making all of them. The counselor at Emerge said if Jerry and I drew near to God, we'd get closer to each other, as points of a triangle, with God at the top. It was comforting being part of a team.

Not long after the wedding, the school board held a meeting open to the public. The rumors spread that they weren't going to renew the principal's contract. One of Jerry's friends, a teacher, came forward and requested the job. That hurt us both.

The gathering was for people to express their opinions. Pete spoke, and no one opposed him. Some people said kind things about Jerry, and others made surprisingly cruel remarks. Some who'd been his friends for years stood against him.

It was a lesson in self-control for me, as I focused on my scribbled notes and bit my tongue. If viewed with spiritual vision, we'd have been seen exiting the building limping and bleeding. Still, God promised to restore us.

Amidst the harsh reality of Christians wounding Christians and then shooting them, figuratively, leaving them to die spiritually, God's unconditional love surrounded us. Although I wanted to run from the caustic people, the thought of running from God didn't cross my mind. He'd proven Himself to me so thoroughly; I knew running to Him was the only solution. He didn't disappoint and brought comfort daily.

∞∞∞∞∞∞∞∞∞∞∞∞

We moved to Rochester, New York, where my new husband worked as the principal of a larger Christian school and we both volunteered in the church.

Star and Samuel love Jerry, who is the best daddy anyone could ask for. He's always loved them as his own and was happy for the opportunity to adopt them.

Thrown into the deep end of Christianity, I learned that, despite decisions to accept Jesus into their lives, the basic personalities of some people remain the same. Those who are unscrupulous before they accept Jesus into their hearts, remain that way if they don't fully commit their lives to God and allow Him to change them.

Chapter Forty-One: Nothing New Under the Sun

Sometimes I doubted my ability to live a clean life. When I saw a woman light a cigarette, I craved one. When I smelled the sweet aroma of marijuana outside, I wanted to smoke a joint. I often felt vulnerable.

Negative feelings about my shortcomings clouded my thoughts. Even without Dace's voice barking in my head, I felt I couldn't do anything right . . . or good enough. It was all self-imposed as Jerry was supportive and loving.

In the Bible it says there is nothing new under the sun. I learned when my thoughts were convicting, they were from God. His sweet Holy Spirit let me know when I strayed off the path.

However, when my thoughts were condemning, they were from Satan. He didn't want to see me happy, and he certainly didn't want me to serve God. If he could get me to feel hopeless and inadequate, maybe I'd walk away from God. He's been doing that since the beginning of time. It's not a fresh ploy.

I studied the Bible for answers to my questions and guidance for my life. I hungered for a deeper relationship with Jesus. I wanted to be closer to Him every day and realized I need Him like I need oxygen. I learned He loves me the same whether I perceive my day as successful or not. I couldn't make Him love me more—or less.

Yet still. Still there were times when I listened to a negative voice in my head, taunting me until I wept.

But you were a stripper. How can God love you? Your sexual sins span years, from losing your virginity at thirteen to allowing your husband to talk you into a ménage a' trois.

How can God forgive that? You love the smell of marijuana. God knows your temptations. Do you really think He overlooks that? You call yourself a Christian? Look at all you've done! You said you became a Christian when you were thirteen and you didn't. You weren't a Christian then and you aren't a Christian now, and God does not love you.

∞∞∞∞∞∞∞∞∞∞∞

One day while I listened to the mocking voice in my head and doubted my salvation, I read about Jesus being our mediator. It's only through Him we can come to God, and He represents us to God, like a lawyer would.

First John 2:1 says, "My dear children, I write this to you so that you will not sin. But if anybody does sin, we have an advocate with the Father—Jesus Christ, the Righteous One."

That night, I wrote this poem:

My Attorney

I stood there waiting to see
just what my Attorney would say.
How would He stick up for me
when so often I didn't obey?

All those times I knew the Law
and refused to obey the commands.
All those times I clearly saw
I was taking it into my own hands.

My Attorney waited patiently for His turn.
I could see the deep love in His eyes.
Fearfully I began to yearn

360

to take back years of lies!

How could He represent me like this?
I had always failed, it seemed.
I'd gone along in disobedient bliss,
often forgetting I was on His team.

So many times I had to cry out again,
because I had strayed away.
But my Attorney had always remained my Friend
all my life—and still today.

"It is her turn now," the Judge called out.
I was petrified as I looked on.
"Please forgive me!" I wanted to shout.
But my Attorney said that would be wrong.

My Attorney approached the bench, and all the while
I sat watching and waiting in fear.
Then the Judge said, "Stand up, My child.
Stand up and come up here."

I looked at my Attorney standing up there.
I slowly came forward too.
He whispered to me, "Don't worry, He's fair.
And remember He loves you too!"

I swallowed hard and began to speak,
but the Judge said to be still.
My legs were shaking and I felt weak
when He asked how I'd handled free will.

My Attorney, with a gentle Spirit so sweet,
shared some unwise decisions I'd made.

361

And as I sat in the judgment seat
I heard of the times I hadn't obeyed.

When He was through with the truth that hurt,
about all the times I had stumbled,
He said the results had made me more alert
and gave me a spirit that was humbled.

As I watched my Attorney tell the Judge about me,
as I saw the genuine love in His eyes,
it was suddenly very clear to see
that He loved me more than I ever realized.

This Friend Who had always helped me out,
Who had always been there when I cried,
was now pleading my case and, without a doubt,
still believed in me—even after I'd died.

Now He was finished pleading my case,
and as we waited for the verdict to come,
my Attorney turned and, face to face,
said, "Well, My sister, I'm done."

He said, "Because you believed in Me
and accepted Me into your heart;
because you strived to live sin-free,
from Me you will never depart."

The Judge pounded His gavel once, then again,
as I stood there as still as stone.
He said, "Because you kept My Son as your Personal
Friend,
welcome My child, you're home."

362

I put my pen down, dropped my head, and wept. Jesus was my Mediator—my Attorney. With Him representing me to God the Father, I knew I was heaven bound. Now my job was to represent Jesus to the world the best I could. Mistakes would happen, but I would always do my best and confess when I blew it. And He would never stop loving me. That's a promise.

Chapter Forty-Two: Reflection—God in the Midst of the Storm

Where had Jesus been when I was in that chaotic lifestyle? Where was His love?

The thought that God loved me didn't cross my mind as I gasped for air when Dace's hands were gripped around my throat. An angry man and a misogynist—he hated women.

If only he'd come with a list of words to avoid or a manual of what not to do in his presence. With such information I might have escaped the damage of brainwashing and the years of bruises and scars that go deeper than the eye can see.

Why didn't God give me a heads-up? Why did He allow me to stumble into situation after situation that just fueled this man's rage?

Nope, I never felt any love—from anyone—during those times.

Growing up in a Congregational church, I'd heard Jesus loves the little children. Being pregnant and unmarried at eighteen is a crash course in growing up. No little children there—just a bride with morning sickness.

Within two weeks of saying "I do," I was ducking swings. Pregnancy didn't change that. A newborn didn't change that. A second pregnancy didn't change it either. One can be hit in the head and told she's nothing for just so long before she believes it and can't think clearly.

When in the throes of abuse, self-preservation and protecting my kids were foremost in my thoughts. If God tried to speak to me, I couldn't hear Him. It was me who was lost, not Him.

I was lost when I screamed for my tormentor to "please stop!" I was lost when forced out of bed to wash dishes at 2 a.m. I was lost when made to sleep on the couch on icy northern winter nights with no pillows or blankets; lost when I begged him to "just kill me and get it over with." I was desperately lost when spitting tooth bits, head was bleeding, and I couldn't raise my arms because of the pain.

I'm a firm believer that often one must be totally off course before finding the way home, and I was adrift.

What finally made me leave? After years of accepting the bait and switch of "I've changed" in hope of a normal life, something in me raised up as a dragon rises out of a misty bog in a fairytale, spewing fire onto a marauding villain.

I fought back. Satan didn't want me to be brave and leave a marriage of disparagement and harm that would crush the spirits and future of my children and me. What made me bold? The sheer will to live? Self-perseveration? Temporary insanity? Call it what you will, but strike back I did. Surely God guided my actions. With one cloudy decision that stuck, I grabbed my babies and fled. I left my abuser. That is how I retaliated, finally putting an end to the notion of murder.

With miles between us, my mind could focus. With months between us, my plans could be established. And with violence behind me, I could hear God. With God in my mind, I could learn about Jesus. And with Jesus in my heart, I could grow in Him.

God had always been with me. I may not have felt Him, but He was there. He saved me from many things and stayed with me through everything.

In the Bible, Proverbs 22:24-25 says, "Do not make friends with a hot-tempered person, do not associate with one easily angered, or you may learn their ways and get yourself ensnared." (NIV)

Proverbs 29:22, "An angry person stirs up conflict, and a hot-tempered person commits many sins." (NIV)

If anyone sins against you in violence or verbal abuse, remember Jesus does not want you in that position. Tell someone. Your Christian sisters will listen to you. Call a friend. Call the church. Call your local battered women's shelter or the Salvation Army. Just call.

Remember, as stated in I Corinthians 13:5, "[Love] does not dishonor others, it is not self-seeking, it is not easily angered, it keeps no record of wrongs." (NIV)

Going from victim to victor is the glorious result of the healing offered through the love of Jesus. I applied the promise God made to His people in Jeremiah 30:17 to myself. "For I will restore you to health and I will heal you of your wounds, declares the Lord." (NASB)

God has great plans for your future and that of your children. Be bold and yield to His will for your life. Remember, "A fool vents all of his anger, but a wise man brings himself under control." (Proverbs 29:11 WEB).

Keep your head. Grab your kids and get to safety. The Lord loves women and wants us to be safe.

Chapter Forty-Three: Your Best Decision Yet

I'd learned about Jesus as a child in Sunday school. I met Him personally as a broke and broken single mother of two preschoolers. When I confessed I needed Jesus to take over the mess I'd made of my family, I found the love I'd longed for all my days. I found peace in knowing I didn't have to do everything all on my own. I found freedom in desiring to please God and not people.

When I could afford to have my chipped tooth fixed, I chose not to. By then I'd come to appreciate the salvation afforded the kids and me; salvation not just from the monster they once called Daddy, but also the salvation of our souls by our loving Lord, Jesus Christ. That chipped tooth stands as a statement of God's goodness in our lives.

While some may not understand the life we escaped, I realize many—too many—do. Countless people know the fear, humiliation, pain, loneliness, and uncertainty of living with someone who is volatile and mean.

If that's you, imagine this: You and I are walking along a road and I'm in front of you. I step into a hole and fall. I turn around and warn you, "Watch out for that hole!"

That's what I'm doing here. If you're dating someone unpredictable and explosive, it's not too late to leave. If you need help to break the relationship off, secure that first. Bring a respected authority figure to accompany you while you officially break up with your partner.

If you're married, seek help. Call someone. Make a plan. Have a trusted person ready to accept you and your children at a moment's notice. Keep pajamas and toothbrushes there.

You do not have to kill your abuser to be free. The way you retaliate is to leave. There is help for you! Please see the list of referrals in the back of this book.

∞∞∞∞∞∞∞∞∞∞∞

Please don't feel that your mistakes or sins are beyond God's forgiveness. It's exhausting trying to be superwoman or supermom. True independence comes when we realize our need for total dependence on God. It's not a weakness to lean on Him. He gives us strength. He's always there for us—just a thought away.

Every person who has ever been born has fallen short of God's best for them. Still, His forgiveness is there for us when we ask. His best is available when we choose to stop making wrong choices and let Him repair our lives. Nothing feels better than living to please God!

Has there ever been a time in your life that you realized it was for your sins/wrong choices that Jesus died on the cross?

Has there been a time when you confessed your sins to God and invited Jesus to come into your heart and life?

If you would like to invite Jesus to come into your life today; if you would like to pray the words below and mean them with all your heart, you can know that your sins are forgiven—a huge weight off your shoulders. As a bonus, you'll never have to face another tomorrow alone. The best part of this decision is that one day you will live forever with God.

Let's pray. (As always, it's your choice.)

God, I'm sorry that so often I fall short. Please forgive me for my sins.

368

Thank you for sending Jesus to die for me.
Jesus please come into my heart right now. I give my life
to you completely.
Please be the Lord over every part of my life, so I don't
have to go it alone anymore.
Thank you for hearing me and for saving me today. In
Jesus, Name, A-Men.

If you prayed that for the first time or you've just recommitted your life to God, please get into a Bible-believing church so you don't fall away and slip back into a destructive or messy lifestyle. I invite you to plug into the Bible studies offered through MentoringMoments.org or your local Stonecroft Ministries group. Find them at Stonecroft.org.

Most of us struggle with forgiveness. Please read on . . .

Epilogue: Forgiveness and Apple Butter

I've heard it said, "Hurting people hurt people."

With Dace's history, it isn't a surprise he lashed out at others. I refuse to perpetuate the cycle. I have forgiven him for what he did to my family and me.

The results of his abuse lingered and took prayer to overcome. Nightmares plagued me for quite a while after we parted.

When Jerry and I were on our honeymoon, I had a frightening episode. I was sweating and crying in my sleep, and he woke me. That show of vulnerability in front of my groom was embarrassing.

He held me and prayed for me—quietly asked God to take away the nightmares. I didn't have much confidence in the prayer because I'd experienced the nightmares intermittently after I left Dace.

Thankfully, even when I had no faith, Jerry's faith carried me through. An emotional healing took place that night. I haven't had one of those terrifying dreams since our honeymoon—over thirty years ago!

Being free of emotional baggage, I've been available for God to use as He chooses. It's almost too simple to comprehend; it started with a single suggestion to "just ask" and a determination to forgive.

It's often said unforgiveness is like sipping poison and expecting the other person to die. Unforgiveness hurts you, not the offender.

Conversely, like sweet and spicy apple butter, the love of God has brought warmth and pleasant excitement as I've sought to follow and obey Him. One such choice has been to forgive.

Medical journals report the harmful effects of unforgiveness. Myriad illnesses are the result of hanging on to old hurts and bad feelings.

My dear friend, Rev. Jean Clark forgave the people who murdered her family. She said, "Forgiveness is a journey. It's a daily decision I make."

When I learned The Lord's Prayer, I got to the part that says, "and forgive us our sins, as we have forgiven those who sin against us." (Matthew 6:12 NLT)

Really? I thought. *Is that really how I want God to forgive me? No. I want Him to forgive me more than I forgive others!*

God forgave many throughout the Bible. Matthew 6, verses 14-15, say, "For if you forgive other people when they sin against you, your heavenly Father will also forgive you. But if you do not forgive others their sins, your Father will not forgive your sins." (NIV)

In Mark 11:25-26, Jesus said, "And when you stand praying, if you hold anything against anyone, forgive them, so that your Father in heaven may forgive you your sins." (NIV)

Jesus also said to forgive seventy-seven times or seventy times seven, meaning to forgive endlessly. (Matthew 18:22)

While dying on the cross, Jesus prayed for those who put Him there, "Father, forgive them, for they don't know what they are doing." (Luke 23:34) (NLT)

I've spent lots of time asking God to help me forgive. When I pray for the person I need to forgive—as difficult as that is—God will eventually let me see that person through His eyes, and I will have compassion on him/her. Also, living as though I have already forgiven can work from the outside in. (Please know forgiving someone doesn't mean that person should be in your life.)

If God can forgive me for the terrible things I've done, I must forgive others. How dare I not?

In the Bible, in Luke 7, a woman with a bad reputation washed Jesus' feet with her tears and wiped them with her hair. Simon the Pharisee thought, "If Jesus were really a prophet, he'd know what kind of woman this is." Jesus knew Simon's thoughts and responded with a parable:

> Two people owed money to a certain moneylender. One owed him five hundred [days wages], and the other fifty [days wages]. Neither of them had the money to pay him back, so he forgave the debts of both. Now which of them will love him more?
> Simon replied, "I suppose the one who had the bigger debt forgiven."
> "You have judged correctly," Jesus said. Then he turned toward the woman and said to Simon, "Do you see this woman? I came into your house. You did not give me any water for my feet, but she wet my feet with her tears and wiped them with her hair. You did not give me a kiss, but this woman, from the time I entered, has not stopped kissing my feet. You did not put oil on my head, but she has poured perfume on my feet. Therefore, I tell you, her many sins have been forgiven—as her great love has shown. But whoever has been forgiven little loves little."
> Then Jesus said to her, "Your sins are forgiven."

The other guests began to say among themselves, "Who is this who even forgives sins?"

Jesus said to the woman, "Your faith has saved you; go in peace." (NIV)

Perhaps the scent of cinnamon was amidst the spicy aromas of the perfume she put on Jesus' feet.

Whoever has been forgiven much, loves much. My heart is forever changed. After decades of poor decisions, God forgave my countless bad choices/sins, when I asked Him to. My love for Him is boundless. How can I not forgive others when I consider how much God has forgiven me?

Let's move into a healthier tomorrow by asking God to help us forgive others today. Remember, like Jean said, forgiveness is a journey, a choice we make each day.

Acknowledgments:

First and foremost, I'd like to thank Christ for keeping His hand on me always. Even before my mother suspected my existence, God knew me. For those few weeks when I was a secret from humanity, He communed with me. Although I don't remember this, it makes me feel special. God's plan for my life would not be thwarted by anyone or anything, seen or unseen. Twists, detours, and interruptions could not upset His map for my life. Thank You, Father, Son, and Holy Spirit!

A special thank you goes to my parents who still love me. Some would question how that can be possible, but you do. Thank you for showing support time and time again, even when logic would say you shouldn't have. You're both the best and I'm blessed to be your daughter!

I'd like to thank my children who, despite a rough toddlerhood, never stopped loving me and are today as adults, not just family, but my dear friends. You were my reason to get up every morning during the darkest time of my life. Clearly, you are both the best I've ever produced!

Thank you to the "Wismon family" (you know who you are) for introducing me to true, unconditional Christian love. Thank you for seeing something redeemable in me, no doubt praying for me and my children, and for being instrumental in introducing me to Jesus Christ and Jerry Stigliano. I can't wait to see (in heaven) how many lives you all changed simply by being yourselves. The ripples are vast.

Thank you, sweet Jerry for not tossing me aside when I told you my darkest secrets. Thank you for putting up with me during the first, nearly unbearable years of our marriage and for being a stable body all three of us so desperately needed. You've always been the Daddy the kids required; always there for them. Your firm but fair discipline and unconditional love helped shape the people they are today and the way they parent our grandchildren. Thank you for loving us. I will cherish you always!

Thank you to the brothers and sisters in Christ across the globe who have loved our family and poured your insight, lessons, and time into our lives.

Thank you to my fellow Word Weavers for listening to my life, chapter by chapter, year after year, and helping me shape this memoir into something readable. Without your insights, expertise, opinions, and encouragement this book would still be a manuscript on the shelf and a document in a computer. It took literally decades to get it out. I value each of you!

Finally, a special thank you goes to my editor and beta readers. Like my writer's critique group, the Word Weavers, you've been instrumental in making this book a tool to help women in at-risk relationships, and single mothers, and those who love them. I pray it brings understanding, help, and hope to each of them.

Endnote 1:

The **Ouija Board** made its debut in 1891, and Parker Brothers reintroduced it in 1967.

Also in 1967, there was a game made of green glow-in-the-dark plastic by Transogram Toy Company. It advertised as **Ka-bala**, the Mysterious Game That Foretells Your Future.

Shaped like a hexagon, Ka-bala had a rounded bottom, requiring two players to put their hands on either side of the unit to stabilize it. It had tarot cards and a clear cobalt marble which circled the parameter in a channel. Players took turns chanting specific words, and the ball would stop at the card that supposedly told his future.

Jutting up in the middle of the game, in the same pale green material, was an eyeball with rays around it like a sun. In the television commercials, the eye followed the marble within the groove. Of course, it didn't actually.

Alabe Crafts invented the **Magic 8 Ball** in 1946. Tyco began producing it in the 1960s. With its shiny black plastic shell, it could be dropped and not spill its dazzling blue fluid. A small window exposed its many-sided ball of nebulous answers.

Endnote 2:

Tagamet was approved in the US by the Food and Drug Administration for prescriptions starting January 1, 1979. Years later a GlaxoSmithKline spokesperson said, "Tagamet is now available as an over-the-counter medicine for heartburn in many countries, this method of purchasing the brand resulting in almost as much sales as those by prescription." (Chemical & Engineering News, 2005)

Endnote 3:

Werner H. Erhard founded **EST** (Erhard Seminars Training) purportedly to help people take control over their lives. The study of Zen Buddhism influenced his personal philosophy.

Organizations that can help you:

National Domestic Violence Hotline website:
http://www.thehotline.org/
If you are at a computer used by your abuser, please call their phone number. It is 1.800.799.SAFE (7233) or for the hearing impaired 1.800.787.3224 (TTY).

For many issues, including abuse, this is a valuable website:
http://helpguide.org/

CPSIA information can be obtained
at www.ICGtesting.com
Printed in the USA
FFHW02n2218231018
48936287-53160FF

9 780692 181621